The Long Journey of the
NEZ PERCE

The Long Journey of the
NEZ PERCE

A Battle History from
Cottonwood to the Bear Paw

Kevin Carson

WESTHOLME
Yardley

Frontispiece: Joseph (left center, in white headdress and garments on a light-colored Appaloosa), White Bird (mounted to the right of Joseph, in a white garment with no headdress), Toohoolhoolzote (center, in black-tipped feather headdress on a dark horse), and Looking Glass (right of center, in a tall white-feathered headdress on a spotted Appaloosa) at the May 1877 Lapwai, Idaho, council meeting with US Army General Oliver O. Howard. (*Northwest Museum of Arts and Culture, Eastern Washington Historical Society, Spokane, Washington, picture L94-7.10s; detail.*)

Westholme Publishing, LLC
904 Edgewood Road
Yardley, Pennsylvania 19067
Visit our Web site at www.westholmepublishing.com

First Printing August 2011
10 9 8 7 6 5 4 3 2 1

ISBN: 978-1-59416-132-2

Printed in the United States of America.

*To my mother and father, and to my wife, Jann,
for making the long journey with me*

Contents

List of Maps

The Patriot Bands of 1877

CHIEF LOOKING GLASS
Alpowai Band
Nez Perce Tribe
Villages:
Asotin, Alpowa,
Sapachesap
Location:
Clearwater River
Idaho Territory

CHIEF WHITE BIRD
Lamtama Band
Nez Perce Tribe
Village:
Lamata
Location:
Salmon River
Idaho Territory

CHIEF JOSEPH
Wallowa Band
Nez Perce Tribe
Village:
Innantoeein
Location:
Wallowa Valley
Oregon

CHIEF HUSISHUSIS KUTE
Palouse Band
Palouse Tribe
Village:
Wawawai
Location:
Snake River
Washington Territory

CHIEF TOOHOOLHOOLZOTE
Pikunan Band
Nez Perce Tribe
Village:
Unknown
Location:
Salmon River
Idaho Territory

Organization of the Military Departments under General William T. Sherman involved in the Nez Perce War, 1877

WILLIAM T. SHERMAN, COMMANDING GENERAL OF THE ARMY
E. D. Townsend, Assistant Adjutant-General
GEN. PHILIP H. SHERIDAN, Military Division of the Missouri
Brig. Gen. Alfred H. Terry, Department of Dakota
BRIG. GEN. GEORGE CROOK, Department of the Platte
Col. John Gibbon, District of Montana
MAJ. GEN. IRVIN MCDOWELL, Military Division of the Pacific
and Department of California
Brig. Gen. Oliver O. Howard,
Department of the Columbia
Maj. Gen. Orlando B. Willcox,
Department of Arizona

Organization of the Department of Columbia during the Nez Perce War, 1877*

BRIG. GEN. OLIVER O. HOWARD
Headquarters Staff, Portland, Oregon

Fort Boise, Idaho Territory, Capt. Patrick Collins, 21st Inf., commanding†

Fort Canby, Washington Territory, Maj. Joseph Stewart, 4th Art., commanding

Fort Colville, Washington Territory, Capt. Moses Harris, 1st Cav., commanding

Camp Harney, Oregon, Maj. John Green, 1st Cav.; Capt. G. M. Downey, 21st Inf., commanding

Fort Klamath, Oregon, Capt. James Jackson, 1st. Cav.; 1st Lt. H. D. W. Moore, 21st Inf., commanding

Fort Lapwai, Idaho Territory, Capt. D. Perry, 1st Cav.; Capt. William H. Boyle, 21st Inf., commanding

Fort Stevens, Washington Territory, Capt. M. P. Miller, 4th Art.; 1st Lt. William Everett, 4th Art., commanding

Fort Townsend, Washington Territory, Capt. E. A. Bancroft, 4th Art.; 1st Lt. E. W. Stone, 1st Art., commanding

Fort Vancouver, Washington Territory, Col. Alfred Sully, 21st Inf.; 1st Lt. G. W. Evans, 21st Inf., commanding

Vancouver Arsenal, Washington Territory, Capt. J. A. Kress, Ordnance Dept., commanding

Fort Walla Walla, Washington Territory, Col. Cuvier Grover, 1st Cav., commanding

Lewiston (temporary), Idaho Terrritory, Col. Frank Wheaton, 2nd Inf., commanding

*Report of the Secretary of War, 1877
†Commanding officer names separated by a semicolon indicate a change of command during the course of the war.

Washington
Territory

Albe

Snake River

Dayton ○

Fort Walla Walla
○

Pataha ○

Oregon

Wallowa
Valley

Lewiston ○

Fort
Lapwai ○

Weippe
Prairie

Lolo Pass

Fort Missoula
○

Fort Fizzle
○

Sapachesap

Kamiah

Clearwater River

Battle of the Clearwater

White
Bird Canyon

Salmon River

Stevensville

Battle of
Big Hole
○

Conti

Salmon ○

Snake River

○ Fort Boise

Idaho Territory

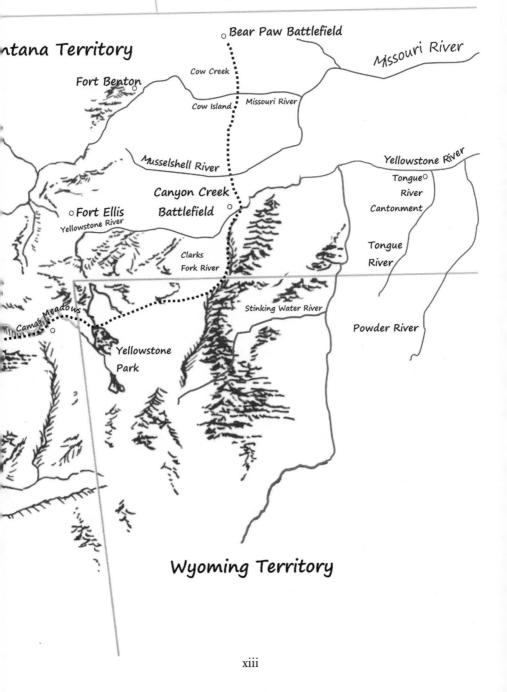

Saskatchewan

Bear Paw Battlefield

Montana Territory

Missouri River

Fort Benton

Cow Creek

Cow Island

Missouri River

Yellowstone River

Musselshell River

Tongue
River
Cantonment

Canyon Creek
Battlefield

Fort Ellis
Yellowstone River

Tongue
River

Clarks
Fork River

Camas Meadows

Stinking Water River

Powder River

Yellowstone
Park

Wyoming Territory

Chronology of Major Events of the Nez Perce War, 1877

May 15	The non-reservation Nez Perce and Palouse bands meet at Fort Lapwai, Idaho Territory, with General Oliver O. Howard and are told they must move to the Lapwai reservation in thirty days or they would face forced relocation.
May 31	After having returned to Oregon, Joseph and the Wallowa band of the Nez Perce ford the Snake River through Hells Canyon on their way to Idaho.
June 3	The five non-reservation bands gathered at Tolo Lake, Idaho.
June 13–15	Disgruntled Nez Perce warriors begin a killing spree against settlers along the Salmon River. Most of the bands' leaders realize that they will now face an attack from the US Army and decide their best course of action is to attempt to reach friendly Crow lands to the east.
June 17	The Battle of White Bird Canyon.
June 22	General Howard marches from Fort Lapwai.
July 1	Captain Stephen Whipple attacks Looking Glass's village, forcing his band to join the rest of the Nez Perce.
July 10–12	The Battle of the Clearwater.
July 11	Nez Perce move along the Lolo Trail.
August 9–10	The Battle of the Big Hole.
August 19	The Battle of Camas Meadows.
August 21	The Nez Perce enter Yellowstone National Park.
September 13	The Battle of Canyon Creek.
September 30	The Battle of Bear Paw.
October 1	Looking Glass killed.
October 5	Joseph Surrenders.
October 9	White Bird meets Sitting Bull in Canada.
October 31	Surrendered Nez Perce taken to Bismarck, North Dakota, by General Nelson A. Miles.

Foreword

In my memory, there was never a time when our family was not fascinated by the saga of the Nez Perce. My family home was filled with antiques handed down from pioneer days, as well as with stories about the people who lived on the frontier in Idaho and Washington.

My great-great-great grandfather, Levi Watrous, served as a scout in the 9th Iowa Volunteer Infantry during the Civil War. He followed various trades until becoming a stockman in Columbia County, Washington, in 1872. When the Nez Perce War flared up in 1877, he left Dayton, Washington, as a lieutenant of volunteers with the renowned frontiersman George Hunter; by the time Levi Watrous was released from service by General Oliver Otis Howard, he was their commander. Generations removed, we now recognize that the war was planned and manufactured by the politicians and the greedy. The history is written, and my ancestor was a part of the violent story of the summer of 1877.

That is my link to the story of the Nez Perce. I wanted to learn more about my ancestor and his part in the war. My family had located documentation for unacknowledged veterans in cemeteries in rural Washington and Idaho, and found many from the rolls of 1877. The Nez Perce—their way of life and the compelling story of their ordeal—spoke to me over the generations. Combined with my interest in military history, these events led to this book.

The kindness and humanity of the tribe in sheltering and saving the members of the Lewis and Clark expedition from certain death in the winter of 1805-06 was remarkable. They took care of the expedition's horses, nursed the ailing explorers back to health, and saved them from starvation and the elements. That is only the first of many examples of their humanity in the historical record.

But beginning in the mid-1800s, the Nez Perce people were confronted by a series of assaults on their traditional lands that increased steadily in scope and intensity until the only response left to them was defiance in the form of warfare. It was a war that they sought to avoid. Today, the men and women of the Nez Perce and allied tribes who resisted the US government's final order to move onto the reservation are known as the Patriots.

Using the term "Patriots" seems appropriate, for there are parallels to America's founders: the precise and rational arguments of the chiefs for human rights, their struggle for freedom from oppression, and the fact that their words fell upon deaf ears. The asymmetrical war they waged was just long enough to awake a nation to the brutal policies of Indian pacification.

Today, the Nez Perce have a thriving and revitalized culture, despite the outrages they suffered as a people. They have maintained their wonderful tradition of creating works of art, including ceramics, textiles, and paintings. Underlying all the qualities of their culture are those of extraordinary mental toughness, fortitude, and courage. These are the attributes these people manifested more than one hundred thirty years ago in negotiations, petitions for justice, and finally, as a last resort, warfare. One of the smallest tribes to oppose the United States, they shocked every force that engaged them in a fierce fight to survive. The Nez Perce warriors revealed their skill in a series of military successes against a vastly larger professional army. Every victory, and every stratagem employed against seemingly impossible odds, allowed the tribe to evade the confinement the government wished to impose.

My purpose in writing this book is to deconstruct the course of the journey of the Nez Perce flight and the battles they fought against the US Army. The book is a work of military history and should be read in that context. But it is also a story with moral and ethical lessons. The bitter lessons of the war were in some strange way a gift to this country. Today, conventional military, special forces, and light infantry all study the hard lessons of the summer of 1877. And they are applied in tough places and in desperate battles by an army that has learned from its mistakes.

In 1877, when the inevitable rebellion erupted, the Nez Perce drove the course of the conflict, making the army constantly adapt and often leaving their pursuers utterly in the dark about their intentions and whereabouts. With a fraction of the number of active combatants to oppose the vast numbers of soldiers at the command of the War Department in the West, the Nez Perce won the majority of the conflicts they fought, by any measure. And the legend of the tribe obscures a lesser-known victory, as we will discover.

A council near Fort Walla Walla, Washington Territory, held on August 4, 1858, between the Nez Perce and US Army. Here, the army discussed their plans to march on Indian groups hostile to the United States north of Nez Perce lands. Three years earlier, the Nez Perce had signed a treaty with the United States reserving their traditional homeland, and they remained peaceful and cooperative with American interests. Five years later, the United States demanded most of the Nez Perce lands, destroying Nez Perce goodwill. (*Library of Congress*)

I

The Grant Peace Policy

In 1877, the Nez Perce were a proud and ancient tribe of American Indians whose traditional lands stretched from the expanses of the mountains and prairies of Idaho in the north to the alpine valleys and lakes of northeastern Oregon to the south. Before the arrival of Europeans in North America, they customarily migrated annually from the Columbia River Basin and Snake River country of Washington a hundred miles west of the Idaho border to the rugged terrain of Montana's Bitterroot Mountains to the east.[1] A nomadic people, they ranged through their lands according to the season and the movements of herds of game. Their mobility was primarily driven by the requirements of forage, hunting, and the seasonal extremes of the land. In 1855, as small settlements of ranches and trading outposts encroached on the edges of their lands, the tribal elders of the Nee-Me-Poo (the Real People, in the Nez Perce language) signed a treaty with the US government that recognized the just right of the People to their homelands. This treaty established a broad reservation of land that encompassed the vastness of their mountains, trails, rivers, and hunting grounds.[2]

Their land was rich, not just in game and fish, but in timber, fertile earth for growing crops, and grasslands for grazing livestock. It was also a treasure trove of mineral wealth, including gold, silver, copper, and precious gemstones. Eventually, gold was discovered on the land of the Nez Perce. In 1860, a gold claim was filed after a find near Lewiston, Idaho. Gold was discovered near the area called Orofino (fine gold), which was the first of many gold-rush camp towns along the Clearwater River and its tributaries. Close on the heels of the discovery came an invasion of prospectors, miners, and speculators. Settlers and merchants began to follow the miners, homesteading in their wake. Lewiston, which grew along the confluence of the Snake and Clearwater rivers, was the gold country gateway.[3]

Despite the severe encroachment on their treaty rights, the Nez Perce did not take up arms, but instead protested the treaty violations peacefully. The tribe could proclaim that it had never killed a white man and that it had honored its treaty with the United States. By 1863, when the Idaho Territory was established over Nez Perce objections, whites could not make the reverse claim that no white man had ever killed a Nez Perce. The following year a chilling event changed the thinking of whites and Indians. In late 1864, Colonel John M. Chivington of the 3rd Colorado Cavalry dispatched his officers with orders that the Indians be "appropriately chastised for their outlawry."[4] In the wake of subsequent events, it appears he was tacitly giving his men permission to kill Indians without quarter or compassion. Chivington himself led an attack on a group of peaceful Cheyenne camped at Sand Creek in the Colorado Territory on November 29, 1864, massacring the elderly, women, and children there, despite a US flag and a white flag of surrender having been flown as signals of peace.

The work of assiduous westward expansion continued unabated, carving out territories in the West. When the surveyors finished, the new territorial area of Idaho contained substantial portions of the Nez Perce land within its borders. The Lincoln administration yielded to powerful interests demanding more access to the Nez Perce land for mining and settlement. A new treaty drafted and presented to the Nez Perce in 1863 reduced their land holdings by more than 90 percent, to 746,651 acres (see map on page 6). The atmosphere soon became tense, with many ancillary tribes ignoring the new treaty. Old Chief Joseph refused to sign the new treaty he had been offered and warned his son about making treaties with the whites.[5] Young Chief Joseph (Heinmot Tooyalakekt, or Thunder Traveling to Mountain Heights) was his oldest son and heir apparent to the tribal leadership. The interests and machinations of the white leaders were too complex to fathom. But Old Joseph believed it probably all boiled down to farming, and he could see that in the future his son would face even more extensive encroachment on their land. The Wallowa homeland in Oregon had been the primary residence of the Nez Perce since the beginning of time and legend. In modern times, after the Nez Perce had left the Lapwai area of Idaho for good, Oregon's high Wallowas became a sanctuary where the tribe did not feel as much pressure from settlement. Of all the lands, Old Joseph warned his son, he must protect the sacred Wallowas for the sake of the Nez Perce. He cautioned his boy that he must not enter into a treaty that relinquished their homeland.

In 1867, prompted by the national outcry over the Sand Creek incident and other outrages against Indians, a peace commission was established to examine the scope of issues raised by the westward expansion. The work of the commission, which was earnest enough in intention, was to become the basis of an initiative known in 1869 as the Grant Peace Policy.[6]

Old Chief Joseph died in 1871 and was succeeded in leadership by his oldest son. Ironically, he died just as the events he had always feared were beginning to transpire. He must have put his faith and the future of his people in Joseph's hands knowing that his son's strong yet moderate temperament and his gift for negotiations and argument were their only hope.

More land was appropriated in 1873, when an executive order by President Ulysses S. Grant divided the Wallowa Valley between settlers and Indians. Grant had hoped at the outset of his administration to be able to establish a new climate of peace in the treatment of Indian people. He had a close adviser in his administration who had particularly influenced his thinking: Ely S. Parker, a former Union general, a trusted aide, and a Seneca Indian.[7]

In 1869, Parker became the first Indian to hold the post of commissioner of Indian affairs. For a short time, the government bureaucracies that administered the fates of Indians in the West were headed by an Indian. In 1873, Colonel H. R. Clum had oversight of the Indian Bureau in Washington, DC.[8] The General Land Office, the Department of the Interior, and the army all had roles to play in what would turn out to be a remarkable, though failed, attempt to try something new.

The original order set aside land for a reservation in the Wallowas to be exempt from settlement and, oddly enough, provided most of the best forest and farmland to the tribe while providing more mountainous areas to the settlers. Most of the settlers wanted to run cattle and establish ranches. The lack of grazing land was certainly a deterrent to this activity. The mountains they were granted would have been largely useless to them for animal husbandry and crops.

In 1873, Edward P. Smith, then commissioner of Indian affairs, drafted a recommendation to the president based on the recommendation of Nez Perce Indian agent John B. Monteith. The area contained in the proposal covered a channel from the confluence of the Grand Ronde River in Oregon and the Snake River some fifty miles uphill and continued onto the prairie, where it abutted the boundaries of the Wallowa River and its west fork at the base of the Wallowa Mountains. This was a corridor to enable the Nez Perce access to their traditional migration trails.

Department of the Interior, Office of Indian Affairs June 9, 1873.

The above diagram [overleaf] is intended to show a proposed reservation for the roaming Nez Percé Indians in the Wallowa Valley, in the State of Oregon. Said proposed reservation is indicated on the diagram by red lines, and is described as follows, viz:

Commencing at the right bank of the mouth of Grande Ronde River; thence up Snake River to a point due east of the southeast corner of township No. 1 south of the base line of the surveys in Oregon, in range No. 46 east of the Willamette meridian; thence from said point due west to the west Fork of the Wallowa River; thence down said West Fork to its junction with the Wallowa River; thence down said river to its confluence with the Grande Ronde River; thence down the last-named river to the place of beginning.

I respectfully recommend that the President be requested to order that the lands comprised within the above-described limits be withheld from entry and settlements as public lands, and that the same be set apart as an Indian reservation, as indicated in my report to the department of this date.

Edward P. Smith, Commissioner [of Indian Affairs].[9]

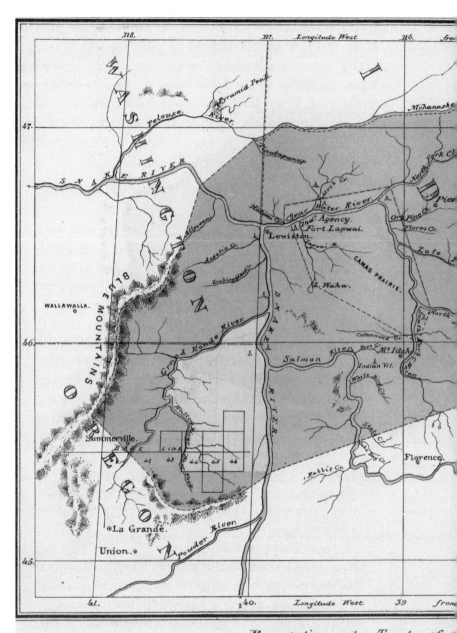

Reservation under Treaty of
"   "   "   "
Wallowa Valley claimed by Your

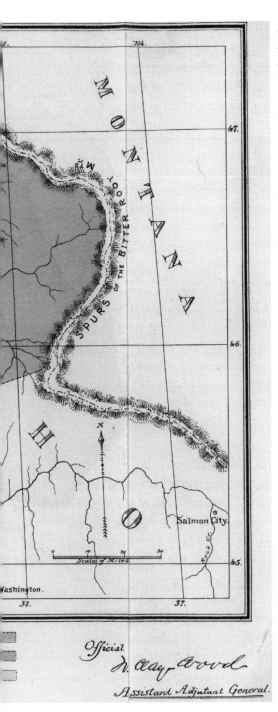

Official
N. Clay Wood
Assistant Adjutant General.

An official map signed by Maj. Clay Wood, Assistant Adjutant General, showing the first Nez Perce reservation treaty of 1855 and the much smaller land allowance of the 1863 treaty (marked by a dotted line around the Camas Prairie). Joseph, the son of Old Chief Joseph who died in 1871, continued to claim the Wallowa Valley. In 1873, the US Indian agent recommended that the valley (shown in a lighter color west of the Snake River and spanning the Washington and Oregon borders) be added to existing, much reduced Nez Perce reservation land. President Ulysses S. Grant agreed. The map also shows land parcels in the valley already surveyed for non-Indian settlements. It was pressure from settlers that led Grant in 1876 to reverse his decision and open the treaty lands up to development, while exiling the Nez Perce and allied tribes. This reversal sparked indignation among the Nez Perce who, up to this point, had been cooperative with the demands of the US government. (*Washington State University Library, MASC*)

Grant had good reason to consider such a proposal. He had little to show for his peace policy, and according to some of his key advisers, this type of compromise could be beneficial to both parties and result in a peaceful settlement. But nothing could have been further from the truth. Grant issued his executive order, dated June 16, 1873, expecting that he was setting a significant milestone in white and Indian relations:

> It is hereby ordered that the tract of country above described be withheld from entry and settlements as public lands, and that the same be set apart as a reservation for the roaming Nez Percé Indians, as recommended by the Secretary of the Interior and the Commissioner of Indian Affairs.[10]

The settlers in the Wallowa Valley immediately began trying to find ways around the order. Initially, the greater portion of the good woodlands and farmland had been given to the tribe. But Governor L. F. Grover of Oregon protested the creation of the new reservation. The Indian Bureau later advocated reversing the order, thinking the creation of additional reserves set a bad precedent. In 1876, the Grant administration reversed itself and encouraged unrestricted settlement in the Wallowas.

A deluge of interlopers in the form of landless settlers, treaty Indians and their chiefs, and the Indian authorities looked for opportunities to seize Nez Perce land with the argument that the native residents had lost their claim to it by not remaining in established settlements throughout the year.[11] This collision of contemporary American Western conventions and indigenous sensibility set spark to tinder in the nonreservation Indian's soul. The influential chiefs were enraged at the final indignity with which they were confronted, a command to move their people to the remaining reservation land in villages at Lapwai and sixty

A stagecoach loaded with prospectors heading for the goldfields found in Nez Perce lands. Settlements and roads were soon found throughout the region, pressuring the native population and their animal herds. (*National Archives*)

miles farther up the Clearwater River at Kamiah in the Idaho Territory.

At this time, an ever-larger number of settlers were seeking homesteads in the new territory. Many had been displaced by the horrors of the Civil War or were driven by a desire to escape from the Reconstruction South. The majority were Anglo-Americans and their families who were interested in establishing a place they could call their own and build a new life. Year after year, a steady stream of emigrants staked claims and built homesteads, initially along the same rivers and streams that the tribe relied upon.

In the hearts of the watching Nez Perce, the tinder was being fanned to flame.

2

Showing the Rifle

At this time, another insult provided fodder for the smoldering native indignation. In mid-June 1876, a settler in the Wallowa Valley named Alexander B. Findley noticed the loss of some of his prize horses from the pastures where they had been grazing. He looked for his horses diligently, combing the surrounding area.

On June 22, 1876, Findley encountered evidence of a Nez Perce hunting camp. He felt nervous about confronting a group of Nez Perce with his accusations and decided to get help. He left to convince other settlers to join him. He found a willing partner in Wells McNall, an avowed Indian hater.

The Nez Perce knew that McNall loathed the Indians and their way of life. Like many settlers, he resented their wealth in horses, land holdings, and gold. McNall castrated any wandering Nez Perce stallions he could catch. His justification was that he sought to preserve the "purity" of his horses.[1]

When the two men returned to the Indian camp, they saw evidence of horse prints in the turf that convinced Findley that the occupants of the camp must have stolen his horses. The two waited, but no one returned to the camp. They decided to come back in the morning, hoping to catch the suspected horse thieves.

The next morning, they found three Nez Perce men at the camp. One was Wilhautyah (Wind Blowing), a close friend of Chief Joseph's. The men had returned from a hunting trip and were hanging a deer in a tree to bleed it before skinning.

The two groups of men had words, and eventually, McNall and Wind Blowing fought for possession of McNall's rifle. McNall called out to Findley to shoot. Findley's rifle fired during the scuffle, and Wind Blowing was killed.[2]

Findley and McNall made a hasty retreat and attempted to lie low, aware that Indian, as well as white, justice might pursue them. They took shelter in the sturdy and defensible home of Ephraim McNall, Wells's father.

General Oliver O. Howard, commander of the Military District of the Columbia, within which the Wallowa band of the Nez Perce lived, insisted to civilian authorities that Findley and McNall stand trial for murder.[3] But by mid-August, they had not been charged and were still free.[4]

War dances and overt hostility in the posture and actions of the Nez Perce began to grow. On September 1, settlers in the valley answered their doors to a Nez Perce delegation that announced that a council would be held in the Indian village. It was clear from the demeanor of the Nez Perce that the white settlers were required to attend. The atmosphere was tense, and the settlers were told they had to surrender the two men and leave the Wallowa Valley. The meeting turned ugly when the settlers refused to produce the two men or to leave.

The next day, September 2, Joseph presented a grim ultimatum at the McNall cabin. If Findley and McNall were not surrendered by Sunday, September 10, his warriors would drive the settlers from the valley and burn their houses. McNall's father, Ephraim, rode one hundred miles to Fort Walla Walla, Washington, to get assistance from the army. He was rebuffed because troops had been requested so frequently that the officers thought the settlers had no credibility.

Joseph's deadline of September 10 was fast approaching. In the meantime, McNall raised a large band of militant volunteers from over the Blue Mountains in the Grande Ronde Valley of northeast Oregon. He recruited riders to accompany him back to the Wallowa Valley to defend the settlers. The men were vocal about their violent intentions.[5] When Lieutenant Albert Gallatin Forse at Fort Walla Walla got wind of the vigilante troop that McNall was recruiting, he rode with a troop of cavalry on the seventh to protect the Nez Perce and keep the peace. Forse was able to negotiate and get the two parties to stand down.[6] Joseph demanded that the two men turn themselves in and that the military compel the civil authorities to bring them to trial.

Forse compelled the two men to go to Union County, in Oregon, and turn themselves in. Findley and McNall traveled to the Grande Ronde Valley and presented themselves to Judge E. C. Brainard in Union. Forse commented, "If McNall and Findley had been arrested, tried and punished . . . there would have been no trouble."[7]

After a quick hearing, McNall was released immediately. Findley was charged with manslaughter and released on bail of $250. Joseph sent two Indian witnesses to the hearing, but for unknown reasons, both refused to testify once they reached Union. A week later, Brainard dismissed the charges against Findley. A grand jury would later be con-

Major General Irvin McDowell, right, was commander of the Military Division of the Pacific and the immediate supervisor of Brigadier General Oliver O. Howard, left, commander of the Department of Columbia. Both of these photographs were taken during the Civil War. (*Library of Congress*)

vened in Union to re-examine the matter, but both men were acquitted in a ruling of self-defense.

Major General Irvin McDowell was the commander of the Military Division of the Pacific. His division included the Department of the Columbia and the Department of California. McDowell was concerned enough about the episode to include the particulars in his annual report to the secretary of war for 1876. This report, and the communications within the Division of the Pacific and the Department of the Columbia, likely focused attention on the question of Joseph and his people and their refusal to move onto a reservation.

Other agencies in Washington took note of what was happening in the Wallowa Valley. The concern over the nonreservation Nez Perce enabled General Howard to take action.

Howard took two initiatives upon hearing of the postac-
quittal rumblings of dissatisfaction within the white and
Indian communities. He dispatched Captain David Perry,
who commanded at Fort Lapwai in the Idaho Territory, to
make a show of force in the Wallowas and to visit with
Joseph with the goal of keeping the peace. Howard also dispatched his adjutant general, Major Henry Clay Wood, to
go to Lapwai and conduct his own investigation and write
a report with his recommendations.[8]

Wood chaired a delegation that traveled to the Wallowa
area in July 1876 to hold council with Joseph; his younger
brother, Ollokot (Frog), also a Nez Perce chief; and other
influential tribal members. The Indians hoped to get a
hearing on the matter of their legal standing and their right
to their land. Howard, though, had the same objective as
the political leaders of Oregon: to ultimately move the Nez
Perce to a reservation and civilize them.[9]

In Wood, Joseph found a white man willing to listen. He
agreed that Joseph's view of the 1863 treaty was correct. He
ascertained that the treaty had no authority to deny the tribe
its homeland. Wood, a lawyer, promised that a tribunal
would investigate the killing of Wind Blowing and that he
would help seek indictments against those responsible. He
also summed up his interpretation of their standing in the
matter of binding treaties: "The non-treaty Nez Perces cannot in law be regarded as bound by the treaty of 1863."[10]
Wood also began to formulate his ideas about a commission
to settle the dispute over the Nez Perce homeland.

After Wood left the valley, the Nez Perce waited impa-
tiently. When nothing happened by early September, they
made displays of aggression that indicated they might pursue their own form of justice if the white men could not.

In the intervening time, Howard had actually acted
somewhat at cross-purpose to Wood. Howard had little
doubt that the Indian Bureau and the commissioner of

Indian affairs were intent on
removing the Wallowa Nez Perce
from Oregon to a reservation.[11]
Howard would co-opt Wood's
suggestion of a commission and
force the issue to a resolution
favorable to the government.[12] In
fact, Howard had already made his
proposal to Washington, DC,
prior to asking Wood to meet with
Joseph.[13]

Wood held a preliminary inter-
view with Joseph regarding the
proposed commission to settle the
issues of land ownership by the
Nez Perce. When Wood asked his
willingness to participate, Joseph
replied, according to Wood, "If
good honest men were sent as
members of the commission, he
would be glad to meet with
them."[14]

Major Henry Clay Wood
negotiated with the Nez
Perce but did not agree
with his superiors' deci-
sion to remove the Nez
Perce to a reservation by
force, if necessary.
(*Battles and Leaders*)

In modern times, General Howard is remembered for
his humanitarian works as administrator of the Freedmen's
Association—a beneficial organization for assisting freed
slaves—and establishing Howard University in Washington, DC. Sometimes called the "Christian General" for his
religious zeal, he was also nicknamed "Uh-Oh Howard"
and "General Day-After-Tomorrow," for two devastating
reversals on the battlefields of the Civil War, where in both
cases he had displayed a marked inability to anticipate the
enemy and had suffered the loss of an arm.

Outmaneuvered and badly beaten by General Thomas
"Stonewall" Jackson at Chancellorsville, Virginia, in early
May 1863, he could not see that his flank was unguarded,

even after being warned by his command staff. Private John Collins of the 8th Pennsylvania Cavalry recounted the pitiful scene he came upon during his retreat from the shattering advance on Howard's right flank:

> In the very height of the flight, we came upon General Howard, who seemed to be the only man in his command that was not running at that moment. He was in the middle of the road and mounted, his maimed arm embracing a stand of colors that some regiment had deserted, while with his sound arm he was gesticulating to the men to make a stand by their flag. With bared head he was pleading with his soldiers, literally weeping as he entreated the unheeding horde.[15]

On the first day of the Battle of Gettysburg, July 1, 1863, Howard's positioning of troops and weakening of his lines to the left and right of his center allowed essentially the same outcome, as XI Corps was routed and retreated, clogging the streets of Gettysburg and allowing the capture of many troops.

In his official report, Howard endeavored to shine a more positive light on the first day's battle than the facts may have indicated: "The First and Eleventh corps, numbering less than eighteen thousand men, nobly aided by Buford's division of cavalry, had engaged and held in check nearly double their numbers from 10 in the morning until 7 in the evening. They gave way it is true, after hard fighting, yet they secured and held the remarkable position which, under the able generalship of the commander of this army, contributed to the grand results of July 2 and 3d."[16] Author and soldier Ambrose Bierce begged to differ and wrote a scathing first-hand assessment of Howard's leadership in his short essay "The Crime at Pickett's Mill."

Howard's warrior résumé was spotty at best, with a history of chances squandered and an evident inability to recognize opportunities and threats on a dynamic battlefield. Ironically, he would be best recognized in the context of his martial endeavors against the Nez Perce.

In 1875, Howard had arranged his own exile in the West at the urging of Grant and General Sherman as a way of shielding his old friends against the taint of scandal. Howard had been condemned in the press for rampant mismanagement and fraud within the Freedmen's Bureau, a federal agency that sought to provide aid and support for freed slaves to transition into a new economy during Reconstruction.[17]

So fortune placed an experienced but tentative general in the position of command to rein in a rebellious people. His foes were leaders whose ability to wage war was burned into their genes and expressed in their brains and sinews. But no one in Washington yet knew the qualities of the native foe they would shortly bring to combat.

During Reconstruction, the US Army had the grueling and unglamorous duty to "pacify" American Indian tribes in the West. The army's role soon shifted, however, to providing security in the frontier for expansion and the achievement of the vision of Manifest Destiny. As a practical matter, this meant supporting the dictates of the civilian Indian Affairs Administration. Much of the day-to-day administration and welfare issues involved the military as well.

In 1876, the army had a significant body of experienced professional soldiers in its officer corps. The ranks of noncommissioned officers were also filled with competent professionals. These individuals were given a principal mission of security. The uncertainty created by government policies that were alternately conciliatory and punitive made duty in the army as an officer challenging and dangerous.[18]

Howard exemplified the political challenges faced by senior army officers. He was directly in the middle of dramatic changes in policies and shifting politics, working to set policy and, as he saw it, to secure the peace.

Howard claimed credit for the idea of creating a peace commission to decide the matter of the Wallowa lands, but he knew the idea was in its early formation in 1876, when Major Wood was seeking the formation of a "commission of politicians." There is little doubt that Howard pushed his subordinate's idea to have the commission formed and to recommend the men to sit on it.[19]

At Howard's urging, and with the support of General McDowell, the secretary of the interior approved the creation of the peace commission.[20] Its members were General Howard, Wood, William Stickney, A. C. Barstow, and David Jerome, who chaired the commission but showed deference to the general throughout the proceedings.[21] Stickney acted as secretary.[22] Stickney was a member of the federal Board of Indian Commissioners in Washington, DC, and had arranged land deals with the Cherokee tribe. Jerome was from Saginaw, Michigan, and was a sitting state senator. Barstow hailed from Providence, Rhode Island.[23] They met on November 13, 1876. Sixty or more representatives of the Wallowa band rode into Lapwai, with Joseph leading the procession. The leaders of the nontreaty tribes represented were Joseph and Ollokot of the Nez Perce; White Bird (Peo Peo Hihhih), leader of the Lamtama; and shaman and Chief Toohoolhoolzote of the Pikunan tribe. Husishusis Kute (Old Bald Head) had come representing the remaining Palouse Indians, while Looking Glass, chief of the Alpowai, made the journey from his main village at the confluence of the Middle Fork of the Clearwater River and Clear Creek. Joseph wanted all his peers to have an opportunity to understand the significance of their predicament. Although Joseph and his Wallowa people were the

Joseph of the Wallowa band of Nez Perce, left, and his younger brother, Ollokot, right (photographed in 1877 by Charles W. Phillips). The two brothers were key representatives for the Nez Perce during negotiations with the American army. (*Library of Congress*)

focus of the commission, he was a somewhat junior member of the group of chiefs assembled from the bands of Indians who did not live on the reservations. There was no head chief over them all.

But Howard felt he needed a single point of tribal authority to deal with among the nontreaty bands. Because of the intense focus on the Wallowa Valley reservation, and because the politicians wanted the area open for settlement, it was convenient for him to seize upon Joseph as the representative and de facto leader of all of the Nez Perce and associated tribes. This misconception was partly due to the lack of understanding that Howard and his staff had of the fundamental nature and composition of political leadership within the Nez Perce and confederated tribes.

It is important to understand that leadership was conferred by the consensus of the entire tribe. Although inheritance of leadership from an influential father was a contributing factor, without shrewdness, tact, strength, and the will of those he led, Joseph never would have risen to prominence within the Wallowa band. But he was a junior chief to the likes of White Bird and Looking Glass. Like all leaders, his hold on power and influence was tenuous. Other prominent men sought his position. Joseph was the chief of a nontreaty band of Nez Perce who called the Wallowa Mountains in Oregon their principal home. Ollokot was also a chief of that tribe and nearly a mirror image of his older brother, slightly taller, handsome, and with the same bearing and style of dress. Ollokot and other subchiefs would make significant contributions throughout the negotiations with Howard, and in the crucial actions in battle and tactical decisions that brought them victory or held the army at bay. Joseph and his brother were two sides of a coin: Joseph represented the olive branch and Ollokot the rifle. While Joseph's talents for negotiations and diplomacy were strongly developed, Ollokot embodied the fighter for both of them, having less patience and interest in politics.

Joseph also had many strong and capable leaders in his senior warriors and his peer chieftains to call upon during the later campaign. He needed their support as the peacetime representative of the Wallowa band. Given his command of language and stature, he was the logical choice to gain consensus among the loosely confederated Nez Perce bands and negotiate with the white authorities. He had been chosen by his father, Old Joseph, to represent the Wallowa band because of the maturity and seriousness of mind he exhibited.[24] Joseph provided continuity with his father's long-held positions in negotiations with the US government. Joseph's relationship and oath to his father bound him to protect his people and the sacred land of the Wallowas.

The most formidable of the tribal chiefs was White Bird. His band of people, the Lamtama, inhabited the Salmon River country of north-central Idaho. He was a serious man, broad-shouldered and six feet tall, who sometimes found himself at odds with Joseph over the issue of diplomacy versus war against the whites. Both chief and shaman, he was respected for his extraordinary physical strength as well as his supposed supernatural powers. White Bird brought neighboring chief and shaman Toohoolhoolzote to the council. The chieftain was described as being possessed of mystical powers and having an aloof bearing. His physical strength and vitality were also legendary, given that he was advancing past middle and

White Bird, the proud and defiant leader of the Lamtama band of Nez Perce, urged the tribe to flee to Canada in order to avoid being forced onto a reservation. (*George Kush Collection*)

into a vigorous old age, perhaps his early sixties.[25] His name was Flathead in origin and meant "Sound." He was to be appropriately vocal in his protestation and oratory with General Howard.[26] He was prominently involved, along with many other chiefs, in a native religion known as the Dreamers.

The Dreamer religion was founded on a prophetic vision of an apocalypse that promised the restoration of stolen lands and annihilation of the whites who occupied them. Partly as a reaction to the aggressive conversion of Indians to Christianity practiced by the Indian agents and missionaries, the tribe needed a new faith to counter the spiritual warfare they were enduring. Their appointed

A group of Nez Perce, possibly during a ceremony of the native Dreamer religion, photographed before the 1877 war. (*Washington State University Library, MASC*)

Indian agent, John B. Monteith, with his excessive proselytizing, was a fly in the ointment. The aggressive conversion of Indians to Christianity had led to a conflict of identity and a schism that divided even families between the treaty and nontreaty factions.

Another factor in the religious mix was the Reverend Joseph Cataldo. A Jesuit priest, Cataldo was a missionary who taught and established churches and schools in the inland Northwest. He wrote religious texts in the Nez Perce language, and in doing so made a significant contribution to its documentation. His goals only superficially aligned with the Protestants' in their struggle for native souls. Both Monteith and Howard took the priest to task for remaining neutral on the issues confronting the nontreaty Indians, which they interpreted as tacit opposition to their efforts to "civilize" the Nez Perce and force them onto the reservation. There is evidence that the Nez Perce were frustrated with the Christian factions' behavior toward each other.

Catholic Nez Perce had contested the choice of Presbyterian Indian agent Monteith, calling it sectarianism.[27] And some of the dialog between Monteith and

Joseph was telling. In 1873, Monteith had made a deter-mined effort to convince Joseph to move to a reservation in order to receive benefits from the government. With him at Lapwai was the superintendent of Indian affairs for Oregon, T. B. Odeneal. Joseph was asked, "Do you want schools or school houses on the Wallowa Reservation?" The chief answered, "No, we do not want schools or school houses on the Wallowa Reservation."

> Superintendent: "Why do you not want schools?"
>
> Chief Joseph: "They will teach us to have churches."
>
> Superintendent: "Do you not want churches?"
>
> Chief Joseph: "No, we do not want churches."
>
> Superintendent: "Why do you not want churches?"
>
> Chief Joseph: "They will teach us to quarrel about God, as the Catholics and Protestants do on the Nez Perce Reservation and other places. We do not want to learn that."[28]

Monteith believed he needed to make good Christians out of his Indian charges along the lines of the dominant white Protestant American culture as part of the govern-ment-sanctioned efforts to reform those whom President Grant had called "the original occupants."[29]

The native faith of the Dreamers (Tooats) stepped into the spiritual void and bridged their traditional beliefs with a messianic vision of a native paradise on Earth. But before this could come to pass, the white invaders had to be driv-en from the Indian land they occupied. Toohoolhoolzote followed the Dreamer teachings of the prophet Smohalla of the Columbia reaches of the river plains, where the Dreamers eked out a living by fishing. Smohalla was a stur-dily built man of modest height. He was a practicing med-icine man who promoted the belief that he had returned from the dead with a potent message from the spirit world.

His followers, the Dreamers, practiced rituals featuring dancing and rhythmic drums that, in all-night ceremonies, promoted individual and group trances and visions. Smohalla emerged from his own waking dream to announce that he had mystical knowledge gleaned from the spirit world. He declared that at some apocalyptic time in the near future, all dead Indians would be resurrected in order to overcome the white intruders. When the original order of things was restored, dead animals killed by long-passed generations of Indian hunters would also rise again, providing plentiful game in the restored lands.[30]

The basic tenants of the Dreamer religion rejected Western materialism and technology. Working, agriculture, animal husbandry, and machinery were to be abandoned in favor of traditional ways of life.[31] The Wallowa Indians did not adopt the Dreamer way wholesale but fused their traditional religion and the Dreamer beliefs, which predated the Lewis and Clark expedition.[32]

The complexities of the situation were probably not evident to the peace commissioners assembled. They could not appreciate the complex religious forces at work, the idea of land being indivisible in the view of the Wallowans. Nor could they appreciate that the land had been consecrated by the blood of Wind Blowing and could not be parted with.

The commission's report was created without the assistance of Monteith, who believed that the commission process was fundamentally flawed and had felt threatened by Ollokot during the meeting that was held with the Wallowa band.[33] During two days, those assembled met first at the Indian agency, where Joseph aired the Wallowans' grievances, primarily focusing on their land rights. The next meeting was the following day at Fort Lapwai. The final report was finished on December 1, 1876, and the commissioners signed it with no uncertainty in their minds about their good service to the Indians.

Among other things, it provided for special removal of those following the Dreamer faith to the Indian reservations. If they objected, they should be transported to the Indian Territories in Oklahoma. One of the final stipulations was that if the Indians did not reach the reservation within a reasonable time, they should be compelled by force.

Major Wood refused to sign the document and tried to append his minority report, to no avail. Nevertheless, Wood sent his own independent report, drawn from his earlier work with Joseph, to the commissioner of Indian affairs.[34]

The overarching recommendation of the commission was that the nontreaty tribes be moved onto the Lapwai reservation in Idaho by April 1. General Howard ordered advanced preparations for a semi-permanent camp to be established near the Grande Ronde River, commanding the western entrance to the Wallowa Valley, both to protect the strategic bridge there from destruction and also to be able to move quickly if trouble broke out in the Wallowa Valley. He ordered Captain Stephen G. Whipple to move from Fort Walla Walla with two companies of the 1st Infantry and occupy the strategic crossing, from which he could also support the troops at Lapwai if needed. Whipple had accrued years of Indian fighting experience as a California militia member and later as an officer of light infantry during the Civil War.

In April 1877, Howard received orders from Washington, DC, to proceed to Fort Lapwai and hold a final council with the Nez Perce tribes. He was directed to be prepared to compel the nontreaty tribes onto the reservation at Lapwai. General McDowell wrote that Sherman "is of the opinion that the Indian Bureau should resolve to remove the Indians or not according to [its] interpretation of the treaty, and that the Army should only aid [it] to execute the resolve when made."[35]

At this point, the Nez Perce had few options other than compliance. Joseph, Ollokot, and White Bird knew well the fates of neighboring tribes such as the Dakota, Cheyenne, and Cayuse, and had seen the decimation of the Palouse Indians to the north firsthand after the Palouse War of 1858. The military rendered extremely harsh penalties, including summary execution for those Palouse warriors who surrendered or turned themselves in to the authorities. The army also killed thousands of Indian ponies as retribution and to take away one of their principal weapons of war.

Joseph took the longer view that his people could be preserved, and the most important of their lands, the Wallowas, would remain in their possession, if he could just work out some kind of compromise with General Howard. Joseph had met Howard several times since Howard had assumed his command in 1875, and the chief had taken the measure of the general and remained uncertain of his intentions. Howard recalled later that at their first meeting in 1875, "Joseph put his large black eyes on my face, and maintained a fixed look for some time." He also noted that Joseph was "endeavoring to read my disposition and character."[36]

Ollokot, acting as ambassador for the tribes, arranged a temporary postponement and set a date for all of the assembled bands to speak with Howard on May 3 in Lapwai. Ollokot briefed his brother regarding his conversations with Howard, and he was clear in imparting to Joseph that the general wanted to move all the tribes onto the same small reservation.[37]

While the brothers deliberated whether they would travel to the next council meeting, Howard decided to make a preemptive move to counter the influence of the Dreamers by putting pressure on Smohalla. The general traveled from Fort Walla Walla west to nearby Wallula on the Columbia River. He took with him Indian agent N. A.

Lapwai, Idaho, where leaders of the Nez Perce and associated tribes met one last time with US army and government representatives to discuss new American demands. The United States ordered the Nez Perce to relocate here on a reservation and relinquish their earlier homeland. (*National Archives*)

Cornoyer, whose own agenda for dealing with the Columbia River Dreamers happened to align with Howard's.[38]

They assembled the prophet and his supporters at Wallula on the banks of the Columbia. Howard threatened them with force of arms if they did not move onto reservations, and when Smohalla broached the matter of the Wallowas, Howard said he would settle that matter with troops as well if it came to that.[39]

The Nez Perce delegation undertook the arduous 120-mile trip through and across two river canyons to reach Lapwai and meet in what was to be the final, fateful council with the white men of the government. Finally, the other nontreaty bands began arriving on May 3. It would be a few days before all the Nez Perce and associated tribes were assembled, making Howard impatient and anxious.

Nonetheless, he began the council talks before the others arrived.

Howard told Joseph that he understood from Ollokot that Joseph had wished to see him and that he was at the meeting to hear what Joseph had to say. Joseph insisted that he had to wait for White Bird, who would join the council the following day. Howard replied strongly that the instructions to go to the reservation were for his people specifically. Howard told the assembled that whatever the outcome of the council, they must obey the orders of the government of the United States. Agent Monteith read his instructions from the government to those assembled. Monteith lectured the Wallowa band that he had sent Nez Perce emissaries from Lapwai to meet with the Wallowa band and deliver the message that they must come along to the reservation.[40] Joseph had refused, saying, as he always did, "All I have to say is that I love my country. We will not sell the land. We will not give up the land."[41]

At Joseph's insistence, Howard eventually adjourned the council until the following day, Friday, by which time Looking Glass, White Bird, and Toohoolhoolzote had arrived. Approximately forty-five years old, Looking Glass stood nearly six feet tall and was muscular. He had brought his Alpowai band. White Bird led his branch of Lamtama people from the Salmon River canyons along with Toohoolhoolzote, whose Pikunan were a branch of the Lamtama band. Two other men followed: Hahtalekin (Echo Red), a subchief, and Husishusis Kute, head chief of the Palouse tribe from the reaches of the Snake River.[42]

The chiefs entered a large pavilion, which was an army field hospital tent, where they would sit in the front. Howard's aides, Lieutenants Melville Wilkinson and William H. Boyle, flanked him and were slightly behind when he sat solemnly facing the chiefs. Monteith and the interpreters were close at hand.

Husishusis Kute and Looking Glass had brought their tribes for a particular reason. Their tribes were not the focus of the government's orders, which were specific to the mainline Nez Perce and the Wallowa band in particular. Since the Palouse Indians were a distinct people, their standing in the matter at hand was unclear to them, and they hoped to understand the government's intentions. And Looking Glass was left wondering what the implications for his people were. The legacy of the 1858 war against the Palouse was always on their minds. Each native man left his rifle and other weapons outside, as was their custom when in serious negotiations. This was

Looking Glass, representative of the Alpowai band of the Nez Perce tribe. He was a brilliant tactician having learned how best to fight the US Army by observing their drills and behavior. (*Library of Congress*)

also a conciliatory gesture, as it was impolite in their culture to introduce warlike gestures in a peaceful ceremony that could be perceived as a provocation to fight.

Waiting outside were the many treaty Indians, curious to hear the result of the meetings. Inside the tent, everyone shook hands and sat down. Father Cataldo opened the meeting with a prayer in the Nez Perce language.

Joseph rose and introduced White Bird, reminding General Howard that this was the first time Howard and White Bird had met, and Joseph wanted him and his band to understand what Howard had been telling the Wallowa band. While Howard conveyed the government's orders to the tribe, White Bird held a feather in front of his eyes in defiance. Howard sharply repeated to all that the tribes had no choice but to comply with the government's orders or be compelled by the army under duress. All those assembled became grim and serious.

Joseph spoke next, recounting the grievances of the assembled people. Toohoolhoolzote became an impassioned speaker for the tribes during this and the ensuing days of meetings, describing the Indians' belief that the earth was the origin of all of them and that it should not be owned or divided. The young warriors nodded in agreement with the old chief as he spoke. The atmosphere became thick with tension as the council progressed. Joseph suggested that they halt until Monday and meet again.[43] Howard readily agreed. Unknown to Joseph, he had troops on the way.

When the council assembled again on Monday, Joseph asked the commissioners, "What person pretends to divide the land and put me upon it"? Howard replied, "I am the man. I stand here for the President. There is no spirit good or bad that will hinder me. My orders are plain and they will be executed."[44]

White Bird spoke from behind his eagle feather: "If I had been taught from early life to be governed by the white men, I would be governed by the white men. Rather, it is the earth that rules me."[45]

When the discussions became heated, Howard had Toohoolhoolzote arrested and taken to the guardhouse as a warning; he was held as a hostage until an agreement was reached.[46] The young men of Toohoolhoolzote's tribe and many of White Bird's followers wished to exact vengeance for the imprisonment. Joseph worked hard to calm the assembled Indians for he, unlike the white men, understood that the warriors might very well kill the commissioners after the insult. Gradually he was able to restore some calm to the meeting.

The chiefs finally agreed to look at the reservation lands. Howard had sent for armed reinforcements, and news of several new army companies reaching the area made the chiefs more amenable to agreement. But the arrest of Toohoolhoolzote was an insult that would not be forgotten, and Howard's "showing the rifle"—threatening to use force— during what the Indians viewed as a peace treaty council was a breach of protocol.

Howard insisted that the principal chiefs—White Bird, Looking Glass, and Joseph—accompany him to look at the land on the Lapwai reservation to pick out places where they could live. The chiefs, however, were discouraged, as the best land was already taken, and sacrifices would have to be made to settle with the already well-established Christian Indians. They all worried about where they would find the land to graze their vast herds of horses and other livestock.

Howard made it clear to the chiefs where he intended to settle them: along the middle section of the Clearwater River, with the Palouse bands. They all had strong misgivings about Howard's plans. The clear threat from Howard was that if they did not report to the reservation on time, Howard would assume they wanted to fight and would use military force. White Bird in particular advised Howard that he could not guarantee that he could bring all of his people in. Howard suggested that he would bring them in if White Bird could not deliver them.[47]

At some point, one of the cavalry officers riding with the party made a disparaging remark about the quality of their Nez Perce ponies. White Bird had had enough talk and challenged the young officer to a horse race with the wager being their freedom to remain upon their lands. Howard was upset by the stratagem and quickly insisted there would be no such wager; instead, he suggested that the bet should be for money. One of the chiefs produced a gold coin from a purseful of other coins and handed it to the general to hold while the race was run. Howard noted later that the race took place in a spirit of good fellowship. However, he did not share the outcome, and he never admitted to losing the wager.[48]

Meanwhile, still in the stockade cell, Toohoolhoolzote struck up a friendship with twenty-year-old trooper John Jones, dubbed "Johnnie Jonesy" by his comrades, who was incarcerated for drunken and disorderly conduct.[49] The young soldier had a record of disorderly conduct and struggled with drink. General Howard would be inclined to give him another chance after his incarceration ended.[50] The old shaman reassured the young bugler that if it came to war, he would personally ensure that no harm came to Jones. Eventually, Toohoolhoolzote was released and made his way back to his tribe.

At the end of the Lapwai council meeting on May 15, Howard gave his final judgment and a warning to those assembled. The bands had thirty days to gather their belongings and holdings and report to the reservation. Any violation of Howard's strict timeline would result in a military intervention. This timetable presented a severe hardship for tribes moving thousands of animals and the very old and the very young across snowy mountain passes and swollen rivers in the most rugged country of the northwest.

On May 21, Howard sent a telegram from Portland to his superiors regarding his efforts to comply with his orders:

> Returned Portland, evening of the 19th. Non-treaty Nez Perces constrained compliance with order of government. Thirty days allowed to gather scattered people and stock. Location on reservation selected and agreed upon. Troops enough left in vicinity under commander Lapwai to enforce agreement case draw back. Some 500 wanderers from Umatillas and Yakima agencies still roaming—would join hostiles case outbreak. Told them to talk their own seeking

government requirement they go upon reservation. Please ask Agent Wilbur be designated by telegram. Indian Bureau cooperate with me for these Indians, as Agent Montieth has well done for Nez Perces.[51]

The Wallowa Mountains in the northeast corner of Oregon are described as the Alps of America. Towering granite peaks reach nearly ten thousand feet, dominating the skyline. Lake basins empty their water into, and beautiful rivers flow from, this rugged wilderness. The Wallowas were only accessible to the Nez Perce during the summer. When they were there, they lived at the foot of the mountains, although still at an elevation of 5,000 feet. At that altitude, nearly a mile high, a blizzard could sweep down on them at any time, even in the summer. Heavy snowfall at the higher elevations in winter made travel there dangerous. The plains around the Wallowas were crisscrossed with rivers and canyons carved from the meandering rivers. The rivers were full during spring from the runoff as the snowpack and deep ice in the high mountains and basins melted. The Wallowa Mountains fed many rivers. The Minam River wound down through the basin toward the vast river valleys to empty with the Wallowa River and Sheep Creek into the Grande Ronde. The Imnaha River flowed on through dramatic gorges to feed the Snake, which flowed at the bottom of its own great ravine, separating Oregon and Idaho. Climbing up onto the prairie in Idaho, the land was sparse of trees and arid, until reaching the banks of the mighty Snake. The waters of the Snake were the lifeblood of the region. Over millions of years, the river had carved its own vast gorge, Hells Canyon, deep and rugged beyond imagining. The Snake gained water from its tributaries, which included the

The Wallowa Mountains in northeastern Oregon remain formidable even in summer, as this recent photograph demonstrates. (*Author*)

Clearwater River, sourced from the Montana Bitterroot Mountains. The tribe knew all of the canyons and rivers well. The Nez Perce bands had lived on the rivers since time had begun.

The Wallowa tribe had thirty days by Howard's unforgiving schedule to gather their widespread livestock, traverse these obstacles and the unforgiving hazards of the terrain, and reach Lapwai for confinement on the reservation. It would take them many days to cross the 130 miles of their difficult trek. No matter how Joseph examined the dilemma, he felt that time was running out for his people. And still he wondered how he could keep his promise to his father. Joseph made the bitterly hard decision to comply with Howard's orders to go to the Lapwai reservation. He brought his people down from the Wallowa highlands into the Snake River country, leaving much of their livestock behind because they could not be located. Even so, they had many thousands of head of horses and cattle that they had to somehow take over two great rivers.

But first they had to cross rough terrain with their stock and possessions. The Imnaha River canyon provided a route to herd their livestock and move along the banks of its sixty-mile expanse, from the falls and the frigid headwaters of the Wallowa River's mountain drainage sourced from its north and south forks to its mouth, which flowed into the Snake River at Hells Canyon. The Imnaha followed a natural geological fault line on its way to the Snake, which the people moved along in their stoic way. The early going was relatively easy for the tribe during the several days it took to make its way downstream.

The people descended to follow the ravine that the Imnaha had carved, and they passed through the opening where the banks widened into Hells Canyon. The Snake River crossings that were practical for the Wallowa band to use were all in the Hells Canyon gorge, the deepest river gorge in North America. The Nez Perce reached the shore of the Snake River, some eight thousand feet below the highest peak abutting the gorge. They chose to cross at a narrow but very deep and swift place. There, with their livestock, they forded the Snake in their first dangerous crossing.

But the danger was only half over. The Salmon River confluence with the Snake River was only four miles away. The raging Salmon, which they called Ta-Mon-ma, was flowing swiftly with the spring runoff.

The Nez Perce were traveling through extremes of altitude and temperature. As they negotiated the difficult trail, they were moving through a region of rugged yet magnificent beauty. Some livestock was lost crossing the swollen Salmon. Once they climbed out of the river canyons, they were exhausted from the rigors of the crossings. They

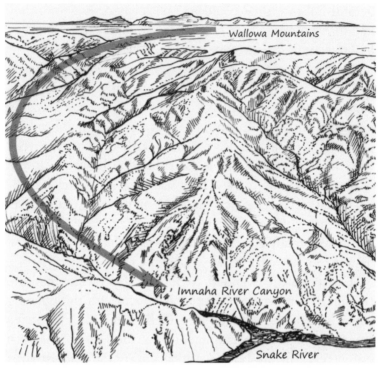

The Nez Perce began their long journey by travelling from the Wallowa highlands to the Snake River. (*Author*)

paused during their difficult trek on the Camas Prairie in Idaho in order to slaughter some of their cattle and to recuperate from the arduous journey in peace. They could not know that events about to be set into motion would allow them neither rest nor peace.

3

The Battle at
White Bird Canyon

On June 12, 1877, White Bird's Nez Perce band of
Lamtama held a tellikleen ceremony at their camp at Tolo
Lake, in the Idaho Territory.[1] Tolo Lake was a favorite
place for a meeting of the bands. The lake was within six
miles of Grangeville on the Camas Prairie. Tolo is the
modern name for the small lake; in 1877, it was called
Tepahlewam (Split Rocks). The ceremony they were con-
ducting was traditionally carried out during times of great
portent, such as war. In this case, the ceremony would com-
memorate the change in their way of life and also serve as
a statement of defiance. It surely included an outcry over
the outrages committed against the Nez Perce bands. The
highlight of the ritual was always a parade of warriors on
horseback in a large circle around their camp.

Foremost among the young Lamtama warriors was
Wahlitas (Shore Crossing). Like a young Achilles, he was
powerful, the best warrior and athlete among the young

men. And he had a nonmetaphorical ax to grind. His father, Eagle Robe, was killed by a white man who suffered no punishment when he was judged by the white man's law for his actions. The recent death of Wind Blowing had caused that wound to fester. During the ceremonial procession, Wahlitas accidentally rode over some camas root being prepared on the ground by women in the village; in anger, an older warrior chided him and questioned his bravery for not avenging his father's death at the hands of the white man.

The old man taunted, "See what you do. Playing brave you ride over my woman's hard-worked food. If you are so brave, why not go kill the white man who killed your father"?[2]

A dark anger rose in the heart of Wahlitas. The murder of his father at the hands of white men occurred in the Salmon River canyons after Eagle Robe had come back to his land after an extended trip. He had discovered that his neighbor, Larry Ott, had enclosed his land and garden with a fence and incorporated parts of Eagle Robe's own homestead. The two men argued and began fighting, with Eagle Robe throwing rocks. Ott retaliated by shooting him with his pistol. Ott was found not guilty of any crime and allowed to return to his land.

Inside Wahlitas, the tightly contained fury burst free. The threats and affronts to his tribe by the US government and the imprisonment of Toohoolhoolzote combined with Howard's threats to use force enraged the young warrior. The insults and egregious crimes against his tribe and family were simply too much.[3] In his rage that evening, during the tellikleen ceremony, he verbally ranted against the settlers who were forcing him and his people from his homeland—and he found a willing audience in his close friends and his cousins. All of the young men had been influenced by the arguments they heard between White Bird and prominent warriors like Yellow Bull and the more moderate men in the Salmon River band, discussing open warfare with the whites.

On the morning of June 13, the still-seething Wahlitas and two of his cousins, Sarpsis Ilppilp (Red Moccasin Tops) and Wetyetmas Wahyakt (Swan Necklace), decided that as they were forced from their lands, they would settle some old scores. Wahlitas decided that their first act would be to kill Ott. As the three made their way to Ott's homestead, tradition maintains that Swan Necklace was unaware of the purpose of their ride. What is consistent in the accounts is that he was a young man and inexperienced, and that his older cousins had brought him along to watch the horses. When they reached Ott's farm, they found it abandoned. Ott had heard that the tribes were being moved and he had gone into hiding, fearing that a tribal member might seek vengeance against him as they passed through the area.

Wahlitas and Sarpsis Ilppilp knew of another white man, Richard Devine, who lived nearby, near Slate Creek. He had been cruel to the Indians in the past and had trained his dogs to attack the Nez Perce. The three cousins rode the eight miles to his homestead. Unlike Ott, Devine was at his house. When he came outside and saw the three young warriors, he quickly ascertained that they intended to kill him. He ran back inside, picked up his gun, and came out shooting at them. Wahlitas fired once and killed him, satisfied with the retribution.[4]

The avengers continued their killing spree, moving on to the John Day ranch. Upon finding that Day was not present, they caught two hired men outside and gunned them down instead.

Three settlers had been killed in the Salmon River Valley—and Wahlitas's rampage had just begun. He and his band of willing young men continued their killing spree for a second day, moving along the John Day Creek, where they murdered three more settlers: Henry Elfers, Robert Bland, and Henry Beckorage.

Farther down along White Bird Creek, Samuel Benedict ran a general store and a small ranch with a fruit orchard. He provided a ferry service and did blacksmithing work. He dealt in whiskey, and as a result he had come to blows with Indians in the past, in one incident shooting and wounding several Indian men, one fatally. Benedict was caught in the open by Wahlitas and his raiders. He was shot through the legs and then followed to his house by the war party, where he was killed. The raiding party allowed his wife, Isabella, and her two daughters, a baby and a five-year-old, to leave. But they killed Benedict's hired man, August Bacon. Their Chinese cook was left unharmed. Isabella Benedict took the children to the Manuel ranch by creeping through the brush along the creek. Her two older children were being schooled and stayed in Mount Idaho. She and her girls reached the Manuel ranch on the evening of the fourteenth.

Jack Manuel was not at the house. Isabella Benedict hid overnight with Manuel's wife, Jeanette, and in the morning started to make her way with her children to Mount Idaho. She had a long trek on foot ahead of her. She and her children avoided the roads and trails, keeping to the brush. It was forty-five miles uphill to the north to get to Grangeville or Mount Idaho over the hot prairie, and there was little shelter from the sun. Mrs. Benedict had to be careful because more angry young warriors were about.

Wahlitas was soon joined by other young men from White Bird's Salmon River band; as many as seventeen extended the violence along the river. Later in the day of June 14, Jack Manuel came upon the war party and was seriously wounded. He was shot through the hips, grazed by a bullet along his skull, and left for dead. James Baker was the last victim that day, killed by Nez Perce arrows.

June 15, the third day of the rampage, saw the deaths of Jeanette Manuel, William Osborne, and Henry Mason at the hands of Wahlitas and his band.[5] On the sixteenth, they set fire to many of the homesteads and ranches they had already raided. Wahlitas shifted his attention from the river to the higher ground above it. The violence was about to move from the Salmon River up onto the prairie.

Jeanette Manuel's baby daughter Maggie was carried away from the trouble by a miner named Patrick Brice. Over time the story became muddled with legend, but the Nez Perce oral tradition holds that Brice encountered several groups of warriors who let him pass on his way, holding the baby girl and heading uphill and out of danger.[6]

Arthur "Ad" Chapman, a settler in the vicinity, arrived in Mount Idaho with news of the outbreak of violence along the Salmon River and warned the settlers to garrison themselves in the town.[7] Another settler, Lew Day, volunteered to take a message to Fort Lapwai in order to alert the authorities and get military help.

Traveling over the prairie, Day passed Benjamin Norton's ranch (also known as Cottonwood House because of the stands of nearby cottonwood trees that had provided the wood used to build it) and was confronted by a band of Indians in the road. The warriors began shooting, and Day was hit twice as he wheeled his horse and rode quickly back to Norton's place to seek shelter and warn his friends.

In 1877, Cottonwood House stood on the high plateau of the Camas Prairie alongside the road from Lewiston to Mount Idaho. It was sixty miles from Lewiston to the ranch, and twenty more miles to Mount Idaho. Because Cottonwood House was the only major structure along that difficult route, almost all traffic and any commerce in the area was conducted among the collection of buildings that made up the station. The structures included a general store, saloon, and hotel. Horses and agriculture were

further served by a smithy as well as stables, barns, and cor-
rals. Norton had acquired the station by the time of the war
and served the freight and travelers who passed along the
road nearby.

Ben Norton must have felt that the station, so far out of
the way, would be vulnerable to the same sort of attacks
that had wreaked such tragedy in the Salmon River area the
previous day. The arrival of the wounded Lew Day on his
doorstep confirmed his fears.

On the night of June 15, Norton decided to leave the
ranch with his family, guests, and employees. He hustled
his charges into his large wagons and made for the safety of
Grangeville, fifteen miles southeast along the main road.
Despite his wounds, Day accompanied the wagons on his
horse. Norton may have hoped that darkness would provide some safety for their journey, but unfortunately they
encountered a band of warriors in the night that attacked
the wagon train. Shots rang out and the horses fell in their
traces. Norton was also shot, and dropped to the road; he
would die of his wounds by morning. His wife, Jennie, was
grievously wounded, as were Lew Day and Norton's ranch
hand, F. Joseph Moore. Day and Moore would die of their
wounds. Two family members, nine-year-old Hill Norton
and eighteen-year-old Lynn Bowers, Jennie Norton's sister,
escaped by running into the darkness. Two others in the
group, John Chamberlain and his baby, were killed in the
attack. Chamberlain's wife was wounded by an arrow and
later raped and killed. Her surviving daughter lay wounded
along the road. A rescue party from Mount Idaho arrived
the next day and collected the wounded.

J. G. Rowton, a citizen who traveled with the relief party
from Mount Idaho, recalled, "The Indians overtook them
about three miles from Grangeville and fired on them. I
helped bring some of the dead next morning. Lew Day
never left his horse when he met and was shot by the three

Indians." Later, Rowton wrote of another killing in the area. "Chas Horton came to Mount Idaho the night of the outbreak—expressed doubts that the Indians were on the warpath. Six days later Horton's body was found a few miles from Ad Smith's house."[8]

Most of the influential chiefs from the Wallowa band, including Joseph and Ollokot, only found out about the killings when they returned to camp from an errand. The camp at the village of Sapachesap was in an uproar. The predominant emotions among the people were disbelief and fear at what might befall them collectively because of the actions of a few. Wottolen (Hair Combed over Eyes), a prominent warrior of White Bird's Lamtama band, later stated, "General Howard had told us we would lose our cattle and horses unless brought in within thirty suns. Seeing that we could do nothing, three young men went out and killed some bad men. Then whiskey was obtained. The warriors, crazed with drink, mistreated and killed a few women and children. This should not have been done."[9]

Back at Fort Lapwai on June 14, General Howard received disturbing dispatches at about 6 p.m. from the Mount Idaho area about the killings along the Salmon River. He suspected that some of the reports were exaggerated, but he also believed that the settlers were in the middle of an Indian uprising. He ordered Captain David Perry, a veteran of both the Civil War and the Modoc Indian War, to lead a force to relieve the settlers. Perry was well liked by his troops; he was a good officer, a little flamboyant, but still untested fighting in the wilds of the Idaho frontier.

Perry was given command of two detachments of cavalry, Troops F and H of the 1st Cavalry, and a troop of infantry. The quartermaster was sent to Lewiston, twelve miles away, to get pack animals loaded with supplies for the mission. As the relief column prepared to depart, General

Howard motioned Perry aside and said, "You must not get whipped." Perry confidently replied, "There is no danger of that, sir."[10]

Howard saw this mission as part of the army's policing role, but the massacre of Lieutenant Colonel George Armstrong Custer and his men at the hands of the Sioux the previous summer was still fresh in everyone's minds.[11] Howard didn't know it yet, but the Nez Perce were even more adept at war in their own terrain.

Pressed for time and sure he could wait no longer for the pack train to return from Lewiston, Perry and his troops left the fort on horseback at 8 p.m., with three days' saddle rations and forty rounds of rifle ammunition per man, bound for Mount Idaho in the evening darkness. If necessary, the pack train would have to trail Perry's force and meet it on the prairie later.

With the news that some young men from White Bird's tribe had exacted revenge on white settlers in the Salmon River area, Joseph and Ollokot decided that the Wallowa band must join with the other tribes for safety. Many of Joseph's people began striking their tipis and making bundles, terrified at the prospect of being blamed for the raids made by the Salmon River band's young men.

White Bird believed that the three cousins would not live to see a fair judgment unless he could arrange to deliver them directly to Fort Lapwai. With their bands combined, White Bird and the other chiefs, with the exception of Looking Glass, believed they would be able to parley from a position of strength and then deliver the men responsible to the authorities at the gate of the fort. Joseph doubted whether giving up the three warriors at this point was a route to peace, but he felt he had to try. On the morning of June 16, fast riders had arrived at Sapachesap with news that a strong force of soldiers was making its way across the prairie toward the village.

Looking Glass and his people wanted no part of the violence that was breaking out, asserting that the fault was with Joseph's and White Bird's bands. They would remain at their village at the junction of the south and middle forks of the Clearwater River, hoping to avoid any trouble.

Chiefs Joseph, White Bird, and Toohoolhoolzote decided they would need a more-defensible area to muster their warriors. Joseph agreed that the Wallowa band must join with the other tribes for safety and led his people to Lama'ta, the village of White Bird's tribe on the Salmon River. The village was at the base of a deep river canyon at the nexus of northern and southern Idaho and close by the confluence of White Bird Creek and the Salmon River.[12] The mountains and basin formed a vast wall with plenty of rugged terrain for defense, ambush, and concealment. The summit above the canyon was nearly a mile in elevation, while at creekside the elevation dropped steeply to one thousand five hundred feet. This was the easiest approach to the village. The surrounding mountains were much higher and impassible for an army. There was no doubt about the trail the soldiers must use. Thus, it would be difficult to approach the village undetected. Captain Perry had experience with Indian combat from the Modoc War, but he did not fully appreciate the challenges he would face fighting the Nez Perce. The Indians would have plenty of warning if the army pursued them.

Nez Perce warriors of the 1870s were capable of fighting semiautonomously, and without direction from commanders. They had spent their entire adult lives learning war craft and the skills that augment its practice. They had to be able to judge terrain and weather in order to hunt and forage. They possessed an uncanny, three-dimensional awareness of the battleground, gained from a harsh and unforgiving lifestyle in the most rugged country in America. They worked together silently in lightning quick horseback raids of rival tribes' horses and staved off those same attacks from other tribes. They learned to judge speed and distance as youths and learned how to fearlessly engage an enemy. Experience counted: many Nez Perce warriors were seasoned by battles against the Shoshone and Blackfoot. In 1863, the Nez Perce and Crow fought as allies against the Dakota in Montana and together defeated that much-stronger Indian nation. Lethal contests like the war with the Dakota kept the warriors of the Nez Perce highly prepared for combat.

In addition, they were magnificent horsemen. Man and animal had long been working together in the horse culture of the Nez Perce tribe.[13] After many generations of selective breeding, the Nez Perce had produced wonderfully strong horses, well adapted to their needs and the environment. The qualities of the Appaloosa made it a perfect horse for canyon, hill, and prairie. The horses were strong, adaptable, and intelligent. This helped in their training and in following the desires of their riders. The Nez Perce possessed many fine warhorses, far better mounts than those of the US Cavalry.

Lieutenant William Parnell, winner of the Medal of Honor for leading the rear guard in the battle at White Bird Canyon, later recounted that the rebellious natives were "armed with shot repeating rifles."[14] Other reliable witnesses report that prior to the Nez Perce War, typical Indian armament varied, consisting of black-powder rifles, shotguns, bow and arrow, lances, and cartridge single-shot and repeating rifles.[15] Some warriors favored sinew-backed bows, often with horn-reinforced nocks. Arrows were fashioned from naturally straight stalks of Syringa. The arrowheads were of razor sharp obsidian stone or sharpened metal.[16]

The Nez Perce have had a long relationship with the horse and are noted for their distinctive Appaloosa breed as well as their horsemanship. The warrior on the left carries a firearm while the other is holding a lance. (*Washington State University Library, MASC*)

Most warriors carried a short stone club called a kopluts and a large knife. Tomahawks were used, but the more traditional kopluts was preferred in battle. When properly built, the weapon had a relatively short handle so that in a close-quarter fight, the opponent could not grasp the handle and contend for the weapon. The head was an oval or round stone three to four inches long and bound to the wooden handle with sinews. It was an extremely effective weapon in close quarters, and its sole purpose was to crush a skull or break an arm bone. Chief Joseph's young nephew Yellow Wolf was said to have built his war club as a young man under the guidance of a wyakin spirit. It was common to name weapons in order to invest them with spiritual power as an extension of the warrior.

The fighting techniques of the Nez Perce horsemen were a marvel. The warriors hung precariously from the sides of their mounts for cover while shooting under the horses' necks. They could turn and shoot arrows and bullets to the rear—if being chased—in their own version of the Parthian shot. They could reload at a full horseback charge. Quirts made with a wooden handle and leather straps were used to urge their horses to greater speed. There were many accounts of warriors moving from a gallop on horseback to becoming dismounted infantry in a split second. They would accomplish this maneuver acrobatically without halting the horse, finally coming to rest prone and firing. When used by a skilled warrior, the horse was not just transportation—it was a deadly weapon.

General Howard later recounted the skill at arms of his enemy:

> The wild Indians were well armed with many breach-loading rifles and pistols. . . . The former were constantly trained by their unceasing racings and firings. . . . The non-treaties had made themselves, like the irregular Cossacks of Russia, the best skirmishers in the world. They are quick-sighted, superior marksmen, and subject to sufficient discipline when following their recognized chiefs to scatter, run to cover, and reassemble without disbanding.[17]

White Bird epitomized the warrior ethos in strength of body and mind. He was on his home ground and in overall command of the defense of his people, the Lamtama, and the other tribes that had joined him. He decided to utilize his greatest advantage against the cavalry when it came. He would use the terrain to prepare strong, hidden positions for his mounted warriors. White Bird was willing to let the enemy have the high ground initially as it advanced into the canyon. He knew that the deeper the cavalry rode into the steep valleys, the easier it would be to flank it from the commanding and higher positions along any of the steep ravines and bluffs that overlooked the approach to the Salmon River. White Bird was confident that if the army fell into static positions, he would surround it and overcome it from all sides. If the cavalry tried to retreat, he intended to break it into smaller groups and drive it into a killing ground in a box canyon or ravine.

To provide early warning, he placed four scouts along the trail into the canyon and sentries on several bluffs. He advised the subchiefs to stay hidden with their men until he gave the order to attack. White Bird respected Joseph's desire to have a parlay and a truce on their terms. But he reasoned that the situation was too volatile not to prepare for war.

The soldiers had ridden overnight to reach Cottonwood House, where they stopped for an hour to feed and water the horses and make coffee for themselves. At 10 p.m., they began the second night of their sixty-hour forced march with no sleep, on their way to the Salmon River, some twenty miles farther ahead. Before the troops reached Grangeville, they were stopped by a group of citizens who volunteered to act as guides and help them defeat the Indians. They also declared that the numbers of the warriors were not great, and they predicted an easy victory.[18]

The typical cavalry soldier in the Columbia command in the mid-1870s was not a veteran of any actions against tribal warriors or any other foe. Some of the troopers barely knew how to ride their green mounts, which were not yet trained to endure close-weapons fire. The cavalry force did contain some veteran officers or noncommissioned officers. Many officers and NCOs earned their spurs in the Civil War and the Indian Wars in fights against the Modoc along the California-Oregon border and the Indians of the Great

Plains. Most of the soldiers had received only basic orientation with their weapons at their initial training depots and barracks. The routine of workaday camp details and guard duties had contributed to a dilution of their basic military training. Their drill was particularly lacking regarding horsemanship and tactical operations. Only a few cartridges were allotted annually for target practice. Marksmanship and range practice were not given high priority in the typical routine of post duties.

Soldiers stationed at Fort Lapwai were serving in a backwater post. The fort was not considered as important as nearby Fort Walla Walla, and as a result, training and preparations suffered. Many of the new men at the fort arrived by riverboat prior to winter with little training. The weather prevented further drills. Most of their garrison time was devoted to maintaining the buildings in the compound. By the time spring came to the area, they had only a few months in which to prepare for a possible conflict.

Each mounted trooper in 1877 had been issued the Model 1873 Springfield Trapdoor single-shot, breech-loading carbine as his primary weapon. It was a serviceable rifle in the hands of a trained soldier. The rifle fired a .45–70 cartridge and was the first breech-loading rifle used widely in the army. On the downside, the weapon was prone to jamming, a fault commonly believed to have played a role in the massacre of Custer's men at the Little Big Horn. A seasoned soldier could do very well with the carbine. Familiarity and practice would ensure that a trooper could load fast, clear a jam if necessary, and do so with the muscle memory from hours of practice even in the dark or poor weather. Alas, weapons maintenance was not a priority, and it was equally unlikely that the soldiers had enough time with the weapon to have its mechanism and operation become second nature to them. The most obvious disadvantage of the weapon was the single shot and complicated

A trooper from Fort Walla Walla photographed in 1898 wearing the uniform and carrying the arms of a typical US cavalryman of the Nez Perce War period. (*Whitman College and Northwest Archives*)

operation of the trapdoor mechanism. It had the advantages of being compact and lightweight for mounted use, and its accuracy in experienced hands was never questioned. The cartridge was powerful, with a fifty-five-grain powder charge. At three thousand yards its accuracy fell off considerably, but the round still had plenty of power left at that distance. Used in disciplined volley fire, the weapon was devastating.

The troopers' sidearm was the Model 1873 Colt single-action army pistol, not the pattern 1860 percussion pistol they had carried before. The Model 1873 .45-caliber handgun was accurate, with plenty of stopping power. With the look of the archetypical Western revolver, it utilized a modern cartridge rather than percussion-fired powder charges and balls in the chambers. Quick to load compared to the earlier weapon, this pistol was also the most powerful handgun in the world at the time. The entire motion of retraction of the hammer and rotation of the cylinder was manual. Once the weapon was cocked, the trigger pull would release the hammer to fire the weapon.

The leader of the quickly assembled citizen volunteers was George Shearer, a former major in the Confederate army, whom Lieutenant Parnell described as a "brave man and a genial good fellow."[19] Shearer had ample military experience, but most of the ten men with him did not.

The exhausted troops reached the edge of the prairie and the beginning of the canyon at 1 a.m. on June 17. At the head of the summit, beginning the descent into the canyon from the north, Captain Perry organized his troops into three groups as they left the established road. The strategy that Parnell and his contemporary officers used when facing a native foe was to attempt to make their forces look larger than they were by deploying in column and spacing out the line so that the perceived size of their host would intimidate the enemy. Perry chose to deploy his troops in this fashion to cause indecision and dissuade any preemptive attack.

Perry ordered Lieutenant Edward R. Theller and a detachment of eight to ten cavalry scouts drawn from Company F to advance in the lead, accompanied by Ad Chapman, who offered his aid as guide into the Salmon River country. Chapman also acted as an interpreter; he was married to an Umatilla woman and spoke the language fluently.

Trooper John Jones, who had been in the stockade with Toohoolhoolzote, was among Theller's advance guard. Perry ordered Theller to advance farther into the valley, halt when the hostile Indians were sighted, deploy in a skirmish line, and then signal Perry. This small detail moved out to a distance of about one hundred yards ahead of the main body. Behind Theller's detail, Perry led Troop F and the small party of citizen volunteers riding in a column of fours. Captain Joel Trimble was leading a rear-guard column, Troop H, fifty yards farther back. Perry's command consisted of ninety-one regulars and eleven volunteers.

Captain David Perry commanded at Fort Lapwai in the Idaho Territory at the start of the Nez Perce War. (*National Archives*)

Perry's guides assured him that the steep trail opened onto a relatively smooth valley. The troops paused at the rim of the canyon to prepare. At this time, Perry did not order the men to dismount and tighten their saddle cinch straps. He gave the order for them to load a round into their carbines. He also ordered them to remove their bulky overcoats. Within a few miles they emerged from the ravine, and the canyon opened before them.

Perry had never been to the White Bird Canyon and relied on Chapman and Shearer to guide the column. Due to fear of ambush in the predawn darkness, the command's approach into the canyon was slow and cautious. Perry ordered his men to wait until the first faint light of dawn to proceed down the steep trail.

The native sentries posted atop several of the buttes and along the trail had heard the movement of men and equipment for some time and were able to see the troopers in the dim light. The sentries made an animal call to rouse the sleeping warriors below and send word to the camp. Lieutenant Parnell heard a single howling coyote call, which he believed must be an Indian scout sounding a stealthy alarm.

White Bird may have destroyed most of the stolen whiskey that the raiding warriors tried to drink the night before, but by morning some were still too sick to fight. He left the hungover to their misery and roused those who were fit to fight. White Bird was assembling his available warriors and calling them to action, and his quirt awakened any man sleeping in an alcohol stupor. The sober warriors who had wisely abstained from whiskey were quietly joining Ollokot and his hidden war party in the deep groove of a butte.

After a quick conference with his brother and White Bird, Joseph mounted his horse and rode into the camp, organizing his people to gather their belongings and make their way to the Salmon River. He planned to return in order to parley with the troopers after calming the panic in the camp and making preparations in case they needed to move.

While the cavalry streamed into the head of the valley, the chiefs stealthily placed men behind the base of two larger buttes near the bottom of the canyon. White Bird knew that these natural formations effectively concealed the artifacts of the disassembled camp, their many horses, and the groups of warriors in hiding. They also screened the movement of children and elders from the area farther down White Bird Creek.

In 1877, the canyon was covered everywhere with native grasses, timothy, rye, and bunch grass, in some places reaching up to a man's waist. Perry was worried about unseen attackers in the grass on his flanks. Although the ground was described to him as most favorable to cavalry once the incline was negotiated, all he saw were inclines, irregularities, and obstacles as they moved cautiously ahead.

Looking down at the White Bird Canyon battlefield in 1932.
(*Washington State University Library, MASC*)

The descent into the canyon began at 3 a.m. The column moved single file down the steep hill, using an old wagon trail. This was the route Chapman would normally take. On the way, the soldiers discovered Isabella Benedict, whose husband had been killed by the rogue band of White Bird's warriors. She was clutching an injured child, with another close behind. She had been making her way cautiously from the Salmon River with her children, trying to get to the settlement at Mount Idaho. The soldiers gave her water and food and found a place for them to hide until a detachment could pick them up later on their return and take them to safety.

As the column approached the two small buttes farther down the canyon, Chapman led them to the left of the formations on an easy trail. In the darkness, there was no effort made to send the scouts onto the high benches for a more complete view of the ground and to ascertain the position of the Nez Perce camp. Perry's knowledge of the potential fighting ground was lacking, as most of his experience had been in Oregon and in California during the Modoc War. He had entered the rugged valley in the very early morning in the dark with cavalry and mounted troops that were only effective as dismounted infantry. And he had yet to measure the strength and capabilities of his enemy.

In contrast, Chief White Bird and his companion, Chief Ollokot, had spent many days at Fort Lapwai taking measure of the fighting methods of their adversaries. They understood very well how the bugle was used to signal the troops to gather in many different fighting formations, to sound the advance, a halt, and a charge. Thanks to White Bird, the Nez Perce warriors knew the meaning of those commands as well as the soldiers did. If it came to battle, White Bird meant to press the attack. He had observed the linear fighting style of his enemy; he would drive for the army's flank when it became overextended and then press his own strong attack when the soldiers, or bluecoats, retreated. He would use the knowledge and observations he had gained while watching the soldiers drill. While at Lapwai, White Bird had never missed the troopers' training as he sat on his horse, smoking and watching, his face impassive. He was determining the methods by which the soldiers could be defeated.

Perry received word from Theller's dispatch rider that he had sighted the enemy. Perry's troop moved into line at a trot. He ordered the citizens to the round knoll on his left. The volunteers skirted the battle line and took a position on the extreme left on a rocky height, anchoring the line and defending against a flanking attack from that side. From that height they could command all approaches. Parnell brought Troop H up in line on the right of Perry. Perry's entire command was committed, with no reserve available.

A small group of six Indians, selected by Joseph, rode out to parley with Theller and his skirmishers in full headdress

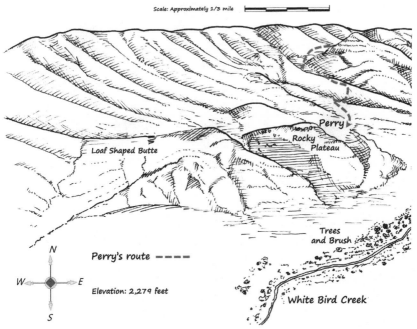

Scale: Approximately 1/3 mile

Perry

Rocky
Plateau

Loaf Shaped Butte

Trees
and Brush

N

Perry's route ‒ ‒ ‒ ‒

W   E

Elevation: 2,279 feet

S

White Bird Creek

Perry's advance into White Bird Canyon, June 17, 1877. (*Author*)

and war regalia, but they also carried a flag of truce. Joseph badly needed to find a peaceful solution to the dangerous confrontation, and he hoped they could come to terms.

The assembled soldiers were quiet as the small band approached. Before the Indian riders met Theller's line, shots broke the calm. The volunteers holding the rocky point had opened fire at Joseph and his companions. The Indians hiding among the rocks returned fire, and dust flew up around the parley mission. Chapman had begun the shooting: he mistakenly believed that skirmishers were moving up to attack the volunteers. Joseph's delegates wheeled their horses sharply and charged back behind the nearest large butte as shots rang out from both sides.

The troops immediately found that the Indians were at a tactical advantage. At the outset, the natives were on foot, using the natural cover of brush grass and the shelter of willows and cottonwood trees.

Down in the creek bed, the diminutive Chief Two Moons (Lepeet Hessemdooks) had gathered some of the best warriors with him to prepare an attack.[20] With him were a number of older men who took cover along the creek bed and loaded their muzzle loaders. A shot from the vicinity of the creek killed Trooper Jones instantly; Toohoolhoolzote had no opportunity to keep his promise. One of the older warriors with Two Moons, shooting from the creek, had made the remarkable shot at great distance. The impact of the well-aimed ball would play heavily in the outcome of the battle. The loss of young Jones, who was a bugler, removed Perry's means of directing his troops.[21] The mounted troopers were easy targets, and several were shot from their horses. Troops began to dismount of their own accord. Sensing the situation, Perry quickly gave an official order to dismount and for horse handlers to take the horses to a depression to the rear. This reduced Perry's effective fighting force, as every fourth man was removed from fighting in order to hold four horses. He then ordered Lieutenant Theller to take command of the battle line.

With most of the soldiers now dismounted, they began to advance directly toward White Bird's front. They could see a chief and his mounted warriors executing a flanking movement to their left. The advance of Troop H had been halted in the face of withering fire by a native skirmish line that appeared on foot from behind the rocky butte. Other warriors rapidly climbed the butte and began firing into the soldiers. The group of older warriors who killed Jones continued to fire their accurate muzzle-loading rifles from farther down the creek.

Trimble instructed First Sergeant Michael McCarthy and six troopers to take and hold a rocky point that overlooked the ravine and the western side of the ridgeline to their front. His instructions were to stop the flanking movements on the left of the line. He saw a strong position on the point with good cover facing the enemy, although it was exposed from behind. He and his men would occupy that spot. But first he had to get there. The formation was contested by a small group of warriors. Trimble rode out with the squad to the position as McCarthy led his men in a fighting charge to clear the way to the rocks. Lieutenant Parnell took over the troop in Trimble's absence. A brief gunfight at close quarters dislodged the warriors barring their way to the point. Captain Trimble then returned to take command of his company. McCarthy surveyed the large formation of boulders half buried in the earth. He set his men in positions with good fields of fire to defend the lines of the men behind who were depending on them.

McCarthy was a good choice for a tough assignment. Born in Newfoundland, his Celtic parents had instilled in him a tough outlook on life in general, and he applied it to combat in particular. He had served with distinction in the US Civil War and the Modoc campaigns, and had skirmished with Apaches and Mexican forces on the US southern border.

Perry rode to the right to confer with Trimble as he returned, observing that he had occupied a high point on the right of the ridge, and told him that if that place could not be held, they needed to find a better defensive position. He also asked if Company H had a trumpet and was horrified to learn it did not. He was having trouble sending commands up and down the line, and his troops were caught up in the din, smoke, and peril of battle. The word was sent for McCarthy to rejoin the line.

Trimble advised Perry that they should summon the troops, call back McCarthy and his men, bring their horses, and charge to the point that McCarthy had just held, as the rocky bluff was a natural fortress and the highest ground. As McCarthy rode back with his men, Trimble ordered him to retake the bluff. Trimble promised he would rally the men and would then reinforce McCarthy.

A disappointed McCarthy wrote later, "The main body of troops, however, did not reach the bluff or apparently even come close to it. The men became scattered in the charge and the column disintegrated. For the second time, the cavalrymen turned to the rear in hasty retreat."[22]

McCarthy regained the bluff, although he and his men were soon cut off from escape. McCarthy got his men together, and they made a desperate charge through gunfire to rejoin the retreating troops.

Perry saw individual men deserting from the line on the left and running to the rear to retrieve their horses. He rode back quickly to stem the collapse of the line.

Chief Ollokot joined the battle as he and his warriors emerged at full charge from behind one of the two largest buttes. They circled and slammed into the right flank, held by Trimble's Company H, which was mostly still mounted. In a few minutes, Ollokot's warriors broke through the line, separating groups of troopers from each other. Trimble rode out from the line in the direction of the volunteers on the left in order to reach a high point to better see the disposition of the enemy and determine what he could do to defend the flank.

Several steady and seasoned warriors had dismounted and were creeping among the depressions and small ravines where they had been concealed. They attacked toward the flank of the line of soldiers on White Bird's extreme right. Native skirmishers made daring charges on foot and horseback to telling effect. These attacks by single warriors were a show of prowess and bravery, and they also demonstrated the strength of their supernatural wyakin powers, which were believed to make a warrior invincible through the presence of a powerful guardian spirit. If there was time prior to battle, warriors prepared themselves for combat through physical and spiritual rites that included painting

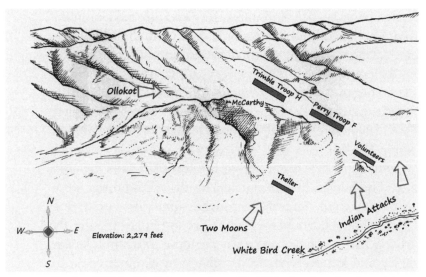

Battle of White Bird Canyon, June 17, 1877, showing the disposition of US forces and Indian attacks. (*Author*)

their bodies, donning charms and amulets, and chanting war and death songs created by the individual warriors.

Before the battle with Perry began, three young warriors—Wahlitas, Sarpsis Ilppilp, and Strong Eagle (Tipyahlahnah Kapskaps)—had put on red coats made from the same fabric, which they wore in battle. Thereafter they were known as the Three Red Coats.[23]

Now, more warriors rode up, dismounted, and climbed up the rocks firing. With a series of fierce attacks by the Indians led by the Three Red Coats, the volunteers were driven from their position on the rocky knoll anchoring the left of Perry's line.[24] Trimble found the volunteers riding past him, away from the battle. Chapman was in the lead on a fast horse. He shouted to Trimble that Norton's ranch was the best place to make a stand. Perry saw the citizens leaving the field in full retreat exposing his left flank. He was now in danger of being flanked on both sides.

Realizing he had no buglers to direct his troops, Perry told Theller to hold his position. The combination of riders leaving the field, exposed flanks, and accurate enemy fire began to have a telling effect on the army formations. Panic began to ripple through the ranks. Trimble was caught up in the flow of the full-blown retreat by the left flank. Lieutenant Parnell assumed leadership on the line of Troop H.

Enfilading fire swept across the left of Perry's exposed line. The horses, held in the depression behind them, were also threatened, and as he looked uphill he noted that Ollokot's attack would soon flank Troop H on the right. By driving hard to their flank and extending to Trimble's rear, they could kill everyone in Trimble's troop, or drive on to take the horses behind them.

In order to halt Ollokot's advance, Perry decided he needed to move higher up the hill. He gave the order to his troops to prepare to move, shouting to his sergeants to shift the men to the rear and their right. The troops reclaimed their mounts and began edging up the slopes to the right, passing behind Troop H, which was actively engaged with the enemy to its front.

More troopers fell from the intense rifle fire. Some of the horse handlers could not control the mounts they were keeping in the ravine, and several horses ran away out of control. In the confusion of seeing Trimble's men falling back and the volunteers in full retreat after being forced from their strong point, many of the soldiers in Troop F began a disorderly dash up the hill in spite of Perry's efforts to rally them and make the withdrawal orderly.

Instead of re-forming up on Parnell's right, Troop F kept on ascending the heights to the west, disappearing from Parnell's view. Parnell saw Theller and his detachment also attempt to climb to the heights, following well behind Troop F. He could also see that they were being overtaken by a formidable body of warriors.

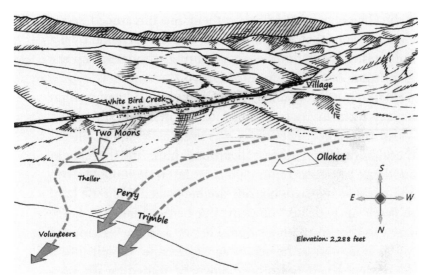

The withdrawal of the volunteers guarding Perry's left flank led to the panic that swept through the troops. As they fled, Lieutenant Theller and his men made two rear-guard stands against the warriors. (*Author*)

Trimble found Theller out of breath, wounded, and on foot. He ordered a stray horse caught for him. Then Perry ordered Theller to make a stand against the flanking attack. Theller grimly accepted his mission and was given twelve men. They managed to deflect the first enemy charge by pouring fire at the mounted attack. Afterward, the intense young officer explained quickly to his men that they would advance up the trail and set up another rearguard position.

The small command was forced off of the trail and into a narrow canyon by a party of warriors. Cornered and cut off, with their backs to a sheer rock wall, they were all killed by Ollokot's young warriors. Indian accounts of the fight describe this small group of soldiers fighting valiantly and dying with honor.[25]

Troop H was in an untenable position. It was flanked on both sides and had been overridden by mounted warriors. Parnell believed it was suicide to follow Theller up to the

right. The enemy had flanked them and threatened encir-
clement from that direction. The soldiers reclaimed what
horses they could and began a fighting withdrawal up the
main route out of White Bird Canyon.

Without reinforcements, McCarthy's squad had to fight
its way from its rocky redoubt back toward its own lines.
Most were killed. McCarthy was eventually unhorsed, but
there were loose horses all around him, and he caught
another. Some accounts indicate he rode double with
another man; perhaps he rode double twice.[26] He rode hard
to catch up with his company, but before long that horse
was also shot from under him. He saw a native warrior firing at him, and as he scrambled to escape, he fell into a
depression. Keeping his head down, he waited for the warriors to finish him off, but he quickly realized that the warriors must have believed him dead from the way he fell
close to the moment of the rifle shot. Once the Indians had
gone, he began to crawl through a brushy ravine to safety.[27]

McCarthy recalled in his journal that he crawled into a
small stream very slowly and lay in the water "about fifteen
minutes allowing the water to flow over my legs and
employing the time planning an escape. It was rather a difficult thing to attempt to leave the creek for the hills were
steep and bare upon both sides and there was no doubt of
there being Indians about." He started slowly moving up
the bank of the stream and heard "the patter of a pony's
hoofs on the road above me. Two warriors returning from
the pursuit. . . . It didn't seem possible that they could avoid
seeing me, but they did not."[28]

In his retreat, Parnell ordered his troops to dash from
knoll to knoll, turning to present defensive fire at the
advancing warriors in order to avoid being cut off. Of his
original command, only fourteen remained. He periodically halted and posted a line of men, calling for fire as the
Indians drew near. He managed to hold his attackers at bay

as the hard-pressed soldiers tried to extricate themselves. At the head of the Canyon, Troop F, then at a strength of twenty men, was holding the mesa above Parnell's Troop H. Behind both was a deep ravine. Perry ordered Parnell to hold the heights while Perry took his troops across. Perry explained that he would provide cover for Troop H as it crossed that dangerous ground under pursuit. Parnell later wrote, "I watched his crossing so as to be ready to move when he had his men in position, but again they tailed him. They had not yet recovered from their unfortunate stampeded condition."[29]

Perry and his men reached the heights above the ravine and once again disappeared out of sight. Feeling forsaken after making a fighting charge to attain the heights, the disheartened Troop H joined the remaining command and regrouped at an abandoned ranch a mile past the ravine. They were quickly dislodged by fierce attacks. It was now 7 a.m., and the troops were badly short of ammunition and exhausted from the steep climb. Parnell called his men to gather the courage to stand, and rallied stragglers to him as he continued to lead the desperate defense of the retreat.

The injured woman and children left on the trail were helped by a citizen volunteer named Charley Crooks; a Sergeant Shaw and an enlisted man from Parnell's fleeing force helped as well. They would all eventually make their way to Grangeville, but not without more drama and danger. The two soldiers took the children and bound them to themselves as they rode. Mrs. Benedict had to ride a spare stray horse that Shaw had found. As they neared the summit, the ride was hard and steep. Mrs. Benedict was not a strong rider and fell behind, trailing the retreat. The cinch strap that held her saddle upright was not tight enough, and the saddle turned, rolling toward the horse's underbelly, and spilled her to the ground. The panicked horse ran on. Exhausted and frightened, she took some solace that her children had been saved. She waited for death. She could hear the drumbeat of the Nez Perce horses' hooves as the riders' speed increased as they pursued the fleeing soldiers.

Seeing that Parnell had organized a blocking force, Perry ordered him to reorganize his command and deploy a larger, reinforced skirmish line as they continued their fighting retreat. This rear guard was larger than Theller's hastily assembled force, and the ground had by now leveled, giving the defenders greater visibility of the enemy and clear fields of fire.

Parnell recalled the desperate struggle:

> With what men I could collect together I now commenced falling back, fighting, by the way we came; that is, up the White Bird Canyon. I saw that it would be suicidal to attempt to reach the bluffs on our right, so we slowly retreated up the ravine, holding the Indians in check from knoll to knoll. I saw that halt must be made pretty soon to tighten up our saddle-girths, so, posting a few men in a little rise in front to hold the Indians, I dismounted and readjusted my saddle, directing the men to do the same. We then took position on the right knoll and from knoll to knoll fell back, waiting at every halt until the Indians came near enough to receive the contents of our carbines. They were swarming in front of us and on the hillsides on both flanks, but the few brave fellows with me obeyed every command with alacrity. I think there were thirteen or fourteen men altogether.
>
> The Indians dared not approach too closely, yet at one time they were near enough for my last pistol cartridge to hit one of them in the thigh. We had several miles of this kind of work up through the can[y]on, but the men were now cool and determined and fully alive to the perilous situation we

were in. When we reached the head of the cañon, we were rejoiced to find Perry's men, who had been falling back in a line nearly parallel with us, on the mesa above. He had eighteen or twenty men with him. I had not seen him since he reached the bluffs two hours before, and neither of us knew anything about the whereabouts or fate of the other. Our meeting no doubt saved the massacre of either or both parties, for we had yet about eighteen miles to fight our way back ere we could hope for succor.[30]

Chief White Bird, along with Two Moons and Ollokot, led several charges with seventy mounted warriors but was repulsed by the concentrated volley fire from the dismounted skirmishers. The men were down to a few rounds of ammunition each when they met a relief party from Mount Idaho. Several times the massed, mounted warriors tried to drive the cavalry off of the prairie into Rocky Canyon and certain destruction. Eventually, White Bird called off the pursuit. The troops had reached safety after a retreat of sixteen torturous miles. By 10 a.m., the soldiers reached the protection of Grangeville. Perry was unhappy to find Trimble already safely ensconced. Trimble seemed unnerved in his first encounter with the Nez Perce.

When Perry checked his troops, he found he had only thirty-eight men. He oversaw the hasty construction of a palisade, and his remaining men dug in, hoping that many others had survived and would eventually find their way back. In the meantime, surrounded and haunted by uncertainty—still in shock at the outcome of the battle—they waited for General Howard to bring reinforcements.

4

The Fight for the Prairie

General Oliver Howard waited anxiously at Fort Lapwai for additional help to arrive from Boise to the south. He knew that the first days of the conflict were critical. If he had the men, he would have put garrisons in the small prairie towns and taken to the offensive immediately. He would also have made another attempt to seek Joseph out through the Christian treaty Indians and see what had caused the outbreak of violence. He was frustrated to be far to the rear awaiting help from the distant army units he called to action. He was thankful that he had positioned some extra troops closer during the meetings with the tribes in Lapwai, but he knew it would be some time before the number of troops that he needed to protect the two towns and go on the offensive could be assembled.

First Sergeant McCarthy, left behind and stranded after the rout at White Bird Canyon, would be days making his way on foot back to Cottonwood House. He later received a Medal of Honor and published his memoirs with commentary on the battle and the ensuing Nez Perce War. This fame in no small part contributed to his later rising from a noncommissioned officer to the first adjutant general of the Washington National Guard.

Perry knew that he had failed by underestimating the formidable enemy he faced. He replayed the battle in his mind, dissecting the failures and what he might have done differently. Scouting the terrain more thoroughly would have changed the direction he took and the course of the battle. He knew enough of Indian warfare to set skirmishers wide on the ridges of his flanks. Extending a strong downhill force of skirmishers while keeping to higher ground on the approach would have been prudent.

Instead, Ad Chapman had led the soldiers by a lower trail, and Perry was unable to see the complete picture with the sloping diagonal ridge and higher buttes ahead of him. The disposition of the forces arrayed against him had been hidden by the mountainous terrain. If his objective was the village, this higher path would have led him directly there with his companies intact, and Ollokot's ambush would have been revealed in the process. He had faced an unfortunate position when he moved his troops into such difficult and unknown terrain. White Bird had picked it for that reason. He had moved the Indian camp from Tolo Lake to an area that he felt confident they could defend.

The men in Perry's command had inadequate training and ammunition for the extended fight at hand. The lack of ammunition nearly sealed their fate during the retreat.

Anchoring the extreme left flank with more-seasoned troops and a senior noncommissioned officer would have strengthened that position.

Inexperience and poor horsemanship also contributed to the defeat. Every officer knew that training and drill were often the answer to a deficit of skill. Trimble and Parnell were excellent riders and could certainly help the less-experienced men with their horsemanship. The unexpected lack of bugles had disabled their ability to communicate among and between companies. When Perry deployed into static positions and chose to fight dismounted—a US cavalry strategy used throughout the Civil War—he provided another key advantage to his adversary. The contest changed from a cavalry battle on horseback to the Nez Perce light horse against dismounted infantry. Only considerable training on horseback, regular patrols, and hard riding on a daily basis could have prepared his men for fighting from horseback. This problem was widespread throughout the Western commands, where the army fought Indian campaigns through attrition and logistics rather than skill.[1]

Perry's noncommissioned officers failed to order the men to readjust their saddle cinch straps, resulting in the saddles turning and causing the men to be thrown from their horses. The failure of the Mount Idaho volunteers to hold their position eventually led to a general rout, with every man scrambling for a horse. Perry had faced difficult situations in the past. But even in tough combat during the Civil War and the Modoc campaigns, he had fought on to victory. Two precise charges by the Nez Perce had startled the troops. The officers and noncommissioned officers had seen a charge by mounted warriors before; an Indian attack would most often wheel about before reaching the army line. In this case, the first charge by Ollokot overran the troops and threatened the rear. Two Moons took the initiative to exploit the situation and hit the left flank with a charge that caused the men to break and run. After the battle of White Bird Canyon, Perry realized he had to learn a new style of warfare against a foe of unprecedented skill at arms. He had been outthought and outfought, and it rankled. He knew he would face severe criticism over the complete Indian victory.

In a court of inquiry later, Perry was not gracious to the memory of Lieutenant Theller, claiming he was "nervous" when ordered to lead the rear guard.[2] By that time, Theller had been wounded at least twice and was still fighting. The young lieutenant knew the danger he and his men were in given the nature of the stand he was ordered to make against a fearsome attack. Theller's valiant defense relieved the pressure on the other two companies long enough for them to gain high ground and regroup. This selfless act in the execution of Perry's orders saved the life of many troopers that day.

Lieutenant William Parnell's sound leadership in his continuous rearguard actions allowed the rest of the cavalry to gain the safety of fortified Grangeville. Parnell had a remarkable military past. He was a forty-one-year-old Irish immigrant, a veteran of the Crimean War and of the American Civil War. And he was one of the few men to survive the bloody charge into the "Valley of Death" at Balaclava, immortalized in Alfred, Lord Tennyson's poem "The Charge of the Light Brigade." Yet Parnell counted himself fortunate to be alive after the battle at White Bird Canyon. He knew what a debacle looked like, and he had survived big calamities before by keeping his head, but Parnell had not been facing cannon and canister this time. He knew he could prevent his troops from being overrun. He was exhausted but calm, and his leadership steadied and reassured the young men around him, many of whom were also Irish. Some were mere boys who had enlisted by falsifying their ages in order to become one of "Custer's Avengers" in the West.[3] Parnell's comrades in arms were fortunate that he commanded the rear guard during their retreat, or they may have all joined Custer in death.

At the close of the battle, the Nez Perce had few, if any, casualties. For the cavalry, the toll was thirty-three men lost in action. In his dispatches, General Howard reported fourteen civilian deaths from the Indian raids on the Salmon River.[4]

White Bird and Ollokot had halted the fighting after chasing the army back to Cottonwood House. The victorious warriors withdrew and rode back to White Bird Canyon. Warriors, women, and children recovered many army carbines, pistols, and precious ammunition from the battleground.

The Nez Perce had routed a US Army force from White Bird Canyon and were able to move at their own speed to the rugged safety of the Salmon River country. This move also gave them access to the Wallowas should they choose to return to Joseph's homeland. More importantly, they controlled the Camas Prairie and the country between there and the approach to Walla Walla.

Edward Robie, a miner in the area, rode tirelessly looking for Isabella Benedict, who had fallen from her horse during the retreat. He chanced going all the way back to the lip of the canyon. Downhearted, he turned around and headed back. Riding toward Cottonwood House, he came upon Benedict—alive. She had been walking for a day, avoiding the road. She was found by Indians after the battle and set back on the trail. Her popularity with the tribe no doubt saved her life, as they remembered many kindnesses in better times. The two rode the rest of the way back on Robie's horse, and she held onto him hard for fear of falling again. He did not object, as he had secretly been in love with the woman for years, admiring her from a discrete distance. Sweet and kind, she had worked hard to raise her children and take care of her husband.

An exhausted courier reached Walla Walla on June 19. He carried news from Lewiston, Idaho, of the army's defeat in the initial encounter with the Nez Perce. He left citizens

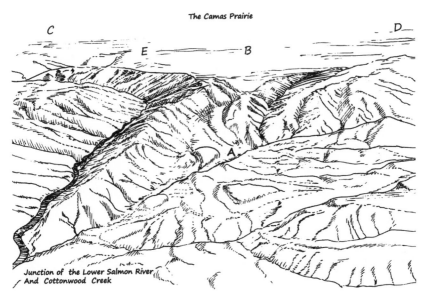

The Camas Prairie

C

D

E   B

A

Junction of the Lower Salmon River
And Cottonwood Creek

A view of White Bird Canyon and the Camas Prairie beyond. A. White Bird Canyon; B. Grangeville; C. Cottonwood House; D. Site of the Battle of the Clearwater; E. Tolo Lake. (*Author*)

with the distinct impression that more than the high prairie was threatened following the battle.

Thomas Page, the Walla Walla County auditor, was concerned enough to start an effort to raise a company of volunteers.[5] The citizenry met at the county courthouse at 1 p.m. That morning, speeches of solidarity had been made proclaiming support for, and the need to help, the people on the far side of the Palouse River and over the Clearwater. To that end, a roster was started at the courthouse meeting to record the names of men willing to go to Lewiston's aid. Soon, one hundred men had volunteered. Those who owned horses set out immediately for Lewiston. Prominent among the volunteers was twenty-year-old Charles Blewett, a good rider and an outdoorsman. He was about to play an important, if tragic, role in the Nez Perce War. Several men who had signed the roster weren't able to retrieve their horses and were absent at the outset; the rest were eager to get underway, and they hoped the others could catch up later. They mounted and rode to the east, heading for threatened Lewiston.

The volunteers arrived in Dayton, Washington, thirty-six miles away, at 1 the next morning. Men and horses slept in the livery until daybreak. The men traveled on at first light, eventually meeting Captain Stephen G. Whipple on the main road to Lewiston. Whipple and his regular troops continued on the main wagon road while the volunteers rode the ridges over a higher trail that gave them a better overview of the terrain.

The volunteers reached Pataha along the mountain trail and stopped for two hours to rest and water the horses. They started up the trail again and made their way to Dan Favor's ranch as the sun was setting. They were about fifteen miles from Lewiston at sundown. The volunteers found places for their horses and themselves to spend the night. Whipple's column rolled in behind them and also quartered on the ranch for the night.

The following morning, the men traveled together and met with Major William F. Spurgeon at Lewiston. The major told the volunteers that there was no immediate threat to Lewiston, but if they wanted to proceed and be of service, it would be in the capacity of auxiliary troops under military command. The men signed their names again, this time for the military roster of temporary duty. Spurgeon gave them orders to report to General Howard for their initial assignment.

The men took a moment to draw aside and choose their leaders. T. P. Page was selected captain and L. K. Grimm, the lieutenant. John McLean would serve as the sergeant of the company. Together, the volunteers rode on to Fort Lapwai.

The creation of the territorial militias in such an ad hoc manor was historic and laid the framework for the future

National Guard organizations of Washington and Idaho. In Idaho, Governor Mason Brayman had been a captain in the Civil War. Armed with this experience and receiving news of the calamitous opening battle with the Nez Perce, he notified the War Department that he would be raising companies of volunteers in Idaho with himself as commander in chief. Companies were raised across the state, but the only ones that were significant actors in the struggle were the ones from Mount Idaho, Grangeville, and Lewiston.[6]

Unknown to the volunteers, news of the catastrophic outcome of the battle had reached both shores of the United States via telegraph. On June 21, the *Oregonian* received a dispatch that was relayed to New York. The *New York Times* ran these headlines on the twenty-second:

Hemmed In By Indians

The Fight With Western Savages

Sad News From Salmon River—List Of The Killed And Wounded—The Troops Repulsed With A Heavy Loss—Cowardice Of The Soldiers—More Help Needed.

At 1 p.m. on the twenty-second, acting as Howard's advance guard, the volunteers led the way to the high Idaho prairie. They were at the head of the column because many were well acquainted with the area. Behind them marched three companies of infantry, two of cavalry, and a company of artillery rolling along in the rear. There were 227 regular army troops in total, along with the volunteers. Some men from Walla Walla who had been unable to find the way easily finally managed to catch up. The new recruits spent the night in shifts, watching over the army's three hundred horses.

The morning of June 23 found the Walla Walla troops beginning the ascent to the Camas Prairie. W. S. Clark, a Walla Walla volunteer, had never seen that country and noted the richness of the prairie; he was amazed at the beauty of the vista before them.

George Hunter did a fine job of describing this land in his book *Reminiscences of an Old Timer*:

> The prairie, or basin is bordered on the west by Craig's Mountain, north and east by other spurs of the Blue Mountains, and south by Salmon River and its mountains; all of the mountains named being covered to a greater or lesser extent with fir, pine, and tamarack timber. Near its northwestern boundary runs the Clearwater River. This beautiful basin is almost level for sixteen or twenty miles across, and about thirty miles long. Through it run several small creeks which form deep canyons as they approach either the Clearwater or Salmon rivers. . . . Craig's Mountain is covered with scattering timber, except where it dips northward toward Clearwater, where it is no more than a fertile, high-rolling prairie. For several miles across the top the land is rolling, being drained by numerous streams of clear cold water. . . . While in the timber are to be found thousands of deer and grouse, and not a few elk and bear. The cougar and mountain wolf semi-occasionally break the stillness of the peaceful air with their music. During the summer this mountain and basin form a panorama of beauty and loveliness that would gladden the eye and heart of any lover of sport, health, and varied scenery.[7]

The army column solemnly noted the location along the road where Lew Day was shot in the first attack. At 1:30 p.m. on the twenty-third, the column reached Cottonwood House, where the Nortons had lived. The men started strengthening the defenses of the improvised fort being built at the Nortons' homestead. The troops occupied the fort and rested there overnight.

In the morning, part of the company was ordered to Mount Idaho, nineteen miles away. Howard needed to relieve his garrison there and get some of his men on the offensive.

As a result, Captain Parnell was able to get his men back on the move, bringing his Troop H of the 1st Cavalry down from Mount Idaho, where they had been stationed to protect the town. They passed through the small berg of Florence and on to the settlement at Slate Creek, which lay close by the Salmon River.

The soldiers were forced to use game trails and blaze their own passage through the mountains, since their native foe held the important established trails. Soon the soldiers found themselves deluged by rain and snow, even though it was summer. By June 25, the expeditionary force reached Slate Creek. A company of volunteers from Lewiston was soon expected, much to the relief of the townsfolk. Also on the twenty-fifth, the Walla Walla volunteers were sent with regular army troops to reconnoiter the area in the vicinity of White Bird Canyon. Once again, at the head of the column, the volunteers passed through the approaches to the battleground. The infantry slogged along on foot behind them. By noon, the column peered down into White Bird Canyon where the first, fateful battle was fought, and lost. The morning progress had been slow with the necessity to bury the many dead. More lay below them in the canyon.

In the afternoon, Chapman led the command onto the high ground of the ridges that divide the Salmon River from the canyon. Chapman saw fresh tracks and signs of Indian horses everywhere and warned the men to be alert for danger. Before long, they could see individual scouts moving about and a large band of Indians moving farther up the heights a great distance away. The men moved down to the homesteads of the Salmon and there unexpectedly found Jack Manuel, wounded but alive. They moved him so he could be taken to the hospital at Mount Idaho. The Walla Walla troops were ordered to escort the supply train safely back to Lewiston. Their brief warrant of service had expired, and they were all heading home with one notable exception. Young Blewett was recognized as an excellent pathfinder and horseman and was given the opportunity to stay on with the army as a scout.

Howard had mobilized every available asset in his extensive command and sent them into the field with the intention of subduing the Nez Perce. Not satisfied with these resources, he requested additional reinforcements from outlying posts. Troops from the California and Arizona commands were hurrying to the area. Other units suddenly found themselves called to action. These included the 2nd US Infantry, being transported by boat and rail from Atlanta to the farthest railhead and then on to Lewiston. The 2nd, 5th, and 7th cavalries in Montana were alerted and ordered spread out in case the Nez Perce took either of the trails in their direction. Planners in Washington, DC, were certainly aware that the potential existed for these rebellious natives to join forces with the formidable thousands who were at Sitting Bull's command in Canada across the border. But to join Sitting Bull and reach Canada, they would have to cross the passes of the Bitterroot Mountains. The forces deployed in Montana would endeavor to prevent this at all costs. Although the army assured the public there was no danger of the Nez Perce and Sioux joining forces, in closed rooms in Washington there was surely fear of a larger Indian uprising involving the Crow, Ute, Blackfoot, and other tribes. If Joseph's two hundred men could beat the army so badly, what havoc would come of three thousand Lakota sweeping down from Canada to join the Nez Perce rebellion? At the time, the issue was foremost in the minds of those in the War Department and others in the administration of President Rutherford B. Hayes, who had succeeded Grant. Howard knew he had to produce results, and soon. His commander, General Sherman, had a short temper and little truck with officers who could not achieve their objectives.

Howard had been keeping his command aware of what was happening in the campaign. General Sherman sent General McDowell, Howard's commander based in San Francisco, a telegram that McDowell forwarded to Howard's Department of the Columbia on June 25:

> Your two dispatches of yesterday are received. I expect to start for the Yellowstone and Montana, Wednesday. Meantime will do all possible to strengthen your hands in the matter of the Nez Perce outbreak. You may instruct Howard to pay no attention to boundary lines of the divisions. Only in case the Indians retreat towards Montana to send word as much in advance as possible.[8]

On June 29, Howard ordered Captain Whipple to seize Looking Glass and take his people prisoner. From the tone of the telegram it is clear that Howard's commanders were not satisfied with his progress, and he needed a victory. On July 1, Whipple's forces stood outside of Looking Glass's village a few miles south of Kamiah with the intent of capturing the chief and bringing his followers to the Lapwai reservation. The troops had to ride down a sloping hill that ran to Clear Creek. The Alpowai village sat on the other side of the creek from the soldiers.

Looking Glass sat in his lodge with Peo Peo Tholekt (Band of Geese) eating breakfast. When the camp became aware of the soldiers, Looking Glass sent Peo Peo Tholekt and another interpreter to parley with a flag of truce. Peo Peo Tholekt was related to Joseph through his mother. He had been a member of the Salmon River Indians and was then living with the Alpowai band. Although he couldn't know it, he was soon to distinguish himself as a warrior of renown.

The two Indians crossed the creek toward Whipple's troop, and gunshots immediately rang out. People in the village fled in all directions. One woman and her baby were killed crossing the creek to get away from the attack. Looking Glass, who had steadfastly distanced himself from the rebellion, found himself being pushed into the fight. After the attack, he believed the army made no distinction between his peaceful people and those who had stirred up the trouble along the Salmon River.

Whipple did not capture Looking Glass or any of his people, who rapidly dispersed during the attack and eventually sought safety at Red Owl's village, Sapachesap, on the south fork of the Clearwater, accompanied by the Palouse band of Husishusis Kute, who had been in the camp as guests. Red Owl (Koolkool Snehee) was an Alpowai subchief of Looking Glass's band who typically stayed at Sapachesap with his followers.

Also on July 1, with the addition of Parnell's soldiers, the column of the Clearwater expeditionary force started a journey into the Salmon River Basin in pursuit of the Nez Perce. They began a tortuous, twelve-mile climb up the rugged slopes of the Salmon River Mountains. Pack mules lost their footing and fell thousands of feet in the rain as the column slogged through mud and over slippery rocks. Leading the way and lightly provisioned, the fast-moving cavalry and foot soldiers reached the summit shortly after 7 p.m. As the weather steadily grew worse with torrential rain and high winds, the artillery, the main body of infantry, and the trailing pack train were forced to camp for the night on the treacherous trail in miserable conditions. Trapped on a small shelf three feet wide in inky blackness, with an unseen drop of two thousand feet next to their bedrolls, the men huddled and tried to control their animals as the storm raged.

On the third, the main force finally attained the heights to join their comrades, fires were built, and troops scouted for signs of the enemy while equipment, uniforms, and animals were dried out and men were revived. On the following day, July 4, there was little celebration as the now-dry column set out early on the trail of the Indians. Moving down the Salmon, it found evidence that the Indians had recrossed the river. The actual crossing had taken place two days previously as the Indians made their way to Craig's Mountain and Cottonwood—back on the prairie. Howard's displeasure at not trapping the Indians must have been detectable by all the troops in his command.

Peo Peo Tholekt (Band of Geese) an important member of Looking Glass's Alpowai band. (*Washington State University Library, MASC*)

In a masterstroke of evasion, the Nez Perce delayed a significant force of their enemy—exhausting its resources and time—while the tribe moved quickly, as agile and elusive as ghosts. The united Nez Perce bands of noncombatants and warriors followed a path that would be long and dangerous, while harassed by enemies at every turn.

By July 2, Captain Whipple, leading Companies E and L of the 1st Cavalry, arrived back at Cottonwood House, which had become the primary base of operations for the defense of the Camas Prairie. Whipple immediately saw to the creation of hasty barricades and rifle entrenchments around the perimeter of the ranch. He was intensely aware that at any time, he could be beset by masses of mounted warriors. He displayed a strong sense of urgency to his men as they hastily dug rough rifle pits and emplacements for their Gatling guns.

On General Howard's orders, Whipple dispatched two scouts, Blewett and William Foster, to try to determine the location of the tribe. Whipple described his orders to the men: "I marched to Cottonwood, July 2, and on the following morning sent two citizens named Foster and Blewett to examine the country in the vicinity of Craig's Ferry, the place where Joseph and his party swam the river, for indications of the presence of the Indians."[9]

On July 3, the two men set out on the main road, eventually turning off to follow the Salmon River Trail toward Lawyer's Canyon. The scouts located an Indian scouting party in the vicinity of the canyon. They attempted to leave to report back to Whipple, but a lone warrior detected them, and firing ensued. At some point Blewett lost his horse, and Foster could not recover the panicking animal as it fled. Returning after chasing the runaway, Foster was too late to help Blewett, who had sought cover in a brushy hillside. So Foster beat a hasty retreat, narrowly escaping from his pursuers.

When Foster arrived back at Cottonwood House, Whipple sent the information the scouts had gathered to General Howard via dispatch rider. Whipple began to ready his forces for an attack in the area where the scouts and the natives had skirmished.

Whipple selected Second Lieutenant Sevier M. Rains of Company L to ride out with ten men as an advance guard for his cavalry, guided by Foster. Rains was an 1876 graduate of West Point, handsome, outgoing, and well thought of by officers and men. His orders were to conduct a reconnaissance of the enemy to gauge its strength and position, and, if possible, to rescue Blewett. He was to stick to high terrain with good visibility and avoid contact with the enemy.

Rains and his men proceeded ahead of the main party, which was still being organized. They advanced to the spine of the ridges and made their way toward Craig's Mountain. Eventually, the rugged terrain forced them into lower country as they moved toward the slopes in the distance. But Indian warriors, led by White Bird, and unseen by the reconnaissance troop, were moving quietly, following from the banks of the creek below. The warriors, among them Two Moons, Five Wounds (Pahkatos Owyeen), and Rainbow (Wah-chumyus), found a draw in which to hide abreast of Rains's route.[10] When the soldiers were at right angles to the warriors, they were ambushed. Rains quickly ordered his men to wheel about and withdraw. He called to them to

Yellow Wolf posed years later with typical Nez Perce armament: kloputs, bandolier, and repeating rifle. (*Library of Congress*)

make for the cover of the forest to their front. No doubt Foster led the retreat, with his strong horse and knowledge of the terrain. But not all of Rains's men were good riders or even cavalrymen. Some were overtaken by their pursuers or shot from their horses. The moment of clarity for their terrible predicament came as Foster drew his horse to an abrupt stop. His sharp eyes noticed warriors along the edge of the trees cutting off their line of retreat. The young officer quickly ordered his men to form a hasty perimeter among some large rocks rising from the rough ground. Accurate fire began to range in from all sides as the men sought cover and found limited options for their defense.

Yellow Wolf recalled the fight against Rains:

> Those soldiers were trapped. They had no show.
> When they began shooting, it was like their calling,
> 'Come on! Come on! Come on!' A calling to death.
>
> Our leader, Pahkatos, threw up his hand, and we
> stopped. The soldiers were shooting at Tipyahlanah
> in the canyon to their left. We dropped back out of
> sight, then circled the hill to the right. A little
> beyond the soldiers we dismounted. Some men
> stayed with the horses, and the others crawled
> toward the soldiers. I was one of the crawlers. The
> soldiers were still firing but not at us. They did not
> see us, and we got close to them. I will not hide it.
> Those soldiers were killed![11]

Whipple rode out to relieve Rains and his small detachment. His advance was tentative over the two miles he
needed to cross to help them. In fact, the relief force did
not advance to contact until all the shooting had stopped.
By the time his men reached the site of the fighting, with
skirmishers deployed, all of Rains's command had perished.
They found Rains dead of multiple gunshot wounds. The
evidence was clear that young Foster must have made a
desperate rush for the tree line to seek help. He and his
horse lay supine on the field beyond the ring of rocks, victims of an ambush. J. W. Redington, one of General
Howard's scouts who later visited the site where Rains
made his stand, remembered of the battleground:

> [T]he ground where the Lieutenant Rains' party was
> killed . . . there were several big boulders there, and
> I think the ground was comparatively level and on a
> bench not far from Cottonwood Creek, and not very
> far from the stage road. I believe there were scatter-
> ing pine trees around there, same as Craigs
> Mountain, but I am not sure. As far as I can remem-

The rock pile where Second Lieutenant Sevier M. Rains of Company L, 1st Cavalry, and the ten men he was leading were killed. (*Washington State University Library, MASC*)

ber, right around the big boulders is where Lieutenant Rains and his troopers and scouts . . . were killed.[12]

General Howard wrote a moving eulogy: "The young officer was of the same mould as the famous Winterfield of history who was killed in just such a fashion under Frederic the Great, prompt, loyal, able without fear, and without reproach. Frederick lost many brave leaders, but only one Winterfield, we lost one Rains."[13]

With adequate support from Whipple's advance, Rains's party could have held its own and made it easier for the attacking force to engage the war party in the rear or flank.

Whipple now directed his force to maneuver and fight the visible Indian foe. After several hours, the conclusion was indecisive as they faced each other above a deep draw. The enemy proved elusive and unwilling to be drawn into a direct fight. They fought a brief holding action and then disengaged, riding away swiftly, whooping in victory. Unknown to Whipple, the Nez Perce chiefs had succeeded in a ruse to draw his troops off target and open a central route from White Bird Canyon in the east to their destination, Red Owl's village, Sapachesap, at the mouth of the Cottonwood River. The fate of Charles Blewett was later confirmed by Yellow Wolf, who remembered that he met his death at the hands of Seeyakoon Illipup (Red Scout).

The Nez Perce ambush was another successful ploy in a strategy that was highly effective for a smaller force against a larger foe. The army studied how to cope with this strategy for some time. The tactics and methods the Nez Perce used were noted by Major Scott Pfau and are included for study in the modern US Army curriculum:

> The success of the Nez Perce against the US military during the numerous engagements shocked the US government and demonstrated how poor logistics, leadership, weapons, and ignorance of culture contributed to the Army's failures during the Nez Perce War. Additionally, this campaign illustrated how effective the Indians were at compensating for inferior numbers and firepower by using deception, flexibility, and guerrilla tactics.[14]

Pfau expanded on the value of the ambushes and skirmishes to the tribe:

> During their ambushes, the natives used variations in the terrain to their advantage. For instance, an ambush might be set up to trap an enemy war party between the raiding warriors and a fast-moving stream, or a cliff, or a steep hill. US Cavalrymen remarked on this tactic's effectiveness and were impressed with the low-casualty rate of Native Americans in this form of combat.[15]

At that moment, the tribes, led by Joseph, Ollokot, White Bird, and Toohoolhoolzote, were evading the army and bypassing Cottonwood as they passed through the Camas Prairie to the South Fork of the Clearwater. They were met at the joining of the Cottonwood and Clearwater rivers by the inconsolable survivors of Whipple's unprovoked assault on Looking Glass's village. The combined bands now numbered more than seven hundred men, women, and children, with what possessions they could carry and their livestock. Howard had unintentionally reinforced his principal adversaries and joined them together with a much larger group of warriors, Looking Glass's, who were now more than willing to fight with the united tribes after the ruthless attack on their village.

While the army and the Indians sparred, getting the measure of each other, the communities around the contested Camas Prairie had been seized with panic. Families from outlying farms and homesteads moved into the closest settlements. In the case of Grangeville, the citizens built a stockade and armed themselves, expecting an assault at any moment from the roving bands of Indians on the warpath.

On the morning of June 15, the day after the murder of his father, young Grant Benedict helped build the fortifications and hauled flour and other grain sacks inside the stockade. Being busy kept his mind from worry and the uncertainty about what had befallen his family. Grant's two younger sisters were with their mother, while he and his sister Caroline lived in Mount Idaho in order to attend school. The stockade was constructed of two rings of fencing with hammered earth and rock in between. Mount Idaho had become a garrison for Howard's troops as well as a safe refuge. Howard rotated his regular troops and volunteers through the community, and they constantly improved the defenses. From there they could also protect Grangeville.

On Slate Creek, palisades of vertical logs were driven into the ground to form a stockade at the Charles Wood ranch. On the near side of the Palouse, the residents of Moscow, Idaho, constructed a stockade around the home of John Russell to stave off the anticipated Nez Perce attack. Over the Snake River and on the far side of the Palouse in Walla Walla, the panic that was sweeping through all of eastern Washington took hold after the murder of a man named Richie on June 23 by an Indian along the Snake River. Rumors and some local newspaper reports linked this death with the unrelated murder of Charles Benedict (no relation to Samuel Benedict), aggravating the general anxiety that had already taken root in the populace. Soon rumors were circulating of wider revolts involving all of the Indian tribes in eastern Washington and northern Idaho. As on the Idaho prairies, people abandoned their farms and ranches and headed for the protection of Fort Walla Walla. Refugees from as far away as Whitman and Stevens counties sought shelter there. Even after a Washington Indian agent brought twenty-eight chiefs from area tribes into the town to reassure the public, the rumors persisted for a short while. They finally receded as life gradually returned to normal.

5

Citizen Soldiers

On July 5, 1877, Captain Stephen G. Whipple sent a lone dispatch rider, Ephraim "Eph" Bunker, from his field position with General Howard to relay a message to Captain Perry at Cottonwood House. While Bunker was making his way there, he stopped briefly at Mount Idaho. Bunker gladly accepted when a group of sixteen citizens volunteered to escort him safely across the prairie. They had a dual purpose in mind. Volunteers Frank Fenn and Luther "Lew" Wilmot felt the situation was in hand at Mount Idaho and that it was simply too dangerous for one man to venture out alone as a dispatch rider to cross the plains. Their commander, Captain Darius Bullock Randall, another Civil War veteran, was eager to help provide relief for the men at Cottonwood House, which he had heard was under siege. On their way, they could also reconnoiter for any movement of the Nez Perce through the area. The men had been doing scout duty in the area for General Howard and were estimating that the movements of the

Indians they had seen would allow them to cross to Cottonwood House. The group left Mount Idaho on July 5 at eight in the morning.

At the same time, Howard had ordered a relief column of volunteers from Dayton and Walla Walla to Cottonwood House to reinforce Perry. It was led by Colonel Edward McConville, Lieutenant Colonel George Hunter, and Lieutenant Levi Watrous. The mounted militia deployed flankers to each side of their column and an advance guard, scouting for trouble as they moved swiftly over the prairie toward the small outpost all the men were calling "Fort Perry."[1]

Also on the fourth and fifth, the tribe were moving their people towards Red Owl's village, Sapachesap, near where the mouth of Cottonwood Creek flowed into the Clearwater River. This meant for two days large herds of horses and cattle were in motion as well. The herds were being driven down to the new camp.[2]

The Nez Perce war council sent its young warriors on a reconnaissance mission (probably to get them out of the way) while deliberations proceeded on what course of action the tribes should take. One group of young warriors included Yellow Wolf. His band was sent out to scout the vicinity for any threats to Sapachesap along the Clearwater. It didn't have far to go before it found some: the seventeen volunteers from Mount Idaho, some distance off on the horizon. The young braves made no attempt to hide; instead they formed a line in the path of Captain Randall and his men, trying to provoke a response and preventing them from reaching Cottonwood House, a mile and a half away.

The Mount Idaho men pulled up and surveyed the Indians before them. "We did not go far when we could see large droves of stock coming off from the mountains. . . . Some of the boys had a small pair of binoculars. . . . I could tell they were Indians. . . . I begged and coaxed Capt. Randall to retreat. This he declined to do. I used all the persuavative power I had. I told him the Indians outnumbered us at least 10 to 1 and so far had not met with defeat."[3]

Despite Wilmot's prudent counsel, Randall, leading the volunteers, ordered his men to charge the war party.[4] The warriors split to the sides of the linear attack into two encircling groups and rapidly lay into the attackers from each quarter, killing several horses. With the loss of the mounts, Randall ordered his men to make a stand in a depression that afforded them some cover. Randall and several other men were armed with Henry repeating rifles, the best magazine rifle in production at that time and a great rifle for long-distance shooting. Most of the men were not well armed. Some had only hand tools for self-defense. Randall was soon mortally wounded. Although dying, he continued to fire until nearly the moment of his demise. With Randall dead and another man mortally wounded, Wilmot assumed command. He was described by a contemporary as "a typical frontiersman. His figure tall and sinewy, a pronounced blond in complexion, with a voice as soft as a woman's, and the best rifle shot in Idaho, he was the cause of more than one Nez Perce biting the dust during the few weeks he hunted them."[5]

With Cottonwood House only a mile away, Wilmot sent two men on fast horses for relief. They rode hard past the war party to Cottonwood House for help from the garrison there. They found Captain Perry anxious and afraid to spare any more men so close on the heels of his disaster at White Bird Canyon.

At Cottonwood House, Perry had overseen the improvement of Whipple's hasty perimeter defense. Perry built a better system of rifle pits and a stockade for the soldiers' protection. Their Gatling guns were set and sighted along the possible avenues of attack. Perry's improvements had been just in time, as Indian skirmishers had made continued assaults the previous evening, the fourth. The high-velocity guns proved a sufficient deterrent and prevented the raiders from getting too close to the defended perimeter. In the morning, Perry had believed the attackers had moved off toward the Clearwater River and he hadn't expected the problem he now faced of the Mount Idaho volunteers under attack.

With Randall's force possibly being wiped out, the issue of relief soon led to a near-mutiny in the camp. George Shearer, a veteran of many battles, exclaimed, "The man who goes down there is a damned fool, but he's a damned coward if he don't."[6] Sergeant Bernard Simpson, a senior noncommissioned officer, mounted twenty-five volunteer soldiers and prepared to go to the aid of the assailed volunteers—with or without orders from his superiors. Perry halted the would-be rescue party and ordered Simpson arrested and charged with insubordination. Then he inexplicably gave orders to Captain Whipple to lead the assembled relief party anyway.[7] The rescuers rolled out, towing a Gatling gun, with an advance party galloping on ahead with volunteer Colonel George Shearer in the lead.

When the advance party made it to the hollow where the besieged volunteers were making their stand, Wilmot told them to dismount quickly. Shearer claimed the danger was gone, the war party having retreated to a distance of a mile. He began to protest the need to dismount. Just then, a bullet sliced through the air and struck his horse, passing through the withers. He rapidly complied and dismounted, now wiser as to the accuracy of Nez Perce marksmanship. Some accounts indicate that the relief party faced a group of Indian fighters of nearly the same strength in number and armed with longer-range .45–70 caliber rifles. Yellow Wolf disputed this claim, saying he had a small number of young warriors. The volunteers from Dayton, along with men from Pataha, could hear the sounds of the battle raging as they tried to cross the Salmon River and come to Perry's aid.[8]

When the main body of the relief party finally reached the area, the Gatling gun Whipple employed discouraged the war party, whose members decided to pull back toward the rivers. They slipped away without further contact. Whipple's party then took the wounded and dead from the group that came to be called the "Brave Seventeen" on to reinforced Mount Idaho, where a doctor, J. B. Morris, had established a field hospital. Randall and Benjamin F. Evans were dead, and D. H. Houser, Charles Johnson, and A. Bledland were wounded. The other members of the group were J. Searly, James Buchanan, William Beemer, Charles Chase, C. M. Day, Frank Fenn, Ephraim Bunker, H. C. Johnson, George Riggings, A. D. Bartley, Frank Vancise, and the dependable Lew Wilmot. Bunker delivered his dispatch safely after all.

Upon arrival in Mount Idaho, Wilmot was furious when he learned of Perry's initial unwillingness to help his besieged force. Wilmot had made his decision about Perry, and in the weeks to come he would challenge Perry on every issue of defense and strategy. Wilmot later wrote a scathing letter to the *Lewiston Teller* newspaper describing what he viewed as Perry's cowardice. The quiet frontiersman had become intolerant of the indecision of Howard and his staff.

Perry gave an interesting summary of the skirmishes from the third to the fifth of July, ending with the movement of the tribe and its livestock: "Shortly after this the whole hostile 'outfit,' families, loose stock, etc., debouched from the foot-hills some six or eight miles from my position and started across the prairies in a furious pace in the direction of the Clearwater, where General Howard afterward engaged them." Perry realized that the demonstrations and attacks against him had the intention of keeping him tied up while the bands rejoined and made their way to the Clearwater to consolidate and hold council. Perry continued:

> Captain Whipple estimated two hundred and fifty warriors while my command of about one hundred had a valuable train to guard, so that to pursue them was not deemed judicious. It was now apparent that their hovering around my camp and their attack was not, as some had supposed, an attempt to capture the train, but to keep us occupied while their families and stock gained the open prairie and prevent our sending out our scouting parties, who, in all probability, would have discovered them.[9]

The confederated tribes crossed the Camas Prairie while Cottonwood House was essentially under siege, making their way to the south fork of the Clearwater River. Screens of warriors ranged out from the banks of the river, moving fast and destroying houses and farms as they passed. They could now roam uncontested between the besieged settlements of Cottonwood and Grangeville at will. The various bands used the clear path to make their way to the camp on the Clearwater River where they were all gathering.

Colonel McConville left a garrison at Grangeville and then set out with the rest of his volunteer command, in coordination with Howard, for a planned attack on the Indian camp. His orders were to drive the enemy into Howard's army forces waiting to the rear of where the tribe was believed to be hiding.

Most of the militia used the older, percussion cap pistols. They had a variety of weapons: some may have been issued so-called needle guns by the army, while others brought their own rifles.[10] The group of volunteers from Pataha began their journey with muzzle-loading rifles and shotguns [11]

The Dayton and Walla Walla volunteers had to wait for the delivery of rifles the army was providing them that shot a paper cartridge and that they regarded as inferior to the native armament of captured Springfield and repeating carbines. When the wagonloads of rifles arrived, however, they were glad to be armed and on the move.

Colonel Edward McConville. A soldier in the regular US Army, McConville led militia volunteers during the Nez Perce War. (*Idaho Military History Museum*)

The Washington and Idaho volunteers, together about sixty-five men,[12] escorted the wagons taking the casualties of Randall's volunteers to Mount Idaho without incident. Then they met General Howard at a place called Craig's Ferry while he was making his way to Cottonwood House.[13]

McConville was tired of garrison duty. He had served with the 13th New York Cavalry throughout the Civil War. Afterward, he went west with the infantry and fought the Apache in the Southwest before mustering out and settling in the Northwest as a civilian. At age thirty-one, he had been out of the military for six years.

Ever the aggressor, McConville boldly suggested a scouting mission with a battalion composed of the volunteer companies. Their orders were to ascertain the location of the Indians' camp and then drive them toward Howard as he attacked from their blind side. The ex-Union officer had a good idea where to lead his men based upon the earlier scouting foray by Blewett and Foster. The joined companies of militia took to the trail, moving quickly toward the enemy. The Nez Perce had moved down Cottonwood

Creek to its confluence with the Clearwater River, and their tipis sat on both sides of the creek.[14]

McConville's seventy-five men were moving down the same valley and spent the night bivouacked, unaware that they were close to the Nez Perce village. In the morning, further scouting located the tribe in force a mile away. The scouts, including Wilmot, closed to within a half mile and observed the village at first light. Meanwhile, dispatch riders were sent to the general.[15] McConville's militia was detected during the day of July 9, and it encountered a significant body of warriors on July 10. Their orders were to hold their ground while Howard maneuvered to place his own regular troops into position for the attack.

Howard was hungry for the intelligence. He had been pursuing the Nez Perce through the Salmon River since July 1, when he was joined by Lieutenant Parnell and his men. The general knew he had an opportunity to end the rebellion with a powerful attack.

McConville sent Wilmot to inform Howard of the enemy's position and to suggest that he detach his cavalry to support the militia's attack. Wilmot dutifully informed the general that without the support of cavalry troops, the mounted militia would most likely be decimated during the fight. Wilmot insisted that an attack by cavalry in concert with the volunteer force and Howard's assault from the north with infantry and artillery could break the enemy. Howard declined to follow this advice and dismissed Wilmot perfunctorily. Howard commented that he knew how to run his own campaign.[16]

Tight-lipped, Wilmot prepared to mount his horse and return to his comrades. Then he saw Perry. Wilmot was still smarting from Perry's indecision at Cottonwood House, which he believed cost the lives of some comrades. He looked the officer up and down, and then dressed him down in the rough language of the frontiersman that he was. Howard, still in earshot, ordered him to be seized. Wilmot broke away, trying to ride around the troops to tell his comrades that no help would be forthcoming. After a brief chase, he was brought down and placed under arrest.

Meanwhile, unaware that the cavalry was not on its way, McConville's attacking militia force was unable to approach closer than a few miles to the camp at Sapachesap near the confluence of the Cottonwood and Clearwater rivers. The aggressive Nez Perce mounted war party was led by the formidable Ollokot and subchiefs Pahkatos and Wahchumyus. The two opposing forces exchanged fire at a distance of one thousand yards. Ollokot circled, looking for an opening, his warriors shooting into the volunteers. Two young men, John Agee and Milton Morgan, were riding side by side in the thick of the fray. They felt the bullets slicing through the air all around them. Over the din of battle, they heard the sharp impact of a bullet strike, and each asked the other if he was wounded. Morgan raised his rifle to display its shattered stock and felt a bullet sliding, loose, in his sleeve.[17] The warriors were now encircling the battalion.

The reconnaissance had ended, and a fight began. McConville's battalion fortified a prominence six miles from the settlement of Kamiah. With the withering fire all around them, the militia dug a ring of rifle pits on a small hillock they would later call "Misery Hill."[18] The Indians called the battleground Possossona (Water Passing). Joseph's twenty-one-year-old nephew Yellow Wolf took part in the attack and later described the action: "We went back over to the hill to where they were. It was . . . about the middle of the afternoon. We surrounded those soldiers. There was fighting until sundown. Near dusk we quit and returned to camp."[19] But Yellow Wolf and a small group of warriors returned in the night and raided the picket of horses after driving the sentry away. Many of these same mounts had been seized by Whipple when he overran Looking Glass's innocent village. With the horses caught by the enemy and his outrider, Wilmot, still absent (and under arrest by Howard), McConville had to decide what action to take, without knowing if he would receive support from the regulars.

Colonel Shearer arrived at dawn, accompanied by a mounted force of fifteen. The Indians did not appear to be renewing their attack. Low on ammunition, supplies, and now unhorsed, the discouraged citizen-soldiers marched back to Grangeville to refit, leaving a disappointed Howard on the opposite side of the Clearwater with no counter-force to hold the tribe in place as he had planned. McConville and his men then took up a position just a few miles outside of Mount Idaho, midway between it and Grangeville, to be able to protect the two communities if necessary. Wilmot met up with his comrades there the following day, after his adventure in the army camp with Perry.

Howard blamed the volunteers under McConville for leaving their blocking position, which the general had envisioned would act as anvil to his hammer. This created an interesting dynamic between McConville, Hunter, and Howard and his officers. The militia was certain it had been poorly used, given faulty weapons and dangerous cartridges—and used as bait. It also believed that, once again, General Day-After-Tomorrow had squandered an ideal opportunity.

All this did not sit well with Howard. He was increasingly under pressure from his superiors, who wanted information they could use to deflect the reports appearing in newspapers and complaints that the army was inept in containing the Indian uprising. A telegram sent July 10 from General McDowell read:

But two dispatches received from you. Please report as often as an opportunity affords, daily if you can. Am greatly in need of reliable information. The papers here are full of reports, damaging to the reputation of our officers and of the army. Report fully as to any thing that occurs, and when nothing occurs, let me hear even this negative information. Gather all the information you can as to the immediate cause of the outbreak, and as to the conduct of officers and troops in every engagement, volunteers as well as regulars. Use the telegraph freely and frequently.[20]

Were it not for the phrase "damaging to the reputation of our officers," Howard might have dismissed the telegram. Instead, he was plagued by doubts about how much support he really had from his superiors. McDowell wanted to know about the performance of his volunteers. Perhaps Howard considered deflecting the criticism onto Hunter and McConville, but although the general had derided the volunteers in the recent action, in the end he wrote a glowing report of the militia's performance in the battle. General McDowell's aide-de-camp, Captain Birney B. Keeler, had spent several weeks in the field with Howard and kept Howard in communication with his headquarters. Keeler was also trying to do damage control in Portland, Oregon, where the Department of the Columbia was headquartered. Keeler must have bridled at Howard's praise for the volunteers, because he declared in a telegram to McDowell, "Volunteers of the character and status of those operating with General Howard would be worse than useless. I am sure you would discourage the use of volunteers in any possible emergency."[21] The *Lewiston Teller* complained that some of the volunteers from Columbia County had "an affinity for stock" and might be helping themselves to horses.[22] There was mutual antipathy between the local volunteers and the regular army, the citizenry and the army, and, apparently, between communities as well. It remained for men like Howard, McConville, and Hunter to sort it out and make their military relationships work as well as possible.

By July 10, all of the nontreaty Nez Perce tribes were gathered at Red Owl's village, Sapachesap, to decide collectively what course to take. A council was held with all the principal chiefs and senior warriors present.

White Bird, Looking Glass, and Joseph found themselves of the same mind: flee to the mountains and hold off the army. Many younger warriors wanted to cross into the buffalo country in western Montana. The Lolo Trail was the logical place to begin either journey; to get there they would have to delay the army and ford the Clearwater River.

The trail followed the natural path carved by the middle fork of the Clearwater River on its way to the Lolo Pass and the gateway to Montana. Beyond the pass lay the land of the Crow. Looking Glass believed that the Crow, united with the Nez Perce and secure in their home ground, would be unassailable. The two tribes had long been allies in warfare against other tribes in the area. Surely, he reasoned, the soldiers would not seek battle with these two formidable hosts.

While the foray of the volunteers did not drive the native enemy into Howard's trap as intended, it unintentionally served his cause. The militia attack caused the Nez Perce to spread lookouts and guards along the western prairie and the approaches along the river. It kept the tribe engaged with the militia and off the prairie for two days, preventing it from engaging Howard with one of its flanking attacks. Colonel McConville was prudent in fortifying their position—had he attempted an attack, it is likely they would have been defeated—given the outcome of the two battles that occurred in this same time period. Howard issued orders thanking the militiamen for their service and released them from duty, now that ample troops were moving in to reinforce the area. Howard ordered Lieutenant Watrous to escort the Dayton volunteers to Mount Idaho to retrieve McConville and then return home after regular army troops had relieved them. Along with the men from Dayton were a smattering of Washington Territory volunteers from Pataha which lay along the road from Walla Walla to Lewiston.

Now that McConville had found the position of the enemy camp, Howard decided to move in from the opposite direction—east—where the Nez Perce had no sentries. The army faced the daunting task of crossing back over the fast-flowing Clearwater River. Whatever bullboats and means the Indians had used to make their passage were later destroyed or hidden. Howard had to find a way to get his men across the river.

Howard resolved to build a large raft to ferry his troops. His infantry did not have an engineer on staff, so the task fell to the dauntless Lieutenant H. G. Otis of the artillery. Otis quickly gathered all the rope that could be spared (mostly lariats) and tied it together end-to-end.

While the raft was being constructed, Hunter mounted his horse, Little Wonder, and swam him across the river to find signs of the rebellious tribe on the far side. He returned with news that he had found signs of recent Indian activity, but that the way was now clear to cross.

Otis's final creation was striking in size, consisting of logs a foot in diameter and forty feet long, and planking from a nearby cabin. Lariats were not only used as the lashings but also served as the anchor lines for the raft as it crossed the river. Unfortunately, the weight of the raft in combination with the fierce current soon carried Otis's effort downriver, where it was spectacularly dashed to pieces like a child's sailboat. Howard ordered the dependable Lieutenant Parnell to swim all of the animals across. He and his men stripped down and faced the cold, swift rapids. Soon, naked men and bareback animals began to move across the river. Eventually the attempted ford was halted because the going was too slow and perilous.

The entire formation had to retrace its steps in quick-time march back to White Bird, nearly forty miles away, and cross the Salmon River by boat. The advance party encamped at Grangeville on July 10. The rest caught up as the slower artillery and supply train made the long cross-ings. On the eleventh, the reunited troops began to ascend the slopes looking for the elusive Nez Perce.

6

The Battle of the Clearwater

Looking Glass assumed the position of war chief and overall leader of the confederated tribes. He had the largest body of warriors to contribute to the struggle and was recognized as an experienced warrior. He had spent much of his time winning the influential subchiefs and warriors over to his side. Believing the tribe was secure in its camp at the confluence of the Cottonwood and Clearwater rivers, he decided to linger in the area before heading up the Lolo Trail. He was in no hurry to stress the weaker folk of the tribe further. Looking Glass was also disappointed that the Crow had pointedly refused his offer of joining ranks. The only material backing they could offer him was a small amount of ammunition as a token of their support. Looking Glass would have to make due with the warriors he had at hand.

In contrast, by July 11, General Howard's growing force consisted of artillery, additional cavalry, and reinforced infantry. The march to the Indian camp was headed by the volunteer militia, scouting the way to the area where it had encountered the Nez Perce. Captain William Winters led Troop E in front of the advancing column. He was followed by Perry's Troop F, Whipple with Troop L, and Trimble's Troop H. An additional battalion of cavalry commanded by Perry trailed Trimble. Following the cavalry was a detachment of four companies of infantry commanded by Captain Evan Miles. Bringing up the rear of the column were four artillery companies, rolling along under the command of Captain Marcus Miller.

Emboldened by his reinforced command, Howard led them through Grangeville and crossed the south fork of the Clearwater over Jackson's Bridge. Reaching the heights of the far side of the river, the column rested as the gun carriages and ammunition pack train lumbered up the incline. The army moved through the dense pine and fir trees and followed a series of high ridges that lay between the two branches of the Clearwater River.

Periodically, Howard sent out mounted scouts to survey the steep ravines to either side, searching for his enemy. Riding ahead of the column, Howard's aide, Lieutenant Robert H. Fletcher, detected Indian activity in a deep ravine close by the point where Cottonwood Creek fed the mighty Clearwater.

Howard's evolving tactical plan was to control the approaches to the camp with his artillery and cut off the tribe from fleeing along the river. His main concern was to keep them from escaping to the Bitterroot Mountains to the north, where they could ford the river at Kamiah and then continue to Weippe and the approach to the Lolo Canyon. By following the Clearwater River and reaching Kamiah, Looking Glass could take his people over the Lolo Pass and into Montana. Howard had no way of knowing that this was, in fact, Looking Glass's intention.[1]

Howard's forces were arrayed upon a large spur that jutted out from the larger mountains at his back. The slope was gradual toward the river to the left. The width was about a mile and a half, and the distance to the point overlooking the camp where his guns were wheeled was a mile. Troop H started forward on the right of the line, guarding the spring it found at the head of the ravine.

Howard ordered his guns deployed to fire on the Nez Perce camp from the position of their overlook. Lieutenant Otis of the 4th Artillery was anxious to perform well after the disastrous raft incident. He positioned his guns and began to lob shells toward the camp. Otis found it impossible to depress the cannon sufficiently, so the rounds did little but frighten the camp and enrage the warriors within. Howard ordered his column about so it could reverse its course to a point where it could descend to attack the village. Between the column and the village was a deep ravine. Howard wanted to move his men to a place where the ravine became a slight depression as the ridge gradually met the mountain. From that place, his downhill charge would be unimpeded with a gentle slope and few obstructions.

Before the firing began, the sharp eyes of a warrior in camp detected Howard's column passing along a high ridge, nearly a thousand feet above the camp. Toohoolhoolzote quickly organized the available warriors into three groups: one to guard the camp, a second to drive the horses and livestock to safety, and a third to ascend to the heights of the ridgeline and deploy at right angles to Howard's column, preventing it from advancing. Toohoolhoolzote and Yellow Wolf were in the first group of about twenty-five mounted men to respond to the threat of the soldiers on the heights above the village. The war party climbed the ridge in front of it on the far side of the river from the village. From the heights, Toohoolhoolzote could see the army moving along the next ridge over. The men rode

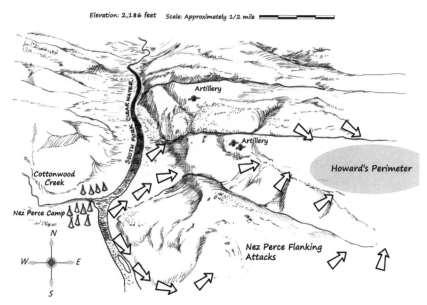

Elevation: 2,186 feet   Scale: Approximately 1/2 mile

The Battle of the Clearwater, July 11, 1877, on the first day. The Nez Perce aggressively attacked the main US Army concentration. (*Author*)

quickly across the depression between the two ridges and tied their horses on the slope of Howard's ridge, out of sight. The warriors ascended quickly to the top of the ridge and piled rocks for cover as they settled in for the fight.[2] They knew that more warriors would soon join them.

Howard tried to extend his force when he saw the Indians driving horses out of the village, but his efforts met immediate and stiff opposition on their flanks, to the front, and finally, to their rear as the trailing pack train was attacked by eighty braves. The Indians swept in from the left, striking Howard's center, killing two packers and several mules. Native warriors were using the deep wooded ravines to move from the river, invisible to the soldiers above, to the perimeter of the army camp without detection. The Nez Perce blocking force had contained Howard's offensive for the time being, and the warriors were confident they could keep the soldiers in place.

By afternoon, from Howard's perspective, the situation was controllable but dire due to the incessant Indian attacks. Because he had a force of four hundred men, he was able to lay out a broad perimeter on the finger-shaped ridge, forming a two-and-a-half-mile front. The ridge itself was several hundred feet wide and reasonably flat on top. He had arrayed his forces in a wide defensive ring, oval in shape. From where he sat at the center, he saw his artillery arrayed directly to the front, loaded with canister shot to prevent any mass attack from that direction. Clockwise from the cannon and Lieutenant Fletcher were Captains Miles and Winters, and Second Lieutenant Hubert H. Bancroft with artillery in his line, then Captain George B. Rodney with more artillery. The doctor's aid station was behind him, protected by a ring of saddles. Completing the left side perimeter was an extended line of Whipple's and Perry's cavalry and infantry. The natives controlled the only water supplies, having taken the spring where they tied their horses and driven away the soldiers guarding the water, and they also had unrestricted access to the two rivers.

Despite Howard's army outnumbering its enemy more than two to one, the Nez Perce completely controlled all the territory around the soldiers. At a critical point in the battle, a cluster of guns—a howitzer and two Gatlings—was in no-man's-land beyond the army's perimeter and threatened with being overrun. Lieutenant Charles F. Humphrey led a squad in a charge to recover the weapons. He and his men dragged them back to their lines before they could be taken.

During the night, the soldiers dug in, improving their hasty positions along the perimeter. The warriors also dug detached trenches and rifle pits from which they could engage their enemy—firing at it on all sides from the many ravines that surrounded the high ground they held.

The morning of July 12 started with more concentrated fire and charges by the Indians. Lieutenants Humphrey and Hobart Bailey noted that Joseph was an active participant in the fighting for the first time. The chief stayed on the ridge for two days during the battle. The soldiers raked the ridge with Gatling gun fire and canister shot as the Indians dug deeper into their rock and earth rifle pits.

Off in the distance, Parnell saw Captain James Jackson's Troop B of the 1st Cavalry escorting a large pack train from Fort Lapwai with much-needed supplies for the besieged camp. General Howard could not afford to lose the train, and he gave direct, urgent orders to make sure the supplies got through.

Under the command of Captain Miller, leading four battalions, the soldiers extended their flank and advanced to protect the mule train. Miller marched his men between the train and the Indian entrenchments. When the packers and their escorts were within the safety of the perimeter, Miller used his initiative to wheel to his right, and with his guns anchoring the pivot point, he flanked the warriors in the rifle pits, breaking the Indian hold on the heights. Supporting fire raked the Indian warriors as they moved from their positions downhill. Simultaneously, an order to attack was given up and down the perimeter of the army camp. Angry troopers complied, launching a vicious fusillade and charge. Trimble moved his Gatling guns to a position where he could fire down the incline into the retreating Indians. The rotary barrel guns did little harm, but certainly encouraged the downhill flight of the warriors.

With no way to regroup, the warriors fell back to the river. The determined counterattack by soldiers along the line was successful and freed the perimeter. Reinforced by another troop under Jackson, thirsty soldiers retook the spring.

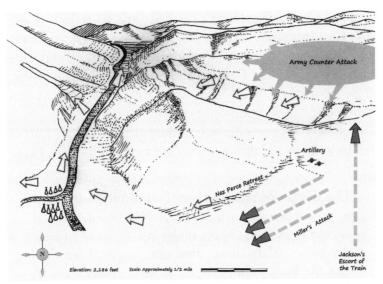

On the second day of the battle, the US Army was able to protect its supply train, but the Nez Perce then escaped to the north on the east side of the south fork of the Clearwater River. (*Author*)

The warriors hurried their families to pack only the items they needed, and they quickly departed the camp, riding along the river valley with their horses.

At the end of the bloody day, the butcher's bill was twelve enlisted men and two officers killed, and twenty-five wounded and in need of care. After the battle, Parnell recalled that he could not account for any Indian casualties. First Sergeant Michael McCarthy thought he had never seen such a pitiful sight as he passed by a wagon filled with dead soldiers, some of them blackened from the sun. He noted that the dead men were mostly infantry and artillery soldiers. If this was a victory, it was a bitter one indeed.[3]

Most warriors were leaving due to disgust with the dug-in fighting, which they regarded as shameful. A warrior gained recognition through face-to-face fighting with an enemy—not on his belly. Howard's foes had suffered the deaths of four warriors.

The exhausted soldiers now had time to reflect. Some officers recognized that the enemy's losses had been minor and that the army never took the initiative until the warriors left en masse.[4] Howard showed no inclination to stay close upon their heels while they were disorganized and riding out, abandoning their camp.

Yellow Wolf's recollection of the battle includes a hint of the indecision and dissension in the ranks of the Nez Perce fighters:

> The Three Red Coats wanted all of the young men to go on horses to fight the left wing of General Howard's soldiers. Make it the last fight. But it was not to be. Many fewer that one hundred warriors met the hard fighting here, as throughout the war. The families were camped across the river from the soldiers. Many of the Indians talked, "Why all this war up here? Our camp is not attacked! All can escape without fighting. Why die without cause? We were not whipped!"[5]

Yellow Wolf suggested that many of the elders and women still in the camp were unaware that the warriors were losing interest in the entrenched fighting and that a withdrawal might occur at any time. As a result, the camp was not packed and ready to move. This could be attributed partly to Joseph's presence on the hill. Absorbed in the battle, he had not been occupied with the administrative duties of preparing the camp to move. In fact, his own wife, Spring Time, was found in peril in the camp, trying to manage a frightened horse and her baby simultaneously. Fortunately, several young warriors helped her onto her horse with her baby. The Nez Perce withdrew from their camp and moved off in the direction of Kamiah, leaving the soldiers to examine and plunder what goods they had left behind in haste.

Back at Howard's headquarters, his aide-de-camp, Captain Keeler, was fighting a battle of his own to protect the reputations of his commander and fellow officers. After Lew Wilmot's struggles with Perry at Cottonwood House, and with Howard and Perry at the Battle of the Clearwater, he had done something that no one expected of the taciturn plainsman: he wrote a scathing account of the prosecution of the war, and it was published in the *Lewiston Teller*. Wilmot was not the only observer of the conflict to put pen to paper and criticize the army generally and Perry in particular. Orin Morrill worked for the Lewiston Stage Company. He began recording his observations of the early battles after he found himself delayed at Cottonwood station with a rifle in his hands during the attack of July 5.[6] Morrill's unflattering observations, as well as comments by Wilmot and the volunteers, were being published in the *Teller* and the *Idaho Statesman*.[7] This was why General McDowell, in his July 10 dispatch to Howard, was so anxiously inquiring about the conduct of the officers.

Keeler composed a reply at the Kamiah base camp and relayed it back for telegraphy from Walla Walla to McDowell in San Francisco:

> Your dispatch of the 10th . . . just received. Have aimed to send all important reliable information as soon as obtained. Difficulties of communication have been great. The country from front to rear has, until now, been infested with the hostiles, and couriers and supplies, in many instances, have failed to get through; none have been lost. I am not aware of the exact tenor of the reports to which you refer, but I infer that they are principally those reflecting upon General Howard and Captain Perry. I have investigated the most important ones, and find them to be false. The statement in the local papers of the affair at Cottonwood on the fifth, to the effect that seventeen citizens were surrounded by Indians and the troops under Perry refused to go to their relief for an

hour and a half, is a wicked falsification. The troops, one hundred and thirteen in number, were themselves outnumbered, environed, and attacked by the Indians, but nevertheless were sent instantly a mile away to the rescue, which was accomplished within twenty minutes. Not only the life of every man in the command was risked, but the safety of a most important position and a large amount of ammunition and other stores. The account as published originated with one Orin Morrill, of Lewsiton, who was at Cottonwood at the time, but who, although armed, remained ensconced in the little fortification there instead of going with the soldiers to the aid of his imperiled fellow-citizens. Other citizens who were present agree with the officers in this statement of the facts. The conduct of the officers and the men has, under the most trying circumstances, been particularly good; they have justified all reasonable expectations. The campaign has been successful. The hostiles have operated skillfully and fought desperately, but they have been defeated and driven from this section with great loss of numbers, spirits and supplies. Unless something unforeseen occurs, General Howard will pursue them but two days longer, when active operations at the point will cease for the present. I believe I can best serve you by immediately thereafter returning to report. This I shall do, unless otherwise instructed at Portland. General Howard reports by this courier the events of the last two days and the present situation. The number of killed and wounded in action on both sides in the action on the eleventh and twelfth turn out to be larger than at first believed.[8]

General Howard wrote that twenty-three warriors were killed, forty wounded, and forty more taken prisoner. Had this been true, he would have destroyed nearly the entire force that assailed his position. The casualties Howard claimed he had inflicted in his victory were refuted by the eyewitness accounts of both Indians and soldiers. Yellow Wolf noted:

> Only four warriors killed. First was Wayakat [Going Across], killed instantly. Second man, his partner in the fight, was Yoomtis Kunnin [Grizzly Bear Blanket], who lived a few hours after shot. Howwallits, also fighting there, was slightly wounded. . . . Third man killed was Heinmot Ilppilp [Red Thunder]. Killed in timber edge at break of canyon, south side of battlefield. Many small bushes there were nearly cut down by soldier bullets. These three men killed and one wounded in earliest fighting. Lelooskin [Whittling] was fourth man killed. Killed in his rifle pit after dark. His partners, Kosooyeen and one other, escaped to safer rifle pits. Wayakat and Lelooskin were so close to the enemy lines. When they were killed . . . both bodies were left. No Indians died on the trail from wounds. Just one man was bad wounded, Kipkip Owyeen [Shot in Breast]. Bullet went in back of shoulder and came out through his breast. That is how he got his name. Had no good name before that time. Pahkatos was wounded in right hand. Three others were lightly wounded, two of them warriors.[9]

Howard had been under constant pressure and the scrutiny of General Sherman. Intentionally or not, his reports inflated the number of Indian dead and wounded. He had hurt the Nez Perce much less than they had him, however, and, with the accounts of Howard's failures printed in the newspapers, his superiors were beginning to feel pressure as well.

Howard had been pinned in place for as long as his adversary wanted to hold him there. The Nez Perce inflicted significant losses and withdrew with minor casualties and minimum impact on their mobility and ability to fight. And suddenly, Howard's enemy had vanished through Clearwater Canyon toward Kamiah. Miller's charge did reveal to the general that he had men in his command who were willing to fight. The one positive action in the battle had been undertaken by a junior officer on his own initiative. Howard reasoned, nonetheless, that it was something he could point to as a success.

The charges brought against Sergeant Simpson for attempting to go to the relief of the seventeen in Cottonwood without direct orders were quietly forgotten after he was wounded in the Battle of the Clearwater.[10] Dismissal of the charges may have also had something to do with the newspaper stories that were circulating. The last thing the command needed was a blow-by-blow account of a court-martial of a noncommissioned officer whose behavior indicated he believed his superior was going to watch seventeen men die without helping them. Simpson lay in the field hospital with twenty-seven other wounded men, two of whom would soon join the thirteen dead soldiers under canvas tarps on the grass. The wounded lay waiting, some moaning and others quietly suffering, knowing their fight was over. They listened to the clatter of hooves and gun carriages as the army prepared to move out again in pursuit of the Nez Perce.

The Nez Perce passed on through the Kamiah Valley and forded the Clearwater River on horseback and in round bullboats. Once across, the men positioned themselves on the bluffs above the river to secure the heights. This was no idle gesture. As pursuing troopers chased the Indians to the river, several volleys by the Indian riflemen stopped the chase and forced the pursuing cavalry to withdraw.

Howard did not immediately renew his attack, but by the thirteenth, the huge army column was poised once again on the banks of the Clearwater. They could see Indians on the far side making a demonstration. In fact, most of the Nez Perce were already far away.

The tribe moved down the river until it neared Kamiah, then crossed to the far side of the river. The Nez Perce held the higher ground, with the river between them and Howard's forces. While sharp-eyed young warriors held the approaches to the ford, a council was held because the principal chiefs had agreed that the leaders would decide what course to take now. Joseph argued that he wanted to go directly north along the Flathead River, and he sent men swiftly up-country to negotiate with the Salish (or Flathead) Indians. White Bird concurred and insisted that accepted form be followed and that the tribe seek permission to pass through its neighbor's land while fleeing north. Looking Glass insisted that they make their way to the buffalo country to the east. Many of the young warriors backed his suggestion because they had never been there before. Perhaps Joseph was reluctant to leave the area of his beloved homeland and remembered his promise to his father. Or maybe he believed that the confederation could only defend itself if it remained together. For whatever reason, Joseph finally voted with Looking Glass to cross into the buffalo country. White Bird was the lone dissenter and became quiet after it was clear that Looking Glass has carried the day. White Bird looked ever north, beyond the walls of his lodge, believing that safety for his people lay in that direction.

July 14 brought no advance for the army, stalled on the Clearwater's banks. Nor was there any prospect of fording the river without significant casualties. The soldiers spent the day assuming the best fighting positions they could while under constant rifle fire from the far side of the river, which they would periodically answer with sweeps of the two Gatling guns and their own rifles.

Frustrated by the strong defense that the warriors offered on the north bank opposite his forces at Kamiah, Howard assembled a force comprising Colonel McConville's forty volunteers and his 1st Cavalry troops, which consisted of Companies B, F, H, and L. The horse-borne force rode out for Durwald's Ferry, some sixty miles downriver, where Howard planned to ford the Clearwater. Once across the river, he could threaten the tribe and drive it to abandon its defense of the far bank at Kamiah. The Nez Perce would be forced to put all their warriors against Howard's attacking cavalry. The troops Howard had left at Kamiah could then cross the river unopposed and attack the enemy from behind. Even if the double-fronted attack failed, the fast moving cavalry would prevent the Nez Perce from taking the Lolo Pass through the Bitterroot Mountains.

Meanwhile, Joseph sent a messenger to Howard. The envoy reached the army troops at Kamiah. An army dispatch rider caught up to the cavalry as it rode downstream and advised Howard of Joseph's intention to parley. Howard had no choice but to reverse his path. But he instructed his men to continue along for a while without him. Howard returned as swiftly as possible to Kamiah, only to find that Joseph had deceived him. The better part of a day was lost. The credulous general soon discovered that the Nez Perce had used the time to seize and hold all of the approaches to the Lolo. Dejected, Howard's horse troops started the ride back to Kamiah.

Howard was not aware that he had a larger problem, as indicated in a telegram that reached Portland on July 14 and was forwarded by his adjutant, Major Wood: "See Associated Press dispatches which state General Howard's removal under consideration by Cabinet."[11]

7

Over the Lolo Pass

Lewis and Clark found it the most trying part of their expedition, a trail so rugged and overgrown that their Shoshone guides had trouble finding and keeping to it.

One of the early explorers who hazarded to venture through the area of the Lolo was Lieutenant John Mullan, an army engineer, surveyor, and explorer. Mullen, at the urging of Governor Isaac Stevens of the Washington Territory, took his surveys into the interior of the Bitterroot Mountain Range.[1]

Mullan, who experienced the Lolo Trail in 1854, declared that he had "never met with a more uninviting or rugged bed of mountains. The whole country is densely timbered, save at a few points where small patches of prairie occur sufficiently large to afford camping grounds; but beyond this it cannot be converted to any useful purpose."[2] It is certain that the trail was a well-used passage. The word Lolo means "to carry."[3] It is likely that trade goods and animal pelts were conveyed across the trail for many generations. The Indians, at least, had put the trail to good use.

For the pursued and pursuer, the formidable Lolo Trail and the pass through the Bitterroots loomed ahead. It was a daunting trek both for the Nez Perce and the army. The two-hundred-fifty-mile-long trail passed from Idaho through the harsh peaks of Montana's Bitterroot Mountain Range of the northern Rockies.

The path was strewn with huge boulders from an ancient upheaval, some the size of houses. Fallen timber blocked any permanent trail with trees broken down during the heavy winter snows. The trail was close, with sheer walls and great piles of shale and loose rock overhead on the heights. Rockslides were commonplace. In wet weather floods often washed away landmarks and created huge, impassable barriers of earth, rock, and timber. In the summer months through October, the many pools of standing water were breeding grounds for hordes of mosquitoes that harassed any traveler to the point of madness. The trail climbed steeply to the mile-high pass through the rugged peaks. This was the route the Nez Perce had chosen, and the army was forced to take it in order to follow them.

On July 17, 1877, the rebellious tribe left the Weippe Prairie and started up the Lolo Trail. General Howard would not follow for ten days. He had other problems, in addition to supply and logistics. A marauding force of about forty warriors had been left behind, and they were raiding for horses and burning homesteads in the vicinity of Weippe and Kamiah. White Bird's purpose with these actions was to pin Howard down and prevent him from committing to a hasty pursuit. The warriors were also watching for signs of pursuit, ambushing small parties and scouts, and providing a credible threat to the rear of any attacking column chasing the main body of the tribe in the narrow canyons. At the very worst, the Nez Perce leadership reasoned, Howard would have no choice but to split his forces, and in any case he would be delayed. As a result, Howard had to counter these guerrilla-style tactics before he could commit fully to the chase.

The long trek through the narrow river canyons allowed the tribe to place obstacles, and ambushes, in the path of the advancing army.

Faced with the daunting trails ahead into the mountains and the country beyond, Howard requested permission from General McDowell, commander of the Military Division of the Pacific, to enroll twenty-five Nez Perce scouts. He closed his request, sent via telegram, with the optimistic comment, "Think we shall make short work of it."[4] After some administrative wrangling, the adjutant general of the army allowed that a company of scouts from the Nez Perce agencies were to be mustered in and given uniforms.[5] Giving the scouts horses was apparently another matter.[6]

Frustration grew stronger among Howard's staff. His men were anxious to take up the trail and pursue the Nez Perce. Early in the morning of July 17, Howard ordered Major Edwin Mason, with his cavalry, light artillery, his Nez Perce scouts, and Colonel McConville's twenty militiamen, to follow the trail of the fleeing tribe.[7] The objective of the mission was a two-day reconnaissance to determine the nature of the terrain and if the Nez Perce were moving toward Montana.

The group set out from Kamiah at 4:30 a.m., led by pathfinder Ad Chapman and twenty Nez Perce scouts from the reservation.[8] The complex terrain the army had to navigate in its pursuit of the Nez Perce presented challenges that only local guides and skilled trailblazers could overcome. Among the Nez Perce scouts were two men the volunteers knew: Captain John, and James Reuben. The residents of the prairie and volunteers had their doubts about the latter, suspecting him of collaboration, or, worse, participation in the Indian uprising. He came armed with a repeating Henry rifle and appeared ready to use it. Being a warrior, he made his disdain for the inexperienced soldiers and volunteers evident, which did nothing to allay their fears.[9]

With the infantry holding the far side of the Clearwater, McConville and his volunteers, followed by Mason's cavalry company, swam their horses across the river without incident.

After a night camped next to fields of Indian grain, the army horses grew testy, as they were not allowed to graze. Howard had given strict orders that Indian crops were not to be touched for forage. But some of the packers and volunteers harvested quantities for their horses in any event.

Back on the trail at first light on the eighteenth, the company of regular cavalry and volunteers began the climbing approach to the Lolo. The expedition moved over the expanse of the Weippe Prairie and eventually uphill into the timber and then onto the Lolo Trail. Within three miles of Orofino Creek near Weippe, the scouts and volunteers encountered evidence of the enemy's rearguard. The treaty Nez Perce scouts were at the head of the column along with McConville and Chapman.[10] Almost all the Indian scouts were in army uniforms, wearing hats with their hair freshly shorn. Each man had been issued three boxes of cartridges, a rifle, and an ammunition belt. They were mounted on their own horses.[11] The column reached the summit, and after marching through a more forested area, they emerged into a clearing at about 3 p.m. McConville directed Chapman and the scouts forward to reconnoiter the open ground before them. Chapman himself rode back to advise Mason of the clearing and the nature of the trail on the far side. Everyone else waited for the cavalry to reach its position at the edge of the clearing.[12]

On July 17, Colonel McConville sent six of his reservation Nez Perce scouts into a clearing near Lolo Creek and Weippe to reconnoiter ahead. About four miles along the way, they encoutered the Nez Perce rear guard on the Lolo Trail. (*Author*)

Abraham Brooks, one of the general's Nez Perce scouts, later told the story of their advance to reconnoiter the clearing a half mile ahead. "Three men were sent out ahead to scout, to wit; Hahats Ilp Ilp (Red Bear), Sam Lawyer, Charley Tlitlkim, and they were captured. Then several of us, James Reuben, Paul Kalla, Captain John, Benjamin Pahatkokoh, Tamalushimlikt, John Levi, and myself went ahead; behind was the soldiers and other Indian scouts; then we ran into the hostiles in the timber; suddenly we were fired upon."[13]

The men were not far into the clearing when shots rang out. The scouts returned fire as they tried to control their rearing horses. John Levi (Sheared Wolf) was killed instantly. James Reuben was soon shot through the hand; Abraham Brooks was shot through the left shoulder at the same moment his horse was shot and killed. The three men who had been captured escaped during the confusion of the gun battle. Two of the men had been stripped of their weapons and clothing.

The incident in that clearing is best understood by the interviews of the men who had been scouts and were involved. Perhaps the most helpful is Sam Lawyer's account. Lawyer was dressed in the same fashion as the Indians they were pursuing. He was wearing a traditional tunic and was wrapped in a robe blanket. He was one of three men captured by the Nez Perce patriot's rearguard. The other two, Captain John and Charlie Tlitlkim, were wearing their army uniforms and were stripped of rifles, hats, tunics, belts, and their horses. Nothing was taken from Lawyer. He was a friend of some of the men who had captured them. As the other scouts rode out to find the three captured men, firing ensued, and when Lawyer heard one of his captors say, "Kill the two men with uniforms on," he escaped and was able to ride back to the army's lines.

Brooks fell to the ground and painfully crawled back to where the volunteers watched the clearing anxiously from the foliage and brush. He left his rifle and hat where he had fallen to the ground by his horse. His new uniform was bloody and torn. The closest men carried him back for aid.

In response to the firing in the clearing, Major Mason's men unslung a mountain howitzer and assembled the cannon.

McConville ordered his men to seek cover just inside the tree line, where they crouched with rifles at the ready behind trees and fallen logs. They passed hardtack and ammunition up and down the line. Some of the men ate while waiting for an attack from the clearing. Some men joked to break the tension, guessing that the howitzer would soon be back upon its mules—its usefulness being questionable in "timber too thick to drag a cat through."[14]

The strain of waiting was at last relieved when Mason ordered Captain Winters to deploy to his right of the trail with the volunteers in advance. Winters moved up to McConville with Mason's orders for the volunteers and troopers to move forward. The men formed a line and advanced into the underbrush.

Captain Trimble's troop was advancing to the left. The volunteers advanced in a skirmish line through the tall grass in the clearing. They soon came upon Levi, hemorrhaging with a bullet through the lungs.[15] He was taken directly to the rear for aid. They pressed on, looking for signs of the ambushers. The cavalry was fighting dismounted, as was usual in this conflict; a few men had not yet dismounted when firing started in earnest again. Mason ordered a skirmish line to each side of the trail to protect their flanks. The troops found themselves under considerable fire from the heights to their front, and increasingly from the flank. Bullets sliced through the air between the advancing volunteers and the cavalry.

Mason ordered the volunteers to return with his regular troops, and they began a retreat back to Kamiah. McConville reminded Mason that he had a responsibility to take care of the injured treaty Nez Perce scouts and could not just abandon them. Mason's indifference enraged McConville; he told Mason that the volunteers would remain with their Indian scouts and see them out of the scrape with or without the army's help.[16] The volunteers cut poles for stretchers and travois to carry the wounded. The now-dead Levi's body was placed upon a travois and lashed to a horse with lariats. By sunset, the wounded were prepared and the volunteers moved out. The regulars were far ahead, and the entire party was on edge as darkness closed in.

Eugene T. Wilson described their journey later in a memoir:

I shall never forget that return march, the Indians silent and grieved over the death of their leader, escorted by the seventeen whites now composing our company, the momentary danger of attack by the hostiles under cover of the almost impenetrable forest surrounding us, the gradually increasing darkness, the accumulating difficulties of travelling over a trail almost impassable in daylight, and the utter unconcern for our safety by the soldiers who had gone ahead secure in the knowledge that we were between them and the enemy.[17]

The small party rode as silently as possible along the forbidding trail until the darkness was relieved somewhat by the rising of the moon over the tree tops. They made slow time uphill in the darkness until midnight, when they reached the summit. It must have been a difficult journey in the darkness, with the wounded and the dead man.[18]

At the request of the Indians, they halted and buried the dead man. Levi's body was laid in a hastily improvised grave. Before he was placed into the grave, the Christian Indians began their service, while those who held to the old faith turned their backs in disapproval. When the Christians finished their prayers, the traditional chants were made and a cairn of rocks was piled over the body.[19]

The rest of the journey was silent and solemn, as each man, white and Indian, Christian and shamanist, imagined that he might have been the one placed in the grave.

The mission had at least revealed a substantial rearguard in the direction that Howard believed his enemy had taken, indicating that Montana was their true objective. And after the reconnaissance, they were informed about what the approach to the Lolo Trail would be like.

As the cavalry and volunteers retreated, they encountered Red Heart and his band of thirty-two people who had returned through the pass from the buffalo lands of

Montana. Red Heart was a minor Nez Perce chieftain who lived not far from the village that General Howard had assaulted during the Battle of the Clearwater. While Red Heart was not a reservation Indian, he was of a similar temperament as Looking Glass and wished to avoid becoming caught up in the fight.[20] Upon meeting the confederated bands at Weippe who were preparing to move through the Lolo Trail, they had learned for the first time about the war that had erupted. Red Heart wished to seek asylum on the agency reservation in Kamiah and not to engage in the troubles. But upon meeting Major Mason, the group was taken into custody for being part of the rebellion, although they probably had nothing at all to do with it.[21]

On July 19, after the small band surrendered peacefully and tried to explain its circumstances, Howard nevertheless detained them and forwarded a dispatch to his division headquarters in San Francisco: "Majority of Hostile Indians have fled on Lolo Trail to buffalo country; forced to go. Thirty-five men, women, and children in my hands voluntary surrender."[22]

Howard committed the thirty-five people to military imprisonment in Vancouver Barracks. Red Heart's band was escorted by several of Howard's new scouts from the reservation. Scout J. W. Reddington later saw them in their confinement.[23]

The Nez Perce rearguard moved back a prudent distance to man some other strong position, while the main body of the tribe moved on at its best pace. Although there was no immediate pursuit by the army, the fifty Nez Perce warriors kept a guarded watch as they moved at the rear of the file of people who moved along the confines of the trail. The vigilant rearguard was quite prepared to turn and hold the narrow trail against any attack.

On its return, the cavalry heard the welcome news that reinforcements had reached Mount Idaho and Lewiston. It also received word that more help was on the way. The 12th Infantry from California was already encamped at Lewiston and would proceed as soon as possible. Howard was under no illusions about the difficulty of the pursuit now that the ground had again become rugged and hostile. In this environment, the Nez Perce were masters of delay, ambush, and attack. He knew that the chase would be perilous for his men. Also, Howard had to be concerned about serious logistics problems.

Napoleon Bonaparte correctly observed that an army marches on its stomach, not on its legs. According to Napoleon, no army relying on wagons for resupply could operate more than one hundred miles from its supply depot; otherwise, the expense of feeding the oxen and horses begins to deplete the supplies. This meant that the army had to set up a series of supply bases for relaying. Foraging off the land was much more difficult in the wilderness than moving through pastures and farmland. The Indian tribe ahead of him would attempt to leave nothing useful to those who pursued them. Their huge herds of livestock would browse and graze the territory all around their route of travel, leaving nothing for the army's horses.

Howard's quartermaster had to transport all supplies from Portland and Walla Walla, which meant they would have to travel hundreds of miles before reaching the men. Days passed with soldiers becoming increasingly more impatient while Howard arranged transport and his supply depots in preparation for the crossing.

Looking Glass had been over the pass to hunt buffalo in Montana many times, and he made the case that he should lead the way. Looking Glass had become the de facto leader of the confederated tribes. Joseph continued to care for his people and clung to the hope that some peaceful outcome could be achieved. Perhaps he would take a more active role in the fighting if it came to battle again. The other chiefs still sought Joseph's wisdom in council, but Looking Glass's status as a warrior gave him the support of the majority of the subchiefs.

The tribes stopped and waited for all the trailing members to reach the hot springs at the pass in order to rest and again hold an important council. By now the tribes had gotten word from the north that the Salish (Flathead) people would help guide them safely through their country, in effect offering safe passage. The Pend d' Oreilles of the northern Idaho Panhandle also visited the Nez Perce and made essentially the same offer. At the council meeting, White Bird made an impassioned argument that they should immediately go north to Canada. But the council tended to favor Looking Glass. During the council, scouts checked the trail ahead from the pass to the Bitterroot River. They reported to the council that the way ahead had been blocked by soldiers and settlers. White Bird was now apprehensive. He considered splitting away from the main band and heading north. He tried to make his case again, that the only sensible way to take was north to Canada, a few days' march away, but his arguments fell on deaf ears. The young men who so badly wanted to hunt buffalo in Montana supported Looking Glass. Joseph had become subdued as Looking Glass gained power. The decision was made to follow Looking Glass into the buffalo land. The Indians were crossing out of Idaho—and, although they did not know it, into another military district and warfare with a new adversary.

8

The Battle of Big Hole

On July 16, 1877, a dispatch arrived at the Pacific Division from John Cunningham Kelton, assistant adjutant general of the Division of the Pacific:

> The general commanding directs that Captain [Harry C.] Cushing's command be forwarded without delay to Lewiston. See that they are supplied for actual field service, leaving all impediments behind. You were notified July sixth (6th) that Second (2d) infantry would be sent via Portland, yet General Howard, on thirteenth (13th) did not know this. This regiment is expected here twenty-third (23d) . . . And will be forwarded without a day's delay. The division commander hopes General Howard has received General Sherman's instructions, forwarded June twenty-sixth (26th), to pay no attention to boundary lines of the division in operating against Joseph's band. He wishes them followed up till they are defeated and surrender or are driven beyond the boundaries of the United States.[1]

On July 19, Howard had dashed back to Fort Lapwai, leaving his troops at Kamiah, in order to attend to personal business. He was shaken to discover that the popular national papers were criticizing his administration of the war. The *San Francisco Chronicle* had featured continuous and critical coverage of the affair at Cottonwood with the "brave seventeen," the debacle at White Bird Canyon, even his current problems at Kamiah. Newspapers from coast to coast were running these pieces, and editorials called for his ouster.[2]

Howard's major problem in his campaign (other than negative press) had been mobility and countermobility. He had so far failed to move his troops with the swiftness of his adversary. Perhaps, he reasoned, he could use communications to limit the maneuverability of his enemy. More troops, better positioned, might be able to intercept the Nez Perce on the Montana side of the Rocky Mountains. He decided to get another dog in the fight. Because Sherman had told Howard to disregard all boundaries of the command, he sent a telegram to Captain Charles C. Rawn, commanding officer at Missoula, Montana, and advised him to move to block up the other side of the Lolo Trail.

> Sir: All reports seem to indicate that what are left of the hostile Indians, with their stock and plunder, have escaped by the Lolo Trail, and may reach you before this dispatch. . . . I shall start the trail . . . on the 26th. . . . If you could move your forces this way as far as the Lolo Fork you could prevent their escape.[3]

Colonel John Gibbon held his post at Fort Shaw on the Sun River to the east of the Rocky Mountains. He was fifty years old, stocky, strongly built, and going grey, and he had a determined countenance and coarse beard. Contemporaries describe him as possessing a good sense of humor and keen wit, with a talent for the tactics of combat. He had plenty of experience in his trade, fighting in Mexico and the Seminole War in Florida. In 1876, he had led troops onto the field in search of the survivors of Custer's cavalry.

Steadfastly loyal, the US Military Academy graduate had supported the Union, even though three brothers went over to the Confederate side. His accomplishments as a commander in the Civil War were legendary. His "black hats"—who looked splendid in the new black felt hats Gibbon procured—proved they were capable of more than sartorial splendor. They made a reputation for themselves at Gainseville, the Second Battle of Bull Run, and Antietam.[4] His men from Wisconsin and Michigan were hailed as among the finest troops in the world. Gibbon now found himself in a smaller theater but up against foes who were every inch the caliber of his nemesis Stonewall Jackson.

There was a lack of a military presence in the land that abutted the pass from the Lolo into the Bitterroot Valley. Gibbon had long intended to rectify this by building a post in the area, but the continual fights with the Sioux the previous year had tied up the manpower necessary for construction.[5] Now, with the Nez Perce coming over the pass, he found he needed to draw all the manpower he could muster from Forts Benton, Baker, and Shaw and bring them west. At this time, only one army unit was in western Montana, the 7th Infantry Regiment, under Gibbon's command.

Whether Gibbon surveyed the map of his command at this point is unknown. Perhaps he reflected upon the many forts across the broad state and the rugged terrain between them. He had already sent Captain Rawn with Company I and Captain William Logan with Company A of the 7th

Infantry from Fort Shaw to the extreme western part of the state near Missoula to construct the long-delayed post. Gibbon could call on those men because they were in the right area, but in the meantime he would need to draw men from the other forts and bring them together into a force with which he could attack decisively.[6]

He called to Company F, from his regiment at Fort Benton, as well as Company D in barracks at Camp Baker, to travel in haste to meet him at Fort Shaw. Gibbon was shuffling troops here and there as he raided the posts for men.

Colonel John Gibbon was a distinguished Union Civil War officer who commanded the 7th Infantry Regiment during the Nez Perce War. (*Library of Congress*)

He had summoned every able man and backfilled as he was able. As soon as he had Companies D and F, he departed from Fort Shaw with 200 soldiers: 168 regulars from Companies D, F, and K, and 32 volunteers and scouts. He moved at a fast pace, as he had 150 miles to traverse. Even so, Gibbon's force wouldn't reach Fort Missoula until August 3.

Gibbon was an artillery officer; he came up in cannon, and he thought like an artillery officer. He wrote the seminal army doctrine for the artillery branch.[7] His professional life had been consumed by judgments about terrain, target, inclination, and angle. He set his mind firmly on his target. Gibbon was a worthy adversary to oppose the Nez Perce. One of his best soldierly attributes was his ability to clearly see his strengths and weaknesses on a campaign, and he immediately realized that time and weight were also his enemy: bringing more equipment and supplies would slow him down, so he had to keep his gear as light as possible. As a seasoned Indian fighter, he knew the Nez Perce were moving considerably faster than any army force could match. He also knew that Howard had been outpaced by the fast-moving native host.

Gibbon needed to accelerate the speed of his troops to have any hope of intercepting the renegade tribe. He intended to move very fast, at a pace of more than thirty miles a day, to possibly catch his adversary off-guard. But his men were foot soldiers, so he couldn't hope to match the speed of his horse-borne opponents with his infantry. So Gibbon decided to load his men into wagons and move as fast as possible with his column.

Gibbon ordered his men to strip away all nonessential gear and pack for speed. Any equipment that could be discarded would be left behind. Blacksmith's kits and sabers could stay in the garrison. As an artilleryman, however, Gibbon could not help but stick to his roots. He would feel naked leaving without cannon.

He elected to take light cannon, called mountain howitzers. Weighing only five hundred pounds, they were easier and faster to move over narrow mountain paths and could be quickly positioned and aimed by a few men without having to use horses. The shot was also lighter to carry.

The Nez Perce began their descent from the highest point of the Lolo Trail. They found the going rougher with the trail carved out of what little ground existed between slopes; the vast river canyons were now looming dark and ominously over them. With every night the forest closed in closer around them, and the light in the canyons dimmed gradually to the absolute obsidianlike darkness, preventing any hope of nighttime progress. In many places, riders were forced to dismount and travel in a single file. While the close quarters of the trail offered the tribe greater security, it also confined it and slowed its travel considerably. A misstep in the darkness would doom anyone of them to a fall of hundreds of feet to the river. On their tenth day of trekking through the river canyon, the angle of descent flattened out, and they finally emerged onto the sandy banks of Lolo Creek, golden in the afternoon sunlight.

A mountain howitzer of the pattern used by Colonel Gibbon in his campaign. This one, and a twin, stand vigil at the entrance to the Columbia County Courthouse in Dayton, Washington. (*Author*)

At the eastern opening of the Lolo Pass, the Nez Perce finally reached the Bitterroot Valley. They were disappointed, however, to find the pass blocked by armed residents and a small number of troops.

Captain Rawn had experienced an eventful summer. On June 5, he had been ordered by his commanders at the District of Montana to take two companies from Fort Shaw to establish a new post at Missoula.[8] With instructions from Gibbon, he left on June 9 with Companies A and I of the 7th Infantry. Company I would form the new garrison for the post. The other company would assist in the hard work of building the fort. After marching 217 miles, they reached their new post on June 25.

Rawn, prominent among the commissioned officers in Gibbon's command, was somewhat in awe of the legendary commander of the "Iron Brigade" during the Civil War. He intended to do well for his commander and himself. He was proud to be part of a very good infantry unit.

Gibbon was part of General Sherman's reform movement to improve the fighting capabilities of all the branches of the army. Gibbon's 7th Infantry was manned by good soldiers who were well trained and equipped. His men enjoyed an esprit de corps due to the influence of their commanding general.[9]

Construction was slow due to supply problems and the lack of skilled workers. Rawn had only begun to worry about his first assignment when he received word of the Nez Perce approaching his vicinity over the Lolo Trail.

He ordered Second Lieutenant Francis Woodbridge and four men to act as scouts to reconnoiter the movements of the Nez Perce as they neared the Lolo Pass. Woodbridge moved out on July 18. After three days with no reports from Woodbridge, Rawn sent another party under First Lieutenant Charles Austin Coolidge consisting of citizen volunteers from the area and a private soldier to check the pass and the approaches. On the twenty-second, Woodbridge, returning to Missoula to report, happened to meet Coolidge on his way up the Lolo Trail.

Earlier that day, Woodbridge had encountered an escaped prisoner from the Nez Perce camp named John Hill who was half Nez Perce himself. Hill informed the officer that the Nez Perce were coming en masse from the west and would emerge from the Lolo shortly. He gave Woodbridge additional information on the tribe's whereabouts and the course it intended to take. Woodbridge then sent a courier ahead to Rawn with the intelligence he had gathered.[10]

Rawn read the dispatch with concern. It was his responsibility to inform the residents of Missoula of the imminent arrival of the warring tribe. Rawn immediately used the telegraph at Deer Lodge, Montana, some seventy miles southeast, to forward the intelligence to Colonel Gibbon at Fort Shaw.

He was expected to obstruct the Nez Perce in the trail and deny them access to the Bitterroot Valley. Rawn wasn't a green officer, as he was in his sixteenth year of service. But he probably had doubts about his ability to threaten or delay the 250 warriors heading his way. Nevertheless, with his few men he began making preparations.

As Rawn informed the local populace, the reactions ranged from moderate concern to panic. The people of the community and the Bitterroot Valley hastily formed volunteer companies to provide for their defense.

To obstruct the tribe's passage, the thirty-five troopers under Rawn's command moved up Lolo Creek. There, on July 25, he chose the ground to fortify their defensive position. The barricade sat astride the trail that led from Lolo Pass, following Lolo Creek, to the Bitterroot River, below present-day Missoula. His soldiers, joined by citizen volunteers in an uneasy alliance, constructed breastworks from earth and logs, and dug a ring of rifle pits. Rawn described the earthworks in his report to the Department of the Dakota:

> The excitement increasing, I, on the 25th of July with every available man that could possibly be spared, proceeded to Lo Lo, intrenched my command in what I considered the most defensible and least easily flanked part of the cañon between the Indians and the Bitter Root Valley. This was about eight miles from the mouth of the cañon, and two miles from the camp of the hostiles. My intentions were with my force (5 commissioned officers and 30 enlisted men), and assisted by the citizen volunteers, to compel the Indians to surrender their arms and ammunition and to dispute their passage by force of arms into Bitter Root Valley.[11]

Rawn had fifty local volunteers nominally under his command. Many of them had deep reservations about fighting the Nez Perce, whom they had regarded as friends. Others, given recent events, were frightened by the presence of the entire tribe and wanted to lend what assistance they could for the common defense. The inevitable opportunists and those with an ax to grind rounded out the citizen volunteers accompanying Rawn.

On July 27, James F. Mills, secretary of the Montana Territory, sent a dispatch to General McDowell in San Francisco from Deer Lodge:

> White Bird with over three hundred Nez Perces, is on the Lolo Trail thirty miles from Missoula; says he wants to go through the country peaceably if he can, forcibly if he must. Captain Rawn has one hundred and ten regulars and volunteers, and is entrenching in Lolo Canon; has just sent for help, and is going to fight them. Governor Potts reached Missoula last night, and courier is just in for men, guns, and cartridges, which are being forwarded rapidly; supply very limited. Company organizing to leave here immediately.[12]

McDowell retransmitted the dispatch in duplicate, via Walla Walla and Dayton in the Washington Territory, to General Howard.[13] On July 29, he sent Mills a wire informing him that General Howard was en route to Montana. He also wrote that he believed "the destruction of the hostile Indians is certain."[14]

When Looking Glass surveyed the state of Rawn's hastily built fort, he smiled at the crude construction and breast-high walls.[15] On the twenty-seventh, Rawn negotiated face-to-face with White Bird and Looking Glass, who sought to pass peaceably through the Bitterroot Valley with their two thousand horses and seven hundred people. Rawn proposed that the Nez Perce surrender their arms—a suggestion that was initially met more with astonishment than

Looking Glass, a leader of the Alpowai band of Nez Perce, was a keen tactician and diplomat. He, Joseph, White Bird, and other Nez Perce warriors astounded the US Army command by their well-designed battle plans. (*National Archives*)

with anger. Rainbow, a hero of many battles, made a Homeric promise:

"Do not tell me to lay down the gun! We did not want this war! . . . General Howard kindled war when he spoke the rifle in the peace council! We answered with the rifle and that answer stands to this sun! Some of my people have been killed, and I will kill some of the enemies and then I shall die in the battle!"[16]

Looking Glass, the spokesman, was more pragmatic. Patting his rifle held in the crook of one arm, he avowed: "Only with these, will we give up our cartridges."[17]

Those assembled were surprised to note that Joseph was not playing a key role in the negotiations as he had done before. Rawn had no way of knowing that Looking Glass was now both administrative and war chief of the combined bands.

Before leaving, Looking Glass cheerfully greeted old friends among the volunteers and invited them to the camp. He singled out a few of the younger men and teased them playfully. "I have two good looking daughters up at the camp. Come up and see them."[18] The boys politely declined.

Rawn was biding his time; he knew that Gibbon was on the march from Fort Shaw and that Howard was in close pursuit over the pass. In either case, he hoped he could extend the time spent in negotiations. Before Looking Glass left the field, Rawn arranged another meeting with just four men: Looking Glass and one warrior, Rawn, and his interpreter, Delaware Jim. Rawn stipulated that they should meet on the open prairie far enough to be out of rifle shot from their camp. The meeting took place the following day.

Rawn repeated his terms that in order for the Indians to pass, he would require them to surrender their cartridges, arms, horses, and livestock. Looking Glass said he had to talk to his people about the arrangements and would return under the same conditions at 9 a.m. the next day. Rawn, not understanding the nature of Nez Perce polity, was distrustful of Looking Glass's motives. Instead, he suggested noon as the time to meet. He returned to his redoubt, expecting an imminent attack on the breastworks.[19]

Looking Glass and the key warriors believed that the best course of action would be to negotiate passage with the white men who held the strong point. The Nez Perce were disheartened at seeing among the volunteers many Salish Indians—the tribe that had offered them assistance. Yellow

Wolf observed that the native men wore white on their arms and heads so they would not be mistaken for Nez Perce.[20] He felt betrayed. He was worried that the markings were so that the Flatheads would not accidentally shoot each other if bullets were to fly. After several meetings, Looking Glass and White Bird reached a separate understanding with the civilians led by E. A. Kenney, captain of a company of volunteers from Missoula. Kenney held the first brief parley with the Nez Perce and seemed a reasonable man to the chiefs. To the volunteers, Looking Glass appeared at ease and not at all concerned with their fortification. He reiterated that his people would not surrender their ammunition.

In the calculus of the settlers, bloodshed could be avoided, and they believed that the natives could be taken at their word. These same people had always visited and traded as neighbors in previous journeys to the hunting ground. Thus satisfied, the volunteers largely dissolved from Rawn's command.

Rawn realized that he couldn't hold the position without them. When the citizen volunteers began leaving after accepting the tribe's promise to pass peacefully, he bristled with indignation at the militia's refusal to submit to his authority. One of his officers threatened to shoot a volunteer officer to prevent "desertion." But the volunteers left anyway, and the tribe had won another, bloodless victory. With only about sixty men left, it was clear to Rawn that he could not fulfill his directive from Howard.

After all the drama, on July 28, the tribe simply disappeared into the surrounding woods and walked around the fort, shielded behind a nearby ridge. As they passed behind the fort, their skirmishers half-heartedly exchanged fire with some troops Rawn has posted to prevent a Nez Perce attack from the rear (and to stem the flow of deserters from his ranks).

Rawn made a desultory demonstration with his regular troops and advanced after the Indians, who continued to outpace him into the forest. But it was simply a face-saving gesture rather than an attack, and the Nez Perce would not be drawn into a real fight after making their promise.

Rawn was obliged to withdraw his small force to Missoula. The fortification was immediately dubbed Fort Fizzle by the locals, since it had prevented nothing.[21] The Nez Perce leadership had reached an understanding with the local folks that in return for safe passage through the Bitterroot Valley, they would guarantee that the settlers would not be harmed by raids or violence.

At Stevensville, Montana, fifteen miles south of the Lolo Trail and twenty miles from Missoula to the north, the volunteer company had reinforced the old trading post and garrison of Fort Owen into a new structure they christened "Fort Brave." The structure had fifteen-foot-high walls that enclosed a well. It contained an imposing thirty-one thousand square feet and would provide shelter for the citizenry if fighting broke out. Families who felt threatened occupied it immediately, while others stayed at their homesteads.

The Nez Perce headmen were still debating the matter of destination. Some argued that the way north might also be dangerous for them now that no one could be certain of the sympathies of the Flathead Indians. In any case, the finality of committing to a northeastern route to Canada was too much for Joseph. He did not want to leave the homeland forever.[22] Looking Glass told the council the way to go was south, to the waters of the Yellowstone and to the country of the Crow tribe, longtime friends of the Nez Perce. The Crow had lived for countless generations in the vastness of the Northern Plains. Occasional brushes with rival tribes sometimes resulted in brief conflicts, even generational enmity. But their relationship with the Nez Perce was different than with other tribes. Living in the shadow of great tribes like the Cheyenne or Sioux was a constant threat, and the competition for hunting grounds and territory made them tough and lean.[23] They formed a bond with the Nez Perce that extended as far as alliances in war, intermarriage, and common fashion. Committed to the southern route and the hope of help from longtime friends, the tribe proceeded in that direction.

The Nez Perce were able to procure much-needed supplies in Stevensville. On July 31, members of the tribe visited the town for supplies. The chiefs and senior warriors imposed order while supplies of flour, salt, coffee, sugar, and tobacco were replenished. Merchants in the town were selling at a high price, but the Nez Perce paid with gold, and without argument. White Bird sat astride his horse in the center of the street. Remembering the incident with the whiskey wagon, he kept order with his quirt and club. One poor soul found enough whiskey to become dangerous and fired off some shots until White Bird's mace knocked him unconscious. No other young warrior called his bluff.[24]

After leaving Stevensville, the tribe passed through the Bitterroot Valley. Believing that all their enemies were now far behind, they became less vigilant. Meanwhile, the determined Gibbon was coming at the pace of a forced march. Traveling twice the distance every day that the tribe did, he was closing in on it quickly.[25]

Looking Glass and his flock were being pursued from another direction, albeit at a slower pace. General Howard was still bringing his troops across the Lolo Trail at his best speed. They had been on the trail for three days. Major Mason believed they would be on the trail for three more when he wrote a letter to his wife from Camp Robert Pollock on August 4. He wrote that they had received bad news in a dispatch from Missoula written by Captain Rawn that said the Nez Perce had bypassed his entrenchments after he had talked with White Bird and Looking Glass, the Indians were purchasing supplies at a high markup from the local merchants, and his volunteers had abandoned him.[26]

The bands of the Nez Perce continued on a southern course for four days, crossing the Continental Divide on August 6, until finally they emerged onto the basin formed by the Big Hole River. Looking Glass ordered lodge poles cut, intending to give his people time to rest. White Bird and Red Owl argued that they should proceed north at once to Canada and not be caught sitting in their camp.

On August 8, while the Nez Perce were making their camp, Howard broke camp on the trail at dawn not far from the Bitterroot Valley and soon reached Rawn's abandoned fortification by the exit to the pass. A citizen showed Howard where the Nez Perce had bypassed the fort and climbed the heights to the right of Rawn's position, thereby avoiding a fight. Howard regretted that the position, which he saw as strong, could not have played a delaying role as he had planned.[27] His intentions had been to capture the Nez Perce inside the narrow trail. Once he had them bottled up in the narrow canyon, they were to be assailed simultaneously by his force at the rear and by Rawn's attack down the trail from the other side. The Nez Perce would have had no escape route out of the canyon. Another of Howard's tactical plans had failed to yield a victory.

Disappointed at the failure of this stratagem, he chose to camp at Stevensville with his cavalry on the eighth, his infantry always just a day or so behind him. He spent a restless night worrying. The rebellious Nez Perce were loose in Montana, and he dreaded what might happen in the days to come.[28]

Meantime, Gibbon concluded his long forced march from Fort Shaw and camped along Trail Creek at the foot of the Continental Divide over the night of August 7. He assigned First Lieutenant James H. Bradley and the 2nd Cavalry to advance to contact with the enemy and to attack its camp if feasible, during the night, when surprise was on their side. Anxious to move out, Bradley pushed on with his mounted force over the mountains. Gibbon roused his men at 5 a.m. to follow at their best speed.

On the eighth, Bradley and Lieutenant Joshua W. Jacobs intended to scout for the exact position of the Nez Perce camp. Bradley picked a handful of reliable men and sent them out in different directions from the advanced camp to canvas the entire valley for signs of the Nez Perce. Two hours later, one of their noncommissioned officers, a Corporal Drummond, returned to report that he had heard voices and movement beyond the dense forest to his front and returned immediately to inform Bradley.

The two lieutenants and the corporal went back on foot, leaving Sergeant Mildon H. Wilson of Company K in charge of the camp. The men advanced about a mile and a half, where Drummond noted the farthest point he had advanced. The men crept forward quietly. First Bradley, then Jacobs, began climbing a tall pine tree to see the area from above. Eventually, they emerged above the tops of the other trees blocking their line of sight. Now they could see a vast herd of Nez Perce horses grazing in a clearing beyond the forest. The horses were under the watchful gaze of several mounted warriors. Beyond the herd, the two men could see the Indian camp and the daily activities: lodge poles being cut, lodges built, and fires maintained. The two men climbed back down the tree as quietly as possible, worried that the sentries might see or hear them.

The three men returned quickly to the advanced camp and immediately sent a dispatch to Gibbon, advising him of their discovery.

Gibbon was now reinforced with Rawn and the two companies from Missoula. His strength was 168 regular army and 32 volunteers.[29] He felt better with a force of two hundred men. But he must have worried that he faced the usual problems of attacking a larger, mobile force. He must have struggled with the problem and reasoned that the only option to even the field was to attack when the warriors were least prepared to fight. In the sleepy hour of dawn, a surprise attack would either carry the day or his men would be mauled like the other troops had been in previous fights with the tribe. It was all or nothing.[30]

Some of the volunteers who accompanied Gibbon were unwilling to attack the camp with women and children asleep. Others had no such qualms. Before dawn on August 9, Gibbon led his troops down a sparsely wooded hillside on the left side of the river. Reaching lower and relatively flat ground, they began spreading out in a broad line formation. The swampy ground hindered their way, however.

Gibbon could finally see the Indian camp ahead in the distance, laid out on the river's right bank. The river ahead was no more than twenty-five feet wide. Beyond, the land leveled out. He was relieved, as it would be easier going for his men after negotiating the swamp and rough ground. The camp was arranged in the shape of a tapered arrowhead, with the point aiming downstream. There were nearly ninety tipis before them.

The men silently prepared for the attack as they crept down the incline in the darkness. About two hundred yards from the village, they could see a few women tending the fires before returning to their lodges in the predawn. The men passed through the Nez Perce ponies and crossed a small creek. Now within striking distance, the line of soldiers lay down in the cold and darkness, watching the fires 150 yards away.

Gibbon surveyed the ground from his overlook. He saw the unguarded village in a wide meadow. Two creeks, Trail

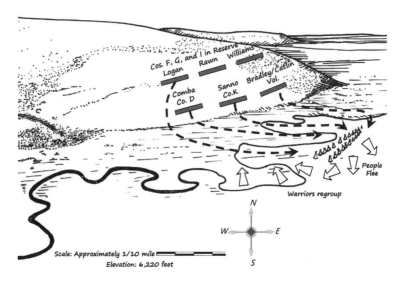

Colonel John Gibbon led a surpise dawn attack on the Nez Perce camp along the Big Hole River on August 9, 1877. (*Author*)

and Ruby, bound the meadow and gave their downstream water to the Big Hole River, lower now at the end of summer. He waited for light. The sleeping camp was to be attacked on Gibbon's command. He ordered his officers, "When the first shot is fired, charge the camp with the whole line."[31]

Some in the camp were early risers, such as Hahtalekin, chief of the Palouse. He was rounding up his horses near the stream when he observed the soldiers in the glimmer of early light. He crept quietly back into camp and alerted his Palouse warriors and the lower end of the camp. Fortunately for the Indians, two warriors, Yellow Bull and Red Elk, were also early risers. They alerted the upper end of the camp as well. But those in the middle slumbered on. An older man, Natelekin, was seeking his horses when he saw the soldiers indistinctly. He was partially blind and uncertain what was afoot, until a volley of shots ended his life. The four shots woke Yellow Wolf, who ran out of his tipi with only a war club. More rifle shots and commotion roused the sleeping. A man running by told Yellow Wolf that stalwart Rainbow had been killed. Yellow Wolf could not believe what had befallen them. He was looking for a rifle and a younger man, John Minthon, offered his. It was loaded with one shell. Within a few minutes, in the confusion he found a Winchester repeating rifle with a full magazine.

The first shots had been fired, and as ordered, the army line charged, firing as it ran through the trees and brush. The initial attack swept through the camp at the tip of the arrowhead made of tipis. Three companies attacked the camp: A company of regular army troops attacked the upper end, led by Captain Richard Comba. The middle thrust was commanded by Captain James Sanno. The lower end of the camp was assaulted by ninety men, a mix of army and militia, under the command of Captain John Catlain. Men, women, and children ran in terror from the mounted soldiers, and many were cut down trying to escape. Many soldiers fired blindly into the tipis to their front. Lieutenant Bradley was killed as he led them toward the village, and his men wavered.

In the middle portion of the camp, Wahlitas and his wife sought shelter in a depression to the front of their tipi. Wahlitas dug in. He told his wife to flee to the rear and hide with the other women. She tried to run but was shot and managed to crawl back to his side in the pit. Wahlitas shot a soldier to his immediate front. Soldiers moving through the willow trees and thickets began to fire in his direction. Wahlitas was shot in the head and died immediately. His wife picked up his rifle and shot the man who killed him. A volley of bullets from the advancing soldiers ended her life.[32]

Inside of twenty minutes, the attack drove most of the occupants out of the village. Many fled to the willows along

Pictographs drawn in 1927 by Peo Peo Tholekt of the Battle of Big Hole. Note the Nez Perce camp below right. (*Washington State University Library, MASC*)

the far side of Ruby Creek. A few men called out to their brother warriors to stand and not run from the army. Sarpsis Ilppilp donned his mystical white wolf pelt robe. He summoned his wyakin guardian powers and charged into the fray firing his magazine rifle.

Sergeant Wilson was part of the force attacking into the tipis. He was running slightly behind Lieutenant Jacobs when a warrior stepped into his path and raised his rifle to shoot Jacobs. Wilson fired quickly and saved the lieutenant's life. The warrior collapsed, and Wilson ran on, following the young officer. The incident seemed to arouse Jacobs, who became fearless, "fighting like a lion" with a pistol firing in each hand.[33]

At the upper end of the camp, soldiers under the command of Captain Logan pushed far into the camp along the river and were at first successful. But soon Logan realized they had advanced too far and their flank was exposed. Warriors, hidden from view along the river bank, rose and began firing deadly volleys into the left flank and rear of the troops. Because there were women and children in the water, Logan had cautioned his men not to shoot randomly. Soon Logan was shot in the head, and he died instantly. He was probably shot by the wife of a man he had just killed.[34] His sergeants rallied the men and charged the flanking force, engaging in vicious close fighting along the bank.

A small group of warriors skirmished with the citizen volunteers as they were trying to drive off several hundred Indian horses. The warriors dispersed the volunteers with rifle fire. They then drove their recaptured horses in a massed herd to safety downriver and out of the midst of the battle.

Gibbon ordered his troops to advance against the largest group of warriors, who had fled across the river, but Chiefs White Bird and Looking Glass had by then collected their men. Exhorting them to defend their families, White Bird declared, "Why are we retreating? Since the world was made, brave men have fought for their women and children. Shall we run into the mountains and let these white dogs kill our women and children before our eyes? It is better that we should be killed fighting. Now is our time to fight."[35] Emboldened, the warriors counterattacked, driving the soldiers out of the camp while flanking and shooting them. The organized warriors supported each other as they advanced and, using concentrated gunfire, stopped Gibbon's attack. The fighting was pitched, hand-to-hand in some cases. The Nez Perce continued to gain ground.[36]

At a distance, the Nez Perce marksmen inflicted heavy casualties, and Gibbon was forced to withdraw, but he was soon taking on fire from two directions and became immobilized in a wooded area not far from the camp. He ordered his men to dig entrenchments along the slopes of a gully that ran transversely through the woods. He dispatched militia member William Edwards on a fast horse to alert the supply base and Howard's command of their dire situation. He arrayed his men back-to-back and ordered charges by the line to clear some room around them.

The Nez Perce decided to try burning the soldiers within the wood. At first the fire raged on, blown by the prevailing winds directly at the surrounded troops, moving uncomfortably close to them. On top of the endless firing from the Nez Perce, Gibbon was afraid that some men might bolt to escape the literal heat of battle. The colonel was considering all of his options. It was not his nature to give up, and he announced his intention to charge and break out rather than see his men burn.

Gibbon recalled the desperate fight: "At almost every crack of a rifle from the distant hills some member of the command was sure to fall."[37] At the last minute, the winds shifted and blew the fire back from their position in the wooded gully. The acrid smoke of burning prairie grass swirled around the indistinct figures and burned the combatant's eyes. Bullets flew indiscriminately through the haze.

A team of warriors reached the high ground behind Gibbon on the bank where the soldiers had retreated. At this point in the fight, Gibbon was sure their collective backs were against the wall. Fighting continued through the afternoon and into the night. He needed to send men back to the wagons to bring up food and water, because his troops had had nothing but meager rations in more than a day. He was certain that exhaustion and hunger would soon sap their will and morale. In desperation, he ordered his famished men to slice steaks from a dead horse, which they ate raw.

As the first light of dawn appeared on the horizon on August 9, Gibbon called in his artillery support. Accompanied by scout Joe Blodgett, a team of six soldiers and noncommissioned officers wheeled the mountain howitzer nearly a half a mile onto a bluff near the front line and prepared to fire. Chief Ollokot led his group of thirty mounted warriors in a head-on assault on the gun. Riding and running as fast as possible, they quickly closed the distance to the gun. Two of the soldiers fled, but the other four made a stand. They were able to load and fire the piece twice at their attackers. The defenders also fired their rifles, but the attacking warriors were not deterred. The three noncommissioned officers pried the gun off the trunnion and threw it to the ground to keep the warriors from using it. The attackers overcame the gun crew and captured the howitzer, leaving Corporal Robert Sayles dead and Sergeants Patrick C. Daly and John W. Fredericks wounded. Both horses pulling the weapon were killed in the close exchange of gunfire. A private named Bennett, who was the teamster, was trapped beneath one of the horses. He escaped and returned to his unit after the Indians left the field.[38]

The natives dismantled the piece, taking the wheels off the trunnion, and hastily buried the parts. Warriors from the same party attacked Gibbon's supply wagons five miles away. The few soldiers guarding the wagon train crawled beneath the wagons. The defenders put up a stiff defense, shooting their rifles from ground level at every threat around them whenever Ollokot's men attacked. Eventually, the war party gave up the assault and withdrew to rejoin the fierce battle. Ollokot's warriors retired with a mule in tow, loaded with two thousand rifle cartridges. All of the ammunition they had bagged could be chambered in the many army rifles they had already acquired.

Gibbon wrote later to the secretary of war: "Just as we took up our position in the timber two shots from our howitzer above us on the trail were heard, and we afterward learned that the gun and pack-mule that were on the road to us were intercepted by the Indians."[39]

A courier from Howard arrived, advising Gibbon that the general was coming as fast as possible, mounted with twenty cavalry troopers and thirty Walla Walla Indians. The colonel asked the courier if he could confirm that his supply wagons were still intact to their rear. The courier informed him that he had not seen the wagons during his approach. Gibbon feared the worst for the men he had left with the wagons.

The Nez Perce had set the wild grass on fire, probably to cover their attacking forces and the families fleeing the battlefield. The fire was not a factor in their advance, but the smoke obscured visibility, and the soldiers were shocked when they realized the native attack was close upon them. The Indian assault also succeeded in shielding those fleeing the fight; in the ensuing combat, Gibbon was wounded in the leg.

Yellow Wolf related part of his battle experience as he crossed the site of the predawn attack:

> At this place I came to a dead soldier [feigning death]. A knife was in his hand. He lay as if he had fixed his position-rifle at right side. When I stooped to get the gun the soldier almost stabbed me. His knife grazed my nose. I jumped five, maybe seven feet getting away from that knife. Approaching, I struck him with my kopluts. He did not raise up. I took his gun and cartridge belt.[40]

Gibbon was unable to dislodge the besiegers from either side. There were reports of enemy to his rear, threatening the supply wagons and baggage. His force was now seriously in danger of annihilation. One more determined Nez Perce charge at their line might be the last that he and his men could repulse. Hungry, thirsty, and short on ammunition, the troops looked to the man who led them.

At this desperate moment, Gibbon reflected that he knew something of men at war. He had forged troops into the Iron Brigade, and he knew he had pushed these men as hard. They would hold, if only he could find a way to bring them the desperately needed ammunition from the supply wagons.

His spirits were buoyed when a soldier arrived through the enemy lines with a report that the supply train was intact and safely in their possession. Gibbon ordered Sergeant Wilson to bring it up to their position as quickly as possible. Wilson picked a detail of six soldiers and led them out of the battlefield. The rest of the soldiers anxiously awaited the arrival of food, blankets, water, and ammunition. As the train moved close to their position, Captain George L. Browning and Lieutenant Woodbridge took another troop of men and met it.

Gibbon was concerned that his original message for help had not made it out of the battle. The colonel asked for a volunteer to carry a dispatch to Deer Lodge. Wilson, just returned from his mission to retrieve the wagon, volunteered to carry the missive back through the lines.

The native stock and horses were already herded from where they had been taken for safety. Many of the horses and most of the remaining cattle had to be abandoned so the tribe could move quickly from the battlefield. Before first light the following day, the tribe was on the move, leaving behind valuable robes and tipis as well. Their movement was painfully slow because they carried their dead and wounded in travois, made from the lodge poles of their broken lodges and tipis.

Yellow Wolf later explained why they didn't finish off the soldiers in the ravine with a final charge: "If we killed one soldier, a thousand would take his place. If we lost one warrior, there was none to take his place."[41]

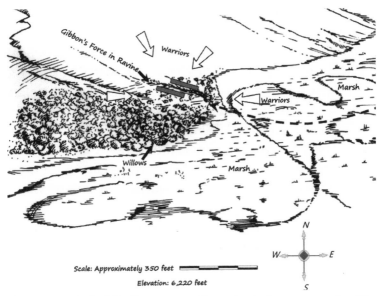

On August 10, the Nez Perce were able to check the army attack at Big Hole and avoid being completely overrun. (*Author*)

A council was held and the warriors and chiefs decided that the soldiers were no longer dangerous to them or their families. The cries of the soldiers' wounded and dying were pitiable. The chiefs and prominent warriors realized that so many of their best combatants had died, and there was no reason to lose more fighters needlessly. They decided to leave some young men behind to hold the soldiers in place while the tribe left the field.

Ollokot and a squad-size group of men stayed behind to pin the enemy in place for as long as they could, denying them the mobility to pursue the tribe. The warriors shot from distant cover and called to the soldiers, deriding their skill at arms and their manhood. No taunts were sufficient to provoke a response, so they watched and listened through the night. The next morning, August 10, Ollokot, who was leading the young men, told the warriors to fire a few volleys to keep the troops in place. Then the warriors began a slow withdrawal as a rear guard to the wounded and sorrowful column of their people.

At 10 a.m., General Howard rode onto the battlefield with his advance party. He had anticipated that Gibbon might have a rough time after attacking the tribe. His fastest cavalry were far ahead of the main body of the army when they encountered Gibbon's dispatch riders and rode swiftly on ahead to the site of the battle. After Howard's troops reached the battlefield to relieve Gibbon, any of Ollokot's warriors still in the immediate area withdrew into the woods.

The battleground was a hellish scene of devastation, with the dead and wounded lying over the entire field. The air was pungent with the stench of death, smoke, and gunpowder.

Now there was time to care for the casualties and to plan the next move. On the eleventh, the soldiers buried the dead and recovered the hidden howitzer, minus the gun carriage.

Medical officers treated the wounded in Gibbon's command throughout the day with what care they could render in the field. The Bannock Indian scouts who accompanied Howard disinterred and desecrated the Nez Perce dead. Howard showed his disgust and dissatisfaction but did not interfere. Mason arrived at the head of the rest of Howard's cavalry late on the twelfth. Before being evacuated, Gibbon detached Captain Browning, Lieutenants George H. Wright and John T. Van Orsdale, and fifty men to continue the pursuit with Howard. The next day at first light, Howard added the men to his battalion and took up the chase in earnest again.

Sergeant Charles N. Loynes would later write about the equipment that was left behind at the camp: "Very little that they might have use for. No doubt the women gathered up everything wanted while the men were busy with us on the hillside. From where we were entrenched the camp could not be seen consequently there was nothing visible to shoot at."[42]

In the battle, Gibbon's forces took 50 percent casualties, with twenty-nine of the attacking soldiers killed in action. The Montana volunteer company suffered 30 percent casualties, with six dead and four wounded. Gibbon had lost many of his officers. First Lieutenants Bradley and William L. English lay among the twenty-five dead. The veteran Captain Logan had seen his last battle and lay with them.[43]

The first of the thirty-four wounded men, including Gibbon, were hauled out in travois ninety miles to Deer Lodge, where better medical care was available. It would be four days before all the men would reach the aid station. Eventually the wounded were evacuated to Fort Missoula to recover.

The Nez Perce had sixty to seventy combatants and innocents killed, including Rainbow and Five Wounds (Pahkatos Owyeen). Their loss was a significant blow to the planning, leadership, and execution of the warriors in battles to come.[44] Also among the dead were Wahlitas and Sarpsis Ilppilp, two of the Three Red Coats who began the war.[45] Young Swan Necklace still lived, and fought on. When his people had reached a safe distance from the battlefield, Ollokot and his men rejoined them.

A new brutality had entered the grim fighting at the Big Hole battlefield. Innocent noncombatants, including many women and children, suffered the most casualties, and hatred on both sides was roused, particularly because many of the dead had been desecrated. Contributing factors to the outrages were the mix of civilian volunteers in the initial attack and the presence of Bannock Indians in the fray after the battle.[46] This particular army engagement was brutal in every aspect. The beginning was intentionally shocking and chaotic; the counterattack by White Bird decimated the army and drove it into a gulch, where it should have died. But the warriors were demoralized and seemed to lack the will to finish the soldiers they had surrounded. They had just fought their way across the wreckage and ashes of their lodges and their loved ones, lying hurt, dead, or dying. Grief, shock, and exhaustion on both sides caused any more significant movement to stall until the Nez Perce withdrawal from the field.

The Nee-Mee-Poo now realized that the army intended to pursue them wherever they went. From this point there was also a marked change in the tribe's treatment of noncombatants. After all, Gibbon's men had killed sleeping women and children in their attack. The tribe that had claimed that no Nez Perce had ever killed a white person now had no qualms about killing whites in its path—whether they were scouts, settlers, or teamsters. Hundreds of white noncombatants directly in the path of the tribe soon found themselves in mortal peril.[47]

Although White Bird made solid arguments why they needed to head north, they instead turned south to the Bighorn River valley on the Montana side of the Bitterroot Mountains. That was probably because Looking Glass still believed that a pact could be made with the powerful Crow Indians and that combined they could come to favorable terms with the U.S. government. White Bird was uncomfortable with the decision. He proposed what he knew to be a better option. The way was clear to the north, and following the Flathead River would be easy going and a fast trek to safety. They could make the border in a little over two days. He knew they should continue on to Canada and join Sitting Bull, with confidence that the very large numbers of his Lakota warriors would guarantee their safety—even from the army.

The Nez Perce may not have fully appreciated the concept of the national sovereignty of Canada, but they certainly knew that the army would not hastily engage a vastly superior and forewarned Lakota force that had destroyed Custer's 7th Cavalry the previous summer. But as they headed south instead, their chosen trail was not a march to freedom, as three large army units maneuvered to encircle them.

On August 14, a telegram was relayed from Virginia City, which lay to the south of Missoula and Helena, to Deer Lodge, and then by dispatch rider to the Big Hole Pass. In the telegram, General Alfred H. Terry, commanding the Department of Dakota, which encompassed Montana as well as the Dakota Territory, attempted to quell fears that the hostile Sioux exiled in Canada might make an alliance with the Nez Perce within his jurisdiction. Terry viewed the Lakota Sioux and their chief, Sitting Bull, as "my band of the hostile Sioux" because they had fled north of his area of responsibility after killing Custer in 1876. Terry wanted to make sure that the commanders involved understood his commitment and that he already had scouts in two major river valleys that might provide an escape route to Canada for the Nez Perce. General Howard understood his meaning:

> Everything in this department that can be of service to you and is within your reach is at your disposal. There are no Sioux west of the meridian of the Tongue River, except those who have fled to the British possessions. It is impossible that the Nez Perces should form a junction with my band of the hostile Sioux: but for the purpose of catching any fugitives who may make their way east I have ordered the Mussel Shell and Judith country to be watched.[48]

On the eighteenth, Lieutenant General Philip H. Sheridan, who commanded the Military Division of the Missouri from Chicago, ordered Terry to be prepared in the event the Nez Perce moved through the newly created Yellowstone Park, which spanned parts of the Montana,

Idaho, and Wyoming territories. Also, he was directed to follow the Stinking Water River, which ran through Yellowstone Park, and be sure to get dispatches to Colonel Nelson Miles to send out as many scouts as he could to determine if they would cross the Big Horn country in Wyoming. If they did, he wanted Miles to "clean them out completely."[49] Sheridan would also dispatch his own scouts from Camp Brown in the Wyoming Territory to watch for the tribe.

The scouts were out, the trap was set, and Miles would ensure that he was in position to spring it on the Nez Perce.

9

The Battle of Camas Meadows

Continuing on their southwest course along the Big Hole River toward Bannock City, Montana, the Nez Perce crossed first Bloody Dick Creek and then Horse Prairie Creek, emerging onto the edge of the Horse Prairie Valley. The Horse Prairie Valley was a plain of undulating low hills on a relatively level plain forty miles east of Salmon City, Idaho, close to the Idaho border. It was good ranching country and sparsely populated in 1877. At the word of the arrival of the fleeing Nez Perce, most ranchers and settlers fled north to Bannock City for shelter.

Moving south, the Nez Perce crossed back into Idaho at Camas Meadows, heading for the Yellowstone River. Their pace had slackened a bit even though they understood the urgency of speed. They were simply unable to travel as far in a day because the dead and wounded they were carrying slowed them down considerably.

At the front of the column setting the pace was the Bitterroot Nez Perce Lean Elk (Wahwookya Wasaaw), acting as leader and guide. Lean Elk had many names; sometimes he was known as Chief Hototo, and also as Little Tobacco. He was a traveler and ranged far across the country in his wanderings. He was short of stature, energetic, and loud, making his commands heard at a distance. He had half French blood and half Nez Perce from the Montana band of Chief Eagle of the Light.[1] The whites in Montana knew him as "Poker Joe," and he was described as being remarkable at games of chance. He and his people were viewed with suspicion and fear. His band met the tribe during its Lolo Trail crossing. With news of the outbreak of violence, the growing and groundless suspicion of the white people in Virginia City, Montana Territory, toward his Bitterroot band may have inclined him to join the tribe. Whatever his motivation, he had decided to throw his lot in with his fleeing friends. He and his six lodges of followers joined the Nez Perce patriots. Lean Elk was wealthy, homely, and very smart.[2]

After the deadly army attack, Looking Glass's influence had diminished, and the people had lost faith in him as their guide and leader.[3] Lean Elk filled the leadership vacuum, and the Nez Perce put their faith in him to guide them to safety. Because he lived among the Bitterroot-area Nez Perce, he knew the country and trails intimately.

Lean Elk intentionally skirted the timberline to the west of the Big Hole Valley. Weaving through the trees cost them time, and it was harder for the wounded, carried in the travois, but he intended to avoid the open spaces as much as possible while traveling. Lean Elk knew that enemy scouts were everywhere, and to avoid them he was bringing the Nez Perce south toward Skinner Meadows.

Approximately fifteen miles from the Big Hole battlefield, they made their first camp along the banks of a small creek at a place called Takseen (willows).[4] The tribe had been gravely wounded emotionally and physically. They wailed and implored the spirits, grieving their losses and unmindful of the threat that any sound presented to their survival. Lean Elk and Looking Glass allowed this as they struggled with their own sorrows. They knew that the living must first mourn for the dead, if there was any hope of finding their way around their enemies—enemies who seemed to be everywhere, and who had attacked in the dawn from nowhere.

Warriors barricaded the approaches to their camp. They dug rifle pits and placed large stones to their front. The solemn fighters spent an uncomfortable night in the cold, crouching near the pits, watching, listening, and waiting.

Throughout the war, the army and Indian horses bore great hardship. Horses have a discrete distance-to-feed ratio, and overdriving them leads to illness and exhaustion, just as with humans. Many horses died because of the extremes of weather, lack of water, starvation, illness, and battle. Gibbon had to leave many horses behind as he chased the tribe; many were played out in the first few days, and those remaining developed a serious hoof disease that spread throughout the herd. Two problems contributed to the condition of the cavalry horses. One was that the army was accustomed to acquiring its horses by means of contractors. Profiteers would supply mounts that were not up to the rigors of rugged terrain and should never have been cavalry horses. The other was that the cavalry troops were not very good at their specialty. An essential job of a frontier cavalry soldier was tending to one's horse. The successful use of cavalry presupposes that the horses are also fit for duty.

With a few exceptions, these cavalry units in Montana and Idaho were not very good. A contributor to the generally poor quality of individual cavalry soldiers and units was the doctrine with which the army chose to prosecute its "pacification" role. The prevailing inclination of thought, which Sherman and Sheridan both supported, was to advance a front of small forts, year after year, deeper into the frontier territories. The presence of these forts, it was felt, would dissuade rebellious Indians from opposing the government. The unintended consequence of this strategy was a dilution of the regimen of drill and training.[5] No thought at all was given to adapting tactics and training to the unorthodox conflicts the army was fighting in the West. And to top it off, General Sherman was presiding over a period of cuts and reductions in an already-lean army. As a result, better mounts and better riders were not a priority.[6]

The Indian ponies were not much better off. The tribe lost many horses in the battle and had not been able to adequately rest and recharge the horses that had already come over one thousand two hundred miles. The Nez Perce were legendary for being able to nurse horses through arduous treks and get the maximum from them in stamina and health. But the adversity of their circumstances was simply too extreme even for their talent with horses to overcome. The Nez Perce hoped to find fresh horses to continue their flight. In the interim, their surviving horses lumbered along, fatigued and hungry. The lack of healthy horses had become a major problem for the tribe.

Their survival depended upon mobility. Losing their freedom of movement meant certain death or capture at the hands of the army. Somewhere, they needed to acquire more horses.

The Nez Perce left their Takseen camp and moved to the southeast. They crossed the Big Hole divide near Skinner Meadows and entered the Horse Prairie Valley in southern Montana. It must have raised their spirits somewhat to be in the beautiful prairie with plentiful grasses and streams bounded by aspens and cottonwood. The area had plentiful game, with large herds of antelope and deer. In the distance, the great mountain ranges sheltered the plain and cast long shadows in the late afternoon.

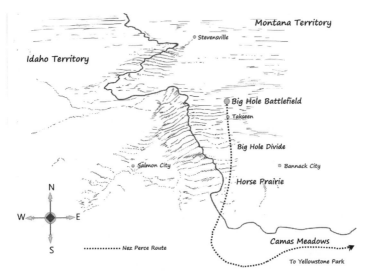

Moving south after the battle of Big Hole, the Nez Perce crossed back into Idaho. Had White Bird been successful in persuading the council of chiefs, Canada would have been a brief two days' march away. (*Author*)

Edging along Trail Creek on August 12, a scouting band of Nez Perce warriors numbering fifty to sixty was hunting for horses in advance of the main host when they saw a ranch house in the distance. It was part of an operation owned by William L. Montague and Daniel Winters. Arriving at the Montague-Winters spread, they found few people working the place. With everyone vigilant for Indian attacks, the women had been taken into Bannock City for protection; six men were still at the ranch. Montague and Thomas Flynn were in the ranch house making dinner, while two ranch hands, James Smith and James Farnsworth, were at the back of the ranch and were not immediately aware of the presence of the war party. Winters and Milton Norris were working out in the distant fields away from the ranch. It was haying time, and the work dispersed the men some distance from the ranch house. Looking up from their labors, Winters and Norris

saw a large party of Indian warriors riding purposefully to
the ranch. An armed William Montague met them on his
porch. Shots were fired, and Montague and Flynn were
soon lying dead in the house. Winters and Norris raced
back toward the house, only to find that it was under attack.
Soon Smith and Farnsworth were also shot dead.

Winters and Norris were able to escape to the cover of
the nearby woods, where they hid until nightfall. They
then made their best time to Bannock City to warn the residents that their worst fears had been realized. Meanwhile,
the warriors collected all the horses at the ranch and rode
south, crossing into eastern Idaho looking for more horses
to replenish their herds.[7]

A party of citizens from Bannock City went to the ranch
the following day.[8] They soon found the bodies of
Montague and Flynn in or near the house, and the other
two victims outside. Mrs. Montague insisted on going into
the house to see her husband's body. With the stoicism of a
hardened frontier woman, she managed her grief better
than Mrs. Winters, who accompanied her and was unaware
that her own husband, Daniel, had escaped and was in hiding. The solemn party took the bodies back to Bannock
City for burial, where Mrs. Winters was joyfully reunited
with her husband.

Immediately after the attack, the warriors moved to
another homestead some five miles away. The rancher,
Thomas Hamilton, raised cattle and employed several men
to run the place. Three of the men, Alex Cooper, John
Wagoner, and Andrew Meyers, and a man named Howard
were confronted by the warriors looking over their horses
and trying to force open the door of their cabin. The men
escaped and ran for the tree line to hide.[9]

The warriors chased the ranchers in close pursuit, but
the men broke into the thick cover of the wood and found
hiding places in the willows.[10] The warriors called out,

promising that if the men surrendered they would be spared any harm. Cooper decided to emerge from the woods and was shot and killed. Meyers and the others burrowed deeper into their hiding place until the Indians left the ranch. After dark, when it was safe, they emerged. A quick search by the men confirmed that the horses had been taken. The three survivors buried Cooper, and Meyers started a long trek to Bannock City, walking and running, to alert the citizens to the threat.[11]

Yellow Wolf described the raids for the horses dispassionately: "We now kept moving for three suns, watching always for horses. While we had many horses, it was good to have fresh ones. . . . We took many horses at places I do not know by white names. Some fighting and a few white people killed where horses were captured."[12]

The tribe moved through the Horse Prairie area on August 13, heading south toward the Continental Divide and the Bannock Pass, where it intended to reenter Idaho.

On the fourteenth, the raiding parties scouting ahead of the tribe encountered men driving freight wagons from the railhead in Utah bound for Salmon City and Leesburg, Idaho. In the ensuing trouble, at least three white men died while two Chinese men employed to cook for the wagoners were spared. On August 27, a letter would reach prominent citizen George Shoup in Salmon City from his shipping agent, L. C. Morse, detailing his concerns about the fate of the three shippers—named Heyden, Green, and Coombs—in what would become known as the Birch Creek massacre. Little remained of the goods from the wagons. Whatever items the warriors did not pillage were destroyed, as the wagons were set on fire and left to burn in the wake of the warriors.[13] Morse wrote:

> The report is here that Heyden, Green & Coombs have been killed by the Indians, but we can't get anything reliable hope it is a false report. One of Jim's

wheel mules & Ian's dog have been found dead near
sand holes and recognize by some freighters also one
of Jim's lead mules found by a man and by him sold
to a traveler. It look[s] dark Wheeler was very anxious to get word from you here and I am waiting for
to day's mail. Can't hear anything from The Salmon
river direct.[14]

The communities in the area reacted much as the communities in the Bitteroot Valley had done. Stockades were
built, and companies of volunteers were raised for defense.

General Howard's scouts reported to him that the Nez
Perce were still within striking distance. They brought the
reports of the deaths of the teamsters killed on the Horse
Prairie. The whirlwind raids on the ranches and wagons
provided the tribe much-needed fresh horses and supplies.
Meanwhile, Howard's weary force moved on to Bannock
City, reaching it on August 14 along with his group of citizen volunteers under the command of Captain William A.
Clark from Gibbon's ordeal at Big Hole. Howard felt
greater urgency than ever to block and fight the tribe after
the deaths on the Horse Prairie.[15]

Lean Elk made camp fifteen miles beyond Camas
Meadows. Ahead, he reasoned, there were only two tenable
passes through the towering and rugged Absaroka Range.
Each was carved by the course of a river from the summit
down to the prairie. One way was the Clarks Fork River,
flowing to the northeast to join the Yellowstone. The way
through the mountains along this route was the Targhee
Pass. The other way was to follow the Stinking Water
River, flowing to the east to join the Bighorn River in its
natural drainage.[16] As he pondered the tribe's course, his
adversary reflected upon his own.

With no special intelligence on the plans of the Nez
Perce and no prescience to divine their course, Howard
had to decide what he thought the tribe would do. Looking

at the maps he had of the area, he came to the same conclusion as Lean Elk: it was one pass or the other. If the Indians went farther east by the Salmon River or past Henry's Lake, he knew they had several options to escape again. If they went farther south, there were political and military considerations. Regardless of his instructions to ignore the bounds of any military district, his men and horses were exhausted. He had chased the Nez Perce through two military departments, and now they looked to cross into a third. If that happened, Howard seriously considered allowing General George R. Crook in the Department of the Dakotas to deal with the problem. His political problem was that the people of the Lemhi area to his south, organized by George Shoup, were literally up in arms. Shoup was demanding that Howard provide relief to the area.[17]

He sought the advice of his Indian scouts, who advised him that they felt the Yellowstone River would be the likely destination the tribe would head toward.[18]

With this counsel, Howard detached a small unit of cavalry commanded by Lieutenant George R. Bacon with orders to sweep in an arc around the Nez Perce in order to reach the Targhee Pass ahead of the tribe, thereby cutting off its retreat through the Absaroka Range and catching it between the two forces. If his plan was executed swiftly, the Nez Perce would have no escape route. Meanwhile, on August 19, Howard moved his forces to the Camas Meadows and made a bivouac. After dispatching his blocking force, guards were set at their pickets for the night, and horses were hobbled and tied to lines to graze.

White Bird and Looking Glass had plans of their own, which they put into effect on the twentieth. Unknown to the soldiers, not far away, a Nez Perce raiding party was moving silently and in the darkness. It had stopped along the way and decided on its plan. Looking Glass, White

Bull, and Ollokot would attack on horseback while their warriors, ahead of the horse riders, crept through the soldiers' pickets to release the army horses from their tethers. The mounted warriors waited quietly as their men crept into the slumbering camp. Wottolen and two other warriors, Left Hand and Five Lightnings, were guarding a key position near the soldiers' tents.

The sentry heard the steady footfalls of horses, perhaps coming into the camp late. The guard issued the routine challenge and was suddenly aware that he was looking at a large group of Indians. A shot rang out, and he knew that he needed to raise the alarm.[19] Suddenly, the group of men on horseback broke apart, with warriors riding in all directions shooting. The sentry heard officers and sergeants calling out orders to their men. Bernard Brooks, the bugler, was calling "boots and saddles," which was the call to prepare to fight and for the cavalry to get their horses ready. The Indian warriors were among the horses and mules that he had been guarding, cutting tethers and hobbles, and stampeding the herd. A significant number of Indians was among the pack animals. Mules and horses bolted through the darkness. The warriors broke off, riding fast in different directions and sowing confusion. The camp erupted in war cries, shots, and panic. Horses began to run wild through the camp, and many were driven by the raiders out of the camp, as were the pack mules. It was only minutes from beginning to end, but the sudden raid had tremendous implications for the immediate course of the war.[20]

The first response came from volunteers from Montana, commanded by Captain Clark. The volunteers ran to the pickets to calm their remaining horses that were panicking and straining at their ropes, and found that some had already been taken. General Howard ordered Major George B. Sanford to pursue the Nez Perce raiders at first light and try to recover what animals he could. Despite the heavy loss of horses, two of Sanford's companies were assembled and ready to go in a short time.

Captain Camillus C. Carr ordered Company I of the 1st Cavalry to mount up and pursue the raiders. First Lieutenant Charles Cresson accompanied him. Cresson was an experienced soldier who had risen from the enlisted ranks to become an officer.[21] Company B, 1st Cavalry, commanded by Captain James Jackson[22] and Lieutenant John Q. Adams, rode out as well, followed by Company L, 2nd Cavalry, commanded by Captain Randall Norwood and Lieutenant Henry M. Benson.[23]

The plan was simple enough: the two companies of the 1st Cavalry would split left and right, while Norwood's 2nd Cavalry would run up the middle. After a ride of thirty minutes through the chilly morning air, the enemy's trail could be seen snaking into the foothills ahead.

With the Nez Perce ahead, Norwood charged up the middle. For a time, seventy-five horses were back in the possession of the cavalry, but the noise panicked them, and all but twenty-five were flushed back to the Indians.

The war party left a blocking force in place on its back trail, and the cavalry was galloping headlong into it. The Nez Perce had occupied rocky cover on the far side of a lava ridge. Their defensive breastworks were natural rock formations that gave them excellent cover and from which they raked the cavalry with withering gunfire. Captain Carr's company was the first to close with the enemy to the front, and it suffered the greatest concentration of fire from the Nez Perce defenders at the outset of the fight. Carr ordered his men to dismount, as did Norwood and Sanford, and the horses were taken to the rear.[24] Carr and Norwood joined their companies in line. Captain Jackson was on the far right. The men designated as horse handlers took their mounts to the rear.[25] The Nez Perce concentrated their fire on the left flank and began to turn it. All three companies

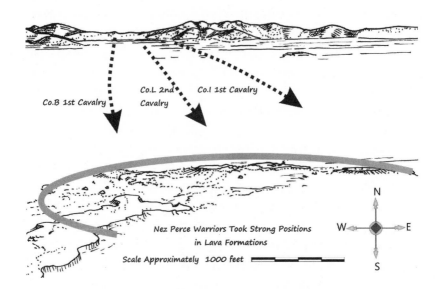

This map from the Nez Perce warriors' viewpoint shows the assault of three cavalry companies on the Indians' rearguard at Camas Meadows on August 20, 1877. From left to right, to the Indian front are: Captain Jackson with Company B, 1st Cavalry, Captain Norwood in the center with Company L, 2nd Cavalry, and on the right, Captain Carr with Company I, 1st Cavalry. (*Author*)

could see warriors moving to flank and surrounding the troopers. Sanford ordered a general withdrawal. At that moment, Jackson was assaulted with a flanking attack on the right. Almost immediately, Jackson saw warriors running along his right trying to get to his rear. He knew that his company would soon be cut off if it didn't follow Sanford's order. His men spaced out on foot as they paced back to the horse handlers with their mounts, pausing occasionally to fire.

Because both Carr and Jackson were extending their flanks as they withdrew on either side, Norwood soon found himself the farthest company forward, with little support on left and right as he stubbornly held his position.[26]

Young Brooks, the bugler in Captain Jackson's company who had sounded the alarm at first attack, was shot from his horse. He tried to regain his mount but failed and sank to the ground, dying on the spot. Seized by remorse at the death of the popular soldier, Major Jackson hazarded an advance to retrieve the bugler's body and returned it to the command. He also recovered Brooks's horse, which had stayed with the fallen trooper, prodding him to rise with his muzzle.[27] Jackson would eventually come to care for the orphaned horse.

Carr and Jackson began to withdraw their companies to the rear. A few minutes later, Norwood's men attempted to reclaim their horses and fall back but were forced to remain in position due to the intensity of the battle. Major Sanford sent Lieutenant Cresson to order Norwood to retreat, but the captain believed he could not withdraw without being encircled and overrun. He finally decided to move his men quickly to the left and rear to a stand of trees where their horses were being held. Norwood ordered his company to retreat to their mounts, tied in a large growth of cotton-wood trees some one thousand two hundred yards to the rear along the trail. The recall order was blown on a trumpet, and it sounded across the field, calling them back. The men fairly sprinted, according to Sergeant H. J. Davis's recollection of the battle.

The dense stand of aspen and cottonwoods was in an oval depression about an acre in size. The position afforded good cover for the retreating soldiers to set up a hasty defensive boundary in the thickets. Once inside the trees, Norwood's soldiers began to exchange fire with the Nez Perce warriors from behind the thick tree trunks. As the firefight continued, the troopers quickly built up breastworks between the trees using native stone. Despite their efforts, Norwood's men were soon taking casualties from the shockingly accurate native fire. Sergeant Henry Wilkins was wounded in the head, while Corporal Harry Garland fell to a slug that struck his cartridge belt and drove several bullets through his body. Private Will Clark slumped next to him, taken down by a grievous shoulder wound from a captured army rifle.[28] A farrier named William H. Jones had been shot and was carried deeper into the grove, while Private Harry Trevor was mortally wounded in the back at close range. Sam Glass, shot in the gut, lay dead. Summoning his courage, Sergeant Hugh McCafferty climbed a tall cottonwood with an angled trunk to a height where he could observe the enemy and relay what he saw to Carr and his troops. The "eye in the sky" reportedly improved the effectiveness of the cavalry's shooting.[29]

Howard was well aware of the battle to his front, and he advanced with his own reinforcements to join the fight. He soon approached Sanford and Carr at the head of their retreating companies. He asked Sanford where Norwood and his men were. Howard was not satisfied with Sanford's answer, nor his retreat, and he quickly rallied the men to resume their advance.

One of the troops of horse cavalry reached Norwood's position and moved rapidly to the other side of the road, advancing to flank the natives. Threatened with concentrated forces and having achieved their delay in order to move the mules, the Indian leaders prudently called for a retreat. In a short time, the soldiers found and relieved Norwood in his defensive lava ring. Wottolen told the Indian side of the ambush years later:

> The soldiers follow and we stop to have a fight. Back of a ridge we dismount to wait for their coming. We do not stop too close to that ridge. Soon some soldiers appear on that ridge top, but do not stay. Immediately they drop back from sight. We do not charge or follow them. Waiting where lined with our horses, shots soon come from hiding places on that

The perimeter of the grove where Norwood and his comand fell back behind a hastily constructed defensive line of lava rocks. (*Washington State University Library, MASC*)

ridge. Long range shooting, nobody is hurt. It is only to hold the enemy that we return the fire.

While exchanging with the hidden enemies, drawing their minds to us, a few good-shot warriors are crawling on them from another part of the hill. Now shots are heard from that direction. Those soldiers become scared. A bugle sounds down in the cottonwoods. These soldiers run like deer for the shelter brush. Then we all join in a fight. The enemies are to the north of us, and have tree protection. But this timber also favors the Indians in crawling up closer to them.[30]

Moments later Wottolen was wounded, struck by a shard of rock. Peo Peo Tholekt climbed down from the ridge with the rest of the warriors as the fighting wore down, and they rode away with the mule herd. Of the Indian casualties little was discovered, but the soldiers later found three dead Indian horses and blood spoor, indicating that natives may have fallen to army fire but were removed with their retreat.[31]

Eventually, most of the army's horses were recovered, but the loss of the mules stopped Howard's logistics and transport in its place.[32] Howard claimed that he had recovered half the mules, but this is disputed by the tribal oral tradition.[33] It's likely that a number of mules recovered had been lost, hurt, or just refused to budge, in typical mule fashion.

Howard's infantry was always trailing his faster-moving cavalry.[34] The following day the infantry arrived, led by Captain Marcus Miller. In twenty-four hours, it had marched a remarkable forty-eight miles. Howard now had a force of six hundred men. They next sheltered on Henry's Lake, at Camp Benson, named after a soldier wounded at Camas Meadows. Miller's reinforcements found the cavalrymen licking their wounds and recovering. About this time, scout S. G. Fisher, along with his Bannock Indian scouts and Captain Augustus Bainbridge, merged with Howard's command, ready to seek the trail of the fleeing Nez Perce.[35]

Howard's army depended on the mule train to support it. The Nez Perce leadership realized this and with their whirlwind raid stopped the advance of the cavalry and disrupted the army supply train. In mere moments, the Indian raid had crippled the mobility of Howard's army, stealing or driving off some of its mounts and most of its pack animals. The army was missing 250 horses and mules, mostly the latter, which were now scattered or serving as replacement animals in the Nez Perce herd. The fleeing tribe had gained some breathing room.

In the morning, following the raid, General Howard was forced to send for resupply. The army was now encamped

Puck satirized General Oliver O. Howard's telegram that he is "still pursuing the Indians." (*Library of Congress*)

at Henry's Lake. Howard rested his troops while he took a wagon the seventy miles to Virginia City, Montana, to acquire horses, pack animals, and supplies. While he was there on August 24, he wired a contrite telegram to General McDowell in San Francisco:

> Dispatches of this date received. Very sorry to be misunderstood. Did not wish to complain of want of cooperation, but to secure in advance that which would make it effectual. My command with jaded animals and men footsore and many of them shoeless, began to show signs of great discontent, and their officers complained to me officially of inability, which I could not ignore. Assure General McDowell that I have not depended upon others, yet I have been unable thus far to get any force ahead of the hostiles. I stated this that eastern commanders might do what I believe they are now doing; that is, inter-

pose some force on the trek of Joseph's advance. Field and Cushing, after the delay named in telegram, are again in route for Corrine via Virginia, Montana. I will, in order to be more independent in my plans, detain them still further, as suggested. The interruption of communication by breaking telegraph wires has prevented my knowing what is now clear. My duty shall be done fully and to the letter without complaint.[36]

Howard's mind was clearly as fatigued as his men. He incorrectly believed he was responding to a telegram sent that very day. The telegram he received was actually from August 17, and was a response to a dispatch he wired on August 14 from Bannock City, Montana.

Pinning his own hopes of redemption in Sherman and Sheridan's eyes on "interpos[ing] some force on the trek of Joseph's advance," Howard was distressed to find out that his latest effort to do so had failed. Lieutenant Bacon's expedition missed its objective when he decided to leave its assigned destination too early, allowing the tribe to slip through the Targhee Pass he had been guarding mere hours earlier.

Moving in a northeastern direction, the Nez Perce crossed over the Targhee Pass unopposed and, on the evening of August 22, camped at the Madison River inside Yellowstone National Park.

Despite checking the army's advance, the Nez Perce were aware that some force was pursuing them. Their own scouts played a deadly game of concealment and stealth, finally detecting the presence of Bannock scouts in their wake. As they traveled along the Madison River, Lean Elk, leading an advance party in search of a safe route to the Crow lands, was cautious, knowing that there were many park visitors and prospectors in the area. Any of the people they encountered could work against them, should they report that they had seen the tribe.

On August 23, the advance party happened upon an old prospector named John Shively in the Lower Geyser Basin in Yellowstone National Park. Shively was a long-time mountain man, and he had explored the area thoroughly, looking for gold. He told Lean Elk that he knew the way to the land of the Crow to the east. He was bargaining his skill as a guide in exchange for his life.[37] Lean Elk's group needed the help. He was intentionally traveling off the more familiar trails because they were too dangerous. The miner began by promising to help Lean Elk pick the best trails for his scouts to explore to the east.

For the next week, he honored the bargain and did his best to guide and familiarize them with the trails heading east. Shivley was absolutely at ease with Lean Elk and his scouts. They sensed no guile in him and treated him with the respect accorded an elder. In the time he was with the Nez Perce, he observed that there was no head chief, and leadership was fluid. Decisions were made in council by the important head men.[38]

It would not be long, however, before the Nez Perce encountered a group of campers.

Frank Carpenter was leading a group of young people from Helena, Montana, and the nearby community of Radersburg who were excited to experience the wonders of the new national park. He had brought his younger sister, thirteen-year-old Ida, and was joined by his friends, William Dingee, A. J. Arnold, Albert Oldham, and Charles Mann. They were joined along the way by Frank and Ida's sister, twenty-four-year old Emma, and her husband, George Cowan. D. L. Meyers was driving their wagon. The party left Radersburg on August 5 and reached the park on the fourteenth through the Targhee Pass.[39]

When they reached the park on August 14, they found a suitable spot in the Lower Geyser Basin to make their permanent camp. As they were settling in for the evening, Frank Carpenter jotted down detailed notes of their adventure in his journal. They spent a carefree evening around a campfire until, tired from the long day, they fell asleep to the sounds of water and the brilliant stars overhead.

During the next week they toured the various falls, geysers, and attractions the park had to offer. By the twenty-third they had returned to their base camp near the Fountain Geyser, an easy landmark to identify. A prospector from Colorado, William H. Harmon, was camped close by and visited with the young people.

On the morning of the twenty-third, other passersby told the travelers the news of the Nez Perce uprising. The campers decided to head out of the park after learning that the potentially hostile Indians were heading into the area.

But they are not swift enough. On the night of August 23, they were observed by a scouting party of four young warriors led by Yellow Wolf who were foraging and becoming familiar with the area.[40] In order not to attract the attention of the campers or others, the scouting party did not build a fire. In the distance, they saw the Carpenter party's campfire and heard the rhythmic crack of wood being split and added to the campers' fire. Yellow Wolf and his followers would wait until morning to move in on them and take them by surprise.

Yellow Wolf was relieved that his group had not found soldiers, as two of the young men with him were little more than boys and he had been worried about their fighting skills. But he was not happy. As he looked at the people sleeping around the fire in the early light, he was aware that all whites were potential enemies. The warriors decided they would take the sleeping travelers back to the Nez Perce camp. Yellow Wolf reasoned that the Nez Perce chiefs would decide what to do with these people.

A photograph taken in 1876 at Yellowstone, the year it was officially designated a national park. In addition to the men and women, the man on the right is holding a young child. The Nez Perce encounterd two similar tourist parties on their way through the park in 1877. (*Library of Congress*)

William Dingee was getting water to make coffee when he saw the young warriors riding up on their horses. The startled campers were apprehensive as they awoke to the warriors around them. A. J. Arnold quickly climbed up on their wagon and began giving the Indians sugar, flour, and some bacon from their stores until George Cowan angrily put a stop to the distribution of their food, engendering some ill will.

Frank Carpenter got up and started asking questions. The women watched from their tent. One of the young men with Yellow Wolf, Henry Tabador (Heinmot Tosinlikt), was the most proficient with English and began to act as interpreter. The warriors at first claimed they were "Snake" Indians but later recanted and admitted that they were Nez Perce. Tabador tried to calm the travelers' fears, telling them the Nez Perce only meant to fight soldiers, not civilians.

Carpenter asked, "Who is the leader here? I see five of you."

Tabador gestured to Yellow Wolf. "There is our leader."

Carpenter offered his hand to Yellow Wolf and asked what the young men intended. Someone asked Yellow Wolf if they intended to kill them. Yellow Wolf replied that they were of two minds on the issue.[41]

Yellow Wolf was worried about another band of restless Nez Perce warriors who had been raiding farms and way-laying travelers on the roads. They had killed some army scouts, and their blood was high: what might they do to these white folks? Yellow Wolf told the captive campers that he would take them to his chief, but that they were in danger. The men from the Radersburg party loaded their two wagons and saddled their horses.

As the Indians began marching the travelers back to the Nez Perce camp, an older group of warriors took the wagon and prisoners from them, as Yellow Wolf had feared. Frank Carpenter asked to be taken to Looking Glass, and he was taken from the party, presumably to see the chief.

A short way down the narrowing trail the wagons could no longer be used, so the warriors stripped them of every-thing they could use while the campers watched. Then they destroyed them. Their draft horses were saddled for Emma and Ida to use.

Eventually they were taken to meet Lean Elk. He told them that they must trade everything they had with them in exchange for some played-out horses. Frank Carpenter rejoined his party. Some accounts indicate that Looking Glass deferred to Lean Elk in the matter of the hostages. In any case, Lean Elk then warned the campers that they must get off the main trail and into the woods because he could

not control some of the warriors who were more inclined
to violence. The party started on its way as Lean Elk had
directed. Frank Carpenter noticed they were being followed by a large group of warriors who seemed extremely
hostile. They found the going inside the tree line very hard
and eventually emerged and passed back onto the trail.
They were immediately surrounded by the warriors who
had been tracking them. At the first opportunity, Arnold
and Dingee decided to make a break for it and dashed off
into the forest. The rest of the travelers were left to face an
increasingly hostile throng of warriors.

The remaining campers were forced back onto the trail
by the warriors, who claimed that the chiefs were not done
with them yet. Several warriors rode aggressively down the
trail toward the campers. There was a struggle, and George
Cowan was shot in the thigh. He fell, grabbing the wound
in pain. Emma jumped down from her horse and tried to
help her husband, but she was dragged away while a warrior produced a revolver and shot Cowan in the head.
Another rifle fired, and Albert Oldham was hit in the face.
The bullet missed hitting any critical structures and passed
through his head. Blinded by the concussion, in shock and
pain, he stumbled into the brush. His friends believed he
was dead.

With muzzles aimed at him and little doubt as to his
probable fate, Frank Carpenter made the sign of the cross,
hoping that some of the Indians may have been exposed to
Catholicism through Father Cataldo's mission.

Three of the party—Meyers, Mann, and prospector
Harmon—dashed off the trail into a low area and found
some reeds and rushes in which to hide. The three men
later escaped into the woods and ran until they were
exhausted.

Dispatched by the other chiefs, Lean Elk arrived just in
time to stop further bloodshed and escorted the survivors

back to the main Nez Perce camp.[42] The travelers spent the night with Chief Joseph in his lodge. Emma Cowan, and Ida and Frank Carpenter watched the fire with a somber silence. Emma was grieving for her husband. Joseph's family offered her what comfort it could. Frank Carpenter tried to speak with Joseph, but he was taciturn. The chief also appeared to be distant and worried.

On August 25, the Nez Perce captured an ex-cavalryman named James C. Irwin who had recently been discharged from Fort Ellis. When questioned, he told his captors about another party of tourists from Helena whom he had seen camped in the park. Lean Elk wished to keep Frank Carpenter to assist Shively and to release the two women with Irwin, but Emma believed Irwin to be a deserter and would have no part of it.

Irwin escaped on the evening of September 1 and was later discovered by scout S. G. Fisher. Scout J. W. Redington, who was one of Fisher's men, recollected that Irwin saved the army considerable trouble in its choice of route through the rough country,

> an unmapped country, and so rough that nobody had as yet been fools enough to try to wiggle through it. It seems to me the old timers then called it the Hoodoo country. The down timber was full of crippled horses when we went through, and it was lucky for the soldiers that they were able to avoid it. The reason they were able to do so was that a man named Irwin was a prisoner among the hostiles, and escaped and took the back track along the main trail. He was a discharged trooper from Fort Ellis, and was exploring the Yellowstone Park when captured, and the hostiles were using him for a guide, and at the same time had another prisoner named Shively, who was enlisted as boss packer for the squaw packtrain. He escaped one dark night and we found his trax in the

mud for quite a way down a creek. . . . Irwin met Captain Fisher on the trail and explained things to him, and Fisher sent him down to Gen. Howard, to whom he explained the course the hostiles were taking, and showed the General how he could go down the river and up the East Fork, and make a cut-off of about 100 miles, and perhaps head off the hostiles on the headwaters of the Clarks Fork.[43]

Some of the Nez Perce people remembered Emma Cowan and her sister from Spokane House, a trading post and way station in the nascent community of Spokane, Washington, and they urged restraint and compassion in their favor. They pointed out that too many innocents on both sides had died already. After a council, the leaders decided to release them. During the evening of the twenty-fifth, Frank Carpenter and the two women were set free near the site of Mud Volcano. The women were given horses, and Carpenter was on foot. Lean Elk directed them to travel down along the river as fast as they could.[44] The three kept inside the timber as much as possible, crossed Sulphur Mountain that night, still in Wyoming, and forded streams on their way to the Tower Falls area the following day, beyond which they encountered a detail of soldiers. Second Lieutenant Charles B. Schofield, who provided for their immediate needs, escorted them out of the park on their way to Fort Ellis and Bozeman, along with Frederic J. Pfister of another ill-fated touring party.[45]

As the family members reached Bozeman, they found Lieutenant Gustavus C. Doane with a group of soldiers and sixty Crow scouts. Emma and her sister planned to travel back to Radersburg. Frank Carpenter bid Emma and Ida a temporary good-bye and joined Doane's soldiers with the intention of finding Emma's husband and burying him.

Carpenter couldn't know that George Cowan was still alive and struggling to survive in the wilderness. He had suffered two bullet wounds, one in his thigh and one in his head. As he dragged himself out of the thicket where he had lain, a roving Nez Perce scout shot him a third time in his left side. He fell back into the brush and waited for the expected coup de grace, but none came.

As night fell, Cowan remained conscious, quietly waiting to crawl out again. He managed to drag himself back to the place where the campers had abandoned their wagon, almost ten miles away. Several times, he avoided Indian scouts that his heightened survival instinct allowed him to detect. When he reached the wagon, nothing remained but Frank Carpenter's diary, and his own dog, still waiting patiently. On the twenty-seventh, Cowan reached their original campground, where he was able to scrounge enough coffee grounds and matches to make a fire and coffee. Afterward he slept for the night, and in the morning he crawled painfully to the adjacent road. Within minutes he met a group of soldiers and Bannock scouts.

He had been found by one of Howard's groups. Among them was Redington, who asked Cowan, "Who the hell are you?"

"I am George Cowan of Radersburg," offered the wounded man.

The glib Redington responded, "You don't say! We've come to bury you."[46]

The scouts treated Cowan's wounds, fed him, and provided him with blankets, fire, and water. They told him they had to move on fast, but that the main force would pass this spot in two days, and he would be cared for by the medical staff in their column. Unfortunately, Cowan's misadventures continued when he fell asleep and was badly seared as his fire burned out of control. He suffered burns on his legs and hands; he escaped by crawling on his forearms, dragging his wounded legs. Within a day, he was in the care of General Howard's surgeon.

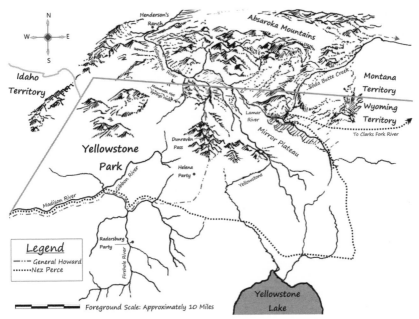

The movements of the Nez Perce and army through Yellowstone National Park. (*Author*)

Redington and his Bannock scouts, already on the lookout for the separated party, also found Meyers and Oldham. Oldham was suffering terribly from his wounds. His tougue was so swollen, he couldn't speak. Redington wrote of the incident, "Our scouting outfit under Gaht Fisher[47] collided with a few of the survivors of the Cowan party, bareheaded and hungry and we gave them some of our rations . . . I think one of them was named Oldham, and they found the command alright—were rather shy of our outfit, as all of us were wild Bannax except three."[48]

While in Yellowstone, the Carpenter-Cowan party was not the only group of tourists to run into trouble with the Nez Perce. Another group from Helena was camped a few miles from where the Radersburg tourists first encountered

Yellow Wolf and his warriors. The Helena party was composed of ten men: Richard Dietrich, Leander Duncan, August Fowler, Charles Kenck, Frederic J. Pfister, Joseph Roberts, John Stewart, Benjamin Stone, Andrew Weikert, and Leslie N. Wilkie. Most of the party had left Helena on August 13, and the other members met up with the main party at a rendezvous near the Mammoth Hot Springs on August 20. At some point the men in the Helena party had crossed paths with the recently discharged Irwin, who was just then a closely held guest of the Nez Perce.[49]

On August 25, the travelers crossed Alum Creek and climbed the slopes of Sulphur Mountain. Upon reaching the summit, they observed Indians on the move through Yellowstone. Gradually, the men became aware that a very large group of Indians was in motion nearby. Realizing that these were the Nez Perce they had heard so much uproar about, they decided to make a hidden camp and wait for the tribe to move on. They spent a restless first night in their secluded campground along Otter Creek. The following day, Weikert and Wilkie rode out to see if the Indians were all moving on from the area.

Informed by Irwin of the presence of the tourists, the Nez Perce sent a scouting party looking for the men from Helena even as Lean Elk led the majority of the tribe into the mountains to the northeast.[50] Later in the day, a party of warriors found the concealed camp and burst into the clearing, firing their weapons at the eight campers who were there. While the men scattered, running into the woods, the camp was plundered. In the melee, camper Charles Kenck was shot twice, as was John Stewart.

Weikert and Wilkie, meanwhile, were on their way back to the camp and ran directly into the war party.[51] They evaded the warriors and circled back to their camp, unaware that the war party had already raided it. They found the clearing in a shambles, with everything of use taken or destroyed. Kenck lay dead of multiple gunshot wounds amid the destruction of the camp. The campers were dispersed from each other. Dietrich, a music teacher, lay in Otter Creek for hours after the attack.

Fowler and Roberts had outrun the attack on the camp and laboriously made their way to Virginia City. Gradually, five of the remaining members of the party made their way back to James McCarthy's hotel at Mammoth Hot Springs: Richard Dietrich was recovered from the creek, and Stone, Stewart, Weikert, and Wilkie reached the hot springs and gratefully entered the hotel on the morning of August 27. McCarthy and Weikert took some of the horses at the hotel back to the camp to look for their missing companions.

Unknown to the Helena campers, one of their missing members, Frederic Pfister, had encountered Lieutenant Schofield's command the previous evening about twelve miles from the springs. Pfister was safe with Schofield's detachment. Along with the detachment was Frank Carpenter of the Radersburg party. Another group of tourists, the party of the Earl of Dunraven, was also with Schofield.[52] They all made their way to the Mammoth Hot Springs Hotel on the 28th. There Stewart and Weikert had their injuries tended; fortunately Dr. Kingsley was there and able to treat them. Duncan and Dietrich finally arrived as well.

Deciding to leave while he could, Pfister was soon en route to Fort Ellis by horse along with the others including the Earl. Lieutenant Doane sent an ambulance to take the wounded Stewart out of the hotel. Dietrich and Stone refused to be transported until they knew that the missing men were safe. Roberts and Fowler were still missing, and their companions could not know that the two would eventually connect with some freighters who took them to Virginia City and out of danger. It was quiet for the next few days with no sign of trouble.

On August 31, Dietrich, Stone, and ambulance driver Jake Stoner were at the hotel. Weikert and McCarthy were out on their horses scouting the area for their comrades.

The two men had a series of close calls and ended up abandoning their horses to the Indians in order to escape. McCarthy returned with Weikert from the Otter Creek camp, where they had found and buried Kenck. But they had another close encounter with warriors and had returned to Mammoth Hot Springs. As the two men finally reached the hotel on foot later in the day on August 31, they found that a war party had been at the hotel while they were out searching. Evidence of the raid was everywhere. Stone, the cook helped them understand what had happened.

A party led by Second Lieutenant Hugh L. Scott, composed of his cavalry and thirty Crow Indians, had broken up the latest raid.[53]

The attack happened after a party of about eighteen warriors had moved on to Henderson's ranch to the north of the park along the road to Bozeman and engaged in a spirited gunfight with the ranch hands there, to little effect. Lieutenant Doane and his men were drawn to the scene by smoke coming from the burning main house, which was made of log construction. The Indians captured nineteen horses from the ranch, but the soldiers chased them back toward Mammoth Hot Springs and eventually retrieved the stolen animals.

With sufficient warning due to Dietrich's seeing men moving toward the hotel that he thought might be Indians, Dietrich, Stone, and Stoner took to the brush and woods to hide. They waited until it was about noon, and Dietrich and Stone, thinking the danger was over, returned to the hotel to get some food. Stone was in the house preparing dinner (he had been the cook for the party), while Dietrich had gone to shift the picket pins for newer pasture for the horses. Through a window, Stone saw an Indian moving from behind a rock as though creeping up to attack. Stone darted out the back door and into the woods, where he climbed a tree to avoid capture.[54]

Dietrich may have come into the house from the fields and then encountered the war party. The music teacher from Helena was surprised at the doorway of the cabin and shot once in the stomach, then again while he lay face down in the doorway. The bullet traversed his body lengthwise.

After scouting the immediate area, six warriors, including Yellow Wolf, returned at dusk to raid the house of supplies, food, and other useful materials. Two men took up a watch. Suddenly, from outside, one of the sentinels shouted to warn the men inside, "Soldiers are coming to attack us!" The warriors burst out of the house and saw a troop of mounted soldiers approaching, firing.[55]

A detachment of ten men from Doane's command, led by Lieutenant Scott, came on the scene and found Dietrich's body a short time after he was killed. These men began to skirmish with the Indians, including Yellow Wolf, at the hotel.[56]

Yellow Wolf had been frantic, as he could not get his horse loose from his lead where it was tied, and it was rearing wildly in panic. Yellow Wolf wheeled and fired as the soldiers rode into a stand of willows. He and two others fired until the soldiers were gone. During the melee, the warriors shot one soldier from his horse after a close-range gunfight. The warriors gathered their plunder and supplies, and rode for their camp. On the way, they happened upon a large camp of warriors and cautiously stopped and observed. The camp was upwind, and Yellow Wolf smelled the air. He looked at his fellows with great concern and then back at the men in the semidark. These were not soldiers. They were not Nez Perce. He and the others could hear muted conversation, and suddenly it was clear. He could tell they were Bannock Indians, riding with the Crow and chasing his people. Yellow Wolf felt the desperation of the hunted.

William Tecumseh Sherman, general of the army, named after a great Indian chief, finished his vacation in the new national park one week before the Nez Perce passed through it. By August 24, Sherman was more than anxious: he felt that he had given Howard more than enough time to "clean out" the Nez Perce. He sent a telegram to Howard's commander, General McDowell:

> It appears that Howard is discouraged in his long pursuit of Joseph. There is no other body of men who can take their places, and I just telegraphed to Howard to give command to somebody else to follow till the Indians can be headed off by troops from the east."[57]

The telegram he had sent from Fort Shaw to Howard outlined what he expected:

> I don't want to give orders, as this may confuse Sheridan and Terry; but that force of yours should pursue the Nez Perces to the death, lead where they may. Miles is too far off and I fear Sturgis is too slow. If you are tired, give the command to some energetic officer, and let him follow them where they may.[58]

Howard had moved far beyond the bounds of the Department of the Columbia. His men were worn out, their horses spent, and he was discouraged.

On August 29, Sherman sent McDowell a dispatch by wire, which the Pacific Division received August 30:

> Am all ready now and shall start for Missoula to-morrow, reaching there September 2d. Have heard

of no one as escort from your side. If you hear nothing more you may take it for granted that I will come via Coeur d'Alene Mission and Spokane bridge, without escort, by horseback and pack train. If Wheaton has got back to Lewiston you might offer him to send some one to meet me on the road, for I find it hard to get reliable intelligence. Howard must be in Yellowstone Park, and Sheridan has three strong detachments to watch on the east of the mountains. I advised Howard to give his command to Lieutenant-Colonel [Charles C.] Gilbert, 7th Infantry, who is familiar with the country, and to overtake me on the road designated.[59]

Sherman was giving his old comrade the boot as gently as possible after he'd suffered a series of squandered opportunities and desperate struggles with the Nez Perce. He was ordering Howard to hand over his command to the older, but more vigorous and ambitious, Gilbert.[60]

The Battle of Canyon Creek

Lieutenant Gustavus Doane, who had happened upon the raid at Henderson's ranch, was making preparations with his men to continue their scouting mission. From the ruins of the ranch, Doane sent General Howard a dispatch on September 1, alerting him that he was making his base there with a company of 7th Cavalry, some volunteers, and his Crow scouts. Although not under Colonel Gibbon's command, he was nonetheless following Gibbon's orders to scout the east fork of the Yellowstone River looking for the Nez Perce.

Lieutenant Colonel Charles Gilbert was rushing to the front to assume his new position as successor to General Howard. Gilbert sent a dispatch to Doane to halt his scouting activity and to await his arrival. Gilbert's message included orders from Sherman to "assume command" of Doane and his men, and that regarding Howard, Gilbert intended to "take the command of his column."[1] Doane sent the dispatch on to Howard, thereby alerting him that Gilbert was coming to join Doane at the ranch and the details of the colonel's intentions.

Armed with this information, Howard gathered other local scouts to augment S. G. Fisher's men, and he sought whatever intelligence the ex-soldier James Irwin possessed. Irwin had unique information after his experience as captive and scout for the Nez Perce. Howard wanted whatever information he could provide about the fastest route to pursue the tribe as it moved out of Yellowstone Park. Howard used Irwin and his scouts to his best advantage and was soon several days ahead of his potential replacement.

The determined Gilbert completed his rendezvous with Lieutenants Doane and Scott on September 3 at the burned-out ranch. Gilbert was carrying orders from General Sherman to General Howard to hand over his command. They read in part, "I don't want to order you back to Oregon, but I do say that you can, with perfect propriety return to your command, leaving the troops to continue till the Nez-Perces have been destroyed or captured, and I authorize you to transfer to him, Lt. Col. Gilbert, your command in the field and to overtake me en-route or in your Department."[2]

Doane suggested moving north to rendezvous with Howard by moving upstream along the Yellowstone River. To the consternation of his junior officers, Gilbert then conducted a retrograde march, out of fear that there were hostile Indians to his front. He led the command in circles for a day before finally getting on the right track. Howard was at least three days ahead and not waiting. Once Gilbert had nearly reached Henry's Lake, he pushed the men and horses at a grueling pace through the difficult trail that Howard had originally taken. With his men exhausted, his horses lame, and chance at glory squandered, he decided to give up his pursuit and his command.[3]

Colonel Miles assigned Colonel Samuel D. Sturgis to move as quickly as possible along the Yellowstone River and intercept the Nez Perce before they could leave the area. He was to direct his cavalry to the Judith Gap area, which lay to the north of the Yellowstone River. The plains of the Judith Gap stretch between the Big Snowies and the Little Belt Mountains.[4] Sturgis was at the head of the reorganized 7th Cavalry, composed of new recruits, men shifted from other commands, and a smattering of reliable veteran soldiers. The unit was eager for redemption in battle, seeking revenge for its destruction the summer before at the Little Big Horn. Sturgis's son, James Garland Sturgis, had been killed in the battle along with the rest of Custer's command.

Despite an endless succession of supply and logistics problems, Sturgis spurred his men on, with their initial destination the old Crow Mission on the Stillwater River in Montana.[5]

The men were somber as they passed through the valley of the Yellowstone and the camp where Custer's ill-fated expedition had embarked in June the previous summer. Their supply problems were developing as word reached the command at the cantonment on the Tongue River via courier that the steamship bringing their rations was "hard aground" on the Yellowstone River and could not proceed without a rise in the water level.

Sturgis, with eight troops of his regiment on the move, had only a day's rations remaining and limited feed for his horse-borne army. Knowing Napoleon's dictum, he immediately dispatched Lieutenant Ezra B. Fuller to Fort Ellis and also to Bozeman, Montana, to establish a supply train to provision the army as it moved. Lieutenant Charles Albert Varnum, the quartermaster, had already ridden ahead with his supply section to meet the steamer at Terry's Landing. He hoped to unload enough rations at the landing to provision the force at least until it reached the Crow Mission. On his route, he was updated about the problem with the steamer. He arranged instead to ship flour three hundred miles from the post supply at Fort Custer, near present-day Hardin, Montana.

Sturgis peeled off a troop to provide transport of whatever rations and feed could be obtained by his quartermaster. In due course, they received wagons of corn and oat feed for the animals from the stores of Fort Ellis, but no food for the men. As the troopers reached the Crow Mission, foraging and fishing helped to alleviate the immediate shortage of rations.[6]

Sturgis was well aware of the two possible exits from the park. The Clarks Fork and Shoshone rivers needed to be covered. He did not want to split his forces, and he did not have enough men to cover both exits.[7] He moved into position on the Clarks Fork. This was the most logical route for the Nez Perce to take, and he anticipated they must pass nearby.

Sturgis sent out scouts to scour the area for any possible passes and trails. His scouting parties returned to report that the steep Clarks Fork Canyon was impassable, even to the resourceful Nez Perce. Armed with this information, Sturgis decided to move east to the Shoshone River in an attempt to block his opponent. Rather than splitting up his forces, he decided to move with all his companies intact. Sturgis was also peeved that he did not have Doane's company, which had first been sent up the Yellowstone scouting by Gibbon and then commandeered and removed from the field of battle by the anxious Colonel Gilbert, Howard's replacement.[8]

Sturgis felt that if he had the additional men of Doane's command, he could either send them ahead or leave them to intercept the Indians if they tried to find a way though the impassable canyon.

Sturgis spent some time at the mission recruiting local Crow scouts as well as some prospectors into service as scouts. He sent the scouts in advance of his column with instructions to scour the adjacent mountain passes and valleys for the tribe and to keep him informed of the position of the enemy if it was located.

Leaving the mission at the Indian agency, Sturgis's command took to the trail again on half rations, crossing the Red Rock and reaching the Clarks Fork River.

The column pressed on, leaving the Clarks Fork behind and marching into the valley of the Stinking Water. It finally came to a halt on the middle branch of the Clarks Fork.

Having no news from his scouts, Sturgis ordered Lieutenant Luther R. Hare and Second Lieutenant Albert J. Russell to reconnoiter the area ahead for the men.[9] Hare moved through the valley keeping an eye on the ground for tracks. He discovered many fresh tracks that appeared to be from Indian ponies, and signs of a struggle. Soon he located the body of one of the prospectors. The man was dead on a hillside, bristling with arrows.

His detachment quickly buried the body and spread out, looking for any sign of the other prospector. They heard a man calling from the banks of the stream below. A sergeant gave the man water and some whiskey from his flask. The man told his rescuers that he and his partner had scouted the mountains for several days after leaving the mission and had not found any trace of hostile Indians. They had been returning to report to Sturgis when, at the very spot he lay, they stumbled into an ambush. His partner was killed, and he was seriously wounded. The miner was sure the men who attacked them were Nez Perce.

Hare suspected that the ambushers were scouts and that the main body of the Nez Perce could not be far off. He ordered his men to make a place to safely ensconce the wounded miner while they returned to camp to make their report.[10]

Lieutenant Russell had climbed the foothills to the right and rear of Hare's position. He and his men were surveying the valleys and ravines from the overlook points on the hills they climbed. They were surrounded by what seemed to be a shield wall of extremely sheer mountains of elevations of ten thousand feet. There seemed to be no pass that the women, children, and horses of the Nez Perce could have traversed. Unsuccessful in any attempt to detect the enemy, they prepared to retrace their steps and locate Hare.

Then Russell saw motion on his periphery. He noticed an intrepid scout, who had crawled to the top of a small ridge, gesturing to him to join him. With one of his sergeants, Russell climbed the ridge and crawled up next to the scout. Peering over the crest, they could see the dust from a large herd of horses headed uphill from the river, driven by young Indian men riding among them. With this intelligence, Russell ordered a quick return to report to Sturgis.[11] But the soldiers had no idea that they were witnessing a ruse, and that the Indian column would retrace its steps in the opposite direction and in the cover of the tree line after misleading the army with a dust cloud and tracks. Sturgis's scouts assured him that there was no way out of the basin the tribe was moving into.[12]

Sturgis's soldiers were now aware that they were in the immediate vicinity of the Nez Perce. The camp was put on a level of heightened alert. During the night, a seasoned sergeant fired steady volleys at indistinct figures in the distance who did not respond to his challenge. The officer of the watch and the sergeant of the guard took the sergeant's report and waited for dawn with some trepidation. The Crow scouts reconnoitered at first light and reported evidence of Indian horses around the camp.

In the morning, a detail, including a surgeon, retrieved the wounded prospector Hare had found. He was placed on a field-improvised travois and taken back to the mission by a squad while Sturgis pushed ahead with the main force deeper into the Shoshone River valley in hot pursuit of his adversary.

Following the trail of Indian horses, the command found itself traveling over extremely steep trails and ravines searching for the phantom tribe. But Sturgis did not know that his men had been deceived.[13] Between the Clarks Fork and the Shoshone rivers, Lean Elk had instructed his men to make a demonstration using their horses by pulling branches behind them to make as much dust as possible and to mill in a circle to give the impression that many Indian horses had crossed over Dead Indian Pass into the Shoshone Valley. Instead, they had gone down a very narrow ravine to the Clarks Fork, which was no longer guarded by Sturgis's command.[14]

This deception drew Sturgis out of his position and got him to concentrate his attention on a phantom movement and a search for the Nez Perce along the wrong trail. When his scouts finally discovered the correct pass, they found that General Howard, who was also chasing the Nez Perce along the trail, had traversed the steep path first and was waiting for Sturgis and his men at the bottom of the sheer trail.[15] Howard drew Sturgis aside and conferred quietly with the colonel.

Howard communicated clearly to Sturgis that he was going to integrate the 7th Cavalry into his command. Sturgis, with his fresh, healthy horses and men in high morale would become the lead element in the pursuit of the Nez Perce.

Sturgis led his exhausted men to the established camp, and they quickly sought out their own camping places. The rumor at the camp was that, with the deception, Lean Elk had managed to put his tribe fifty miles ahead of the army and even then was fleeing for the Canadian border and to the very rendezvous with the Sioux that Sturgis had been ordered to prevent. Sturgis could see that Howard's men and horses were all on the verge of exhaustion and collapse, and he wondered whether the Nez Perce were in a similar state at this point.

In fact, the Nez Perce were also exhausted, and they had no chance to fully recover from their grief after the Battle of Big Hole before being pushed farther and faster. The elderly and children especially suffered.

Forced to leave behind their lodge poles and many robes and hides was a serious loss that was beginning to tell on the tribe. The lack of proper shelter was becoming a bigger problem every day. The nights in the mountains had become increasingly damp and cold. The first breath of chill wind from the heights promised that winter was coming.

The last thing the troopers heard as they fell into an exhausted sleep were the explosive expletives shouted by Sturgis at his officers that he would overtake the Indians before they crossed the Missouri River if he had to go afoot and alone. Sturgis ordered reveille for half-past three and for the officers to be prepared to be on horse and ready to move out at 5 a.m. on September 12.

As ordered, the 7th Cavalry resumed the pursuit at five sharp, through drizzle and mud. Howard's soldiers, moving like men in a daze, set out hours behind Sturgis, and because of exhaustion, they were much slower.

In contrast, the men in Sturgis's command were in for a grueling but fast-paced day. They pushed through the rough trail overland with only an occasional and brief pause. At the end of the long day, at midnight, after sixty miles in the saddle, their forced march came to a temporary halt.

At dawn on September 13, the men of the 7th Cavalry were on the Indian trail again. They forded the Yellowstone River and tied their horses on pickets. They began to lay their gear out to dry in the sun. Abruptly, one of their scouts, Pawnee Tom, appeared on the slope to their front, running pell-mell down the hill while yelling, "Indians, Indians!"[16]

Lieutenant Harrison Otis quickly assumed his place at the head of the 1st Battalion. Major Lewis Merrill assembled the 2nd Battalion, consisting of Companies F, I, and L. Company L, under the command of Lieutenant Melville Wilkinson, was in the lead of his battalion. Company F was under Lieutenant James Montgomery Bell, and Company I was commanded by Captain Henry J. Nowlan.[17] Captain Frederick W. Benteen commanded the 3rd Battalion, composed of Companies G, M, and H, which were initially held in reserve. (Benteen had formerly commanded a battalion at the Battle of Little Big Horn.) Benteen was attended by Captain Thomas F. French. The three battalions rode quickly down the valley toward the area where the Nez Perce had been seen. The 3rd Battalion, moving north to south, went to a place called Canyon Creek.

After a ten-minute ride, the Nez Perce were visible to Benteen's front. Colonel Sturgis watched the Indians streaming with their livestock toward the canyon some two miles in the distance. His efforts to get his troops in position to cut the tribe's escape route were about to yield a final resolution to the long pursuit. Sturgis knew that he had to get his men to the canyon mouth first, or the tribe would escape again. He ordered his commanders to take the canyon at all costs and stop their escape.

The Nez Perce people, horses, and warriors were crowded together and heading quickly for the canyon's entrance. The entrance was broad, with most of the high ground forming the opening only at the mouth of the

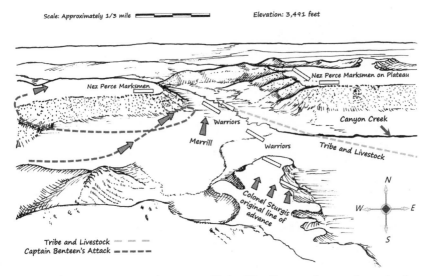

Scale: Approximately 1/3 mile   Elevation: 3,491 feet

The army attempted to cut off the Nez Perce advance through the mouth of Canyon Creek on September 13, 1877, but were thwarted by Indian marksmen who controlled the heights. (*Author*)

canyon. The ravine gradually leveled out in the deeper reaches of the canyon as it opened onto the Yellowstone Valley plain beyond. Nevertheless, the high shield walls adjacent to the mouth offered a fine position for Nez Perce marksmen, who had gained the heights.[18]

Just ahead of Benteen's troops, Major Merrill ordered his 2nd Battalion forward to the center of the prairie, buttressed by Company L under Lieutenant Wilkinson. He intended to secure the canyon entrance and prevent the escape of the Nez Perce. Merrill's men knew that the long struggle could be ended with a victory in the fight they were entering. Captains Bell and Nowlan, commanding Companies F and I, fell in behind Merrill.

Captains Benteen and French were held in reserve and had to watch the advance for the time being. From where Benteen sat, he could see the entire skirmish unfolding. The troops were racing forward, almost at a charge. The

A Nez Perce warrior armed with a repeating rifle surveys the trail below from his commanding position. The Nez Perce were excellent marksmen. (*Washington State University Library, MASC*)

first rifle shots from the bluffs on either side of the canyon revealed the presence of Indian sharpshooters. Also, warriors were positioned between the fleeing people and the advancing troops. Their close, accurate firing cut into the advancing cavalry. Soldiers were shot from their saddles, easy targets for the native marksmen. As men become apprehensive at the number of casualties, the speed of the advance slowed considerably. The officers finally ordered the men to dismount and continue the attack on foot. Some men were frustrated that their officers did not order them to charge en masse for the canyon and sweep the skirmishers out of the way.

Benteen received orders to attack and secure the canyon's mouth. He sent out skirmishers and organized his command for an attack. When he gave the order, his men pushed on for the canyon's mouth at a charge. Soon, the army skirmishers were under devastating fire from the bluffs. Indian warriors were well placed to control and guard the entrance to the canyon. The 1st and 2nd battalions also encountered stiff resistance from Indian skirmishers, who were protecting their people as they dashed into the mouth of the canyon.

Yellow Wolf was one of the warriors defending the canyon entrance. Finally, at the urging of an older warrior, he rode inside and climbed the ravine and the adjacent high ground to fire from a height on the attacking cavalry.[19] Two other warriors, fighting dismounted, used their accurate firing to hold the advancing cavalry companies at bay for at least ten minutes.[20]

The Indian fire coming from the bluffs above and the mouth of the canyon successfully deflected the cavalry charge. Benteen was forced to break off his main attack on the opening to the canyon and instead directed his men at the main body of Nez Perce as they neared the pass. Private Goldin described the action:

> On we galloped and a little later, sheltered from the enemy on the bluffs, we were dismounting in a deep ravine. Our loss so far had been only two men. Leaving our horses in charge of the horse holders, we scrambled up the bank, deployed as skirmishers and were soon hotly engaged. In the meantime, so far as we could see the other two battalions, as dismounted skirmishers, were moving up the valley, keeping up a running fight with the Indians. Just about this time up came Lieutenant Otis with his "jackass" battery.*
>
> Pushing well out to the front, he opened fire on the enemy, apparently doing considerable damage. By this time, the first and second battalions had joined us and the fight was raging fiercely, the Indians gradually drawing into the cañon in spite of our efforts to restrain them. The first and second battalions had been pushed out toward the hills, and from the incessant firing in that direction, we knew they had their hands full.[21]

---

*A "jackass" battery was a small howitzer with a shortened barrel. It was a field piece designed to be disassembled and carried on several mules. One animal would bear the howitzer barrel and the other the trunnion and carriage. It could be towed on its carriage by a team of horses and mules, but mountain trails often required dismantling and packing. Other mules would carry shot, artillery, and blacksmith tools.

The troops were unable to prevent the Indians from escaping through the canyon, and as they pursued, they were subjected to severe fire from the heights on both sides. Finally, the reserve companies charged, with Captain French leading the way. The troopers cleared the shooters from one bluff as the men charged up the hillside. Some soldiers, still on horseback, rode up the steep incline, while others ran uphill on foot. Having been rebuffed at the canyon mouth, Benteen charged the heights to the left side of the canyon where Nez Perce sharpshooters were raining down a fierce counterfire. He ordered his men to advance as rapidly as possible. When the top of the heights were taken, no defenders remained. The Nez Perce rearguard had broken off and moved across the valley to another defensible ridge. The cavalry soldiers reformed and moved across the wild grass of the plateau and saw the warriors at a distance. The men attacked downhill on the far slope of the bluffs and were soon being fired on from the Nez Perce positions on the far side of the valley. A group of Crow pressed the army's attack farther into the canyon, ahead of the soldiers. The Nez Perce warriors had defensible cover in the interior of the canyon and put up a stiff defense.

Yellow Wolf described this portion of the fight: "Chief Ollokot, my uncle, was not far away. He dismounted and I, too, got down from my horse. We both fought from the ground. In short time, Ollokot sprang up, leaped on his horse and galloped away. He hurried with others to drive back the Crows now fixing to flank the moving families."[22]

Yellow Wolf, with the reckless abandon of youth (and his faith in his wyakin), fought a deliberate battle with what he described as "a hundred Crows and Snake Indians" before he and his horse sustained wounds that forced them to retire. He reported that soldiers had killed multiple horses and wounded three Nez Perce men, while the Crow had killed three Nez Perce men.[23]

The steam had gone out of the attack, the soldiers' horses played out. Leaving their Crow scouts to continue to track the Nez Perce, the men went into camp to rest. Sturgis had lost his opportunity for revenge and redemption for the 7th Cavalry.

The tribes continued to hurry on to the north. The forces in pursuit now included six companies of the 7th Cavalry under Sturgis, five companies of the 5th Cavalry under Major Verling Hart, and ten companies of cavalry under Colonel Wesley Merritt from Wyoming. The Crow Indians who were allied with the 7th Cavalry, as well as the Bannock scouts, persisted in hounding the fleeing Nez Perce and were soundly rebuffed by their rear guard.

Most of the casualties had been sustained by Benteen's men as they charged into the enfilading fire at the mouth of the canyon. Three soldiers were killed and eleven wounded in the fight.[24] His Indian adversaries had broken away in good order, conducted a strong rearguard defense, and then disappeared, crossing over the Musselshell River. Sturgis claimed that the Nez Perce lost twenty-one men in the engagement. Yellow Wolf's figure of three men killed and three wounded was probably closer to reality. The army surgeon, Dr. Jenkins FitzGerald, tried to examine all the Nez Perce dead and stated he had examined only two.[25]

The Nez Perce moved on farther to the Missouri River and looked for a natural ford to cross.[26] The ford was occupied by a considerable body of soldiers, civilian engineers, and workers who were shaping the flow of the river and removing obstructions to navigation near the Dauphin Rapids. Company B of the 7th Infantry, out of Fort Benton with Captain T. S. Kirtland commanding, had been assigned to guard the engineers.[27] Kirtland had detailed a few soldiers to guard the provisions stored in the commissary tents. The tents and a large ditch were the only structures at the landing. The construction area where the civilian engineers were working was upriver from a supply depot.

Fifteen "bull" wagons of freight and supplies had reached the depot on the nineteenth. These large wagons were hooked together in series of three and then pulled by teams of oxen.

At the same time, the steamboat *Peneniah* was unloading freight at the depot. Two days later, on the morning of the twenty-first, the steamer *Fontenelle* brought more supplies for the freighters to take overland. Supplies accumulated at the Cow Island depot because the seasonal water level would not allow steamboats to navigate all the way to Fort Benton. From the Cow Island depot, the goods would be freighted to Fort Benton overland or farther north to Canada, even west over the Mullen Road to Walla Walla, Washington Territory.

In addition to the tons of supplies which were intended to be freighted via the Cow Creek trail, there was also a significant stockpile of supplies accumulating at the depot to support the engineering work. As provisions or equipment were needed they were hauled to the work site. The work on the rapids had gone so well that most of the supplies for the men working at the rapids, including food, had optimistically been transferred back to the Cow Island depot in anticipation that the job would soon be done.

Upon finding later that the work was taking longer than anticipated at a difficult section of the river near the Dauphins Rapids, it was determined that the men would need more rations if they were going to stay and work on the site. First Sergeant William Moelchert decided to take a detail of men back to Cow Island some eighteen miles

Bull wagons of the type used to resupply the US Army in their pursuit of the Nez Perce. (*Library of Congress*)

downstream for additional rations. He had a squad of three men with him. Before he left, Captain Kirtland warned Moelchert to be careful of the Nez Perce in the area. The sergeant and two men floated downriver in a borrowed boat, while another soldier followed along the shoreline using the captain's horse. The horse would be used to pull the loaded boat back upriver on their return trip. Moelchert and his men had been at the Cow Island landing long enough to stack what supplies they needed and were waiting for the horse to arrive along with the detail guarding the supply depot. A soldier observed Indians on horseback on the far side of the river. It appeared to Moelchert that the Indians were looking for a ford to cross. He sorted out the men he had at his disposal and put them in defensive positions.

Two chiefs or influential warriors rode up to the depot with twenty of their men, and Moelchert signaled that they should stop and advance no farther.

Behind the twenty warriors, the seemingly endless stream of native people made the crossing over the river.

The column of families and ponies crossed over and made its way to the mouth of Cow Creek Canyon. There they camped.

After the procession over the river was safe, the two leaders of the warriors advanced and made signs that they wanted to parley. Leaving his rifle, Moelchert advanced to confer with one of the Indian leaders, who spoke perfect English and, after shaking hands, offered silver and gold coin for supplies.[28] Three times he asked, and three times the sergeant refused to sell anything. Finally, he selected some hardtack and meat, hoping it would appease them. The Indians gave thanks for the gift and rode off. A short while later, the men heard a shot and were filled with foreboding. They were certain that their comrade riding the captain's horse had been shot and killed.

At sunset, the Indians began a series of attacks from the willows on the shore. This went on until sunrise. The supply tents were looted and burned. The following morning, the Nez Perce left the depot, moving along Cow Creek Canyon after raiding and destroying fifty tons of government provisions.

In the morning the firing wore down, and the tribe moved out of the area, leaving Private Martin's body beside the river along with that of a citizen volunteer, Edmund Bradley. Two other civilians were wounded.

On September 21, troops from Fort Benton took to the field heading for the area of Fort Clagett, a trading post on the Missouri River below the confluence with the Judith River, one of its tributaries. Word had reached Fort Benton that the station was being threatened by Nez Perce. Major Guido Ilges, who was commanding a meager force at Fort Benton, brought a unit of 7th Infantry downstream commanded by Lieutenant Edward E. Hardin. Ilges initially had under him Lieutenant Hardin, one enlisted man, and a company of thirty-six citizen volunteers. He was also towing a mountain howitzer. They reached the area on the twenty-fourth, arrived at Cow Island, and found the supplies still burning.[29] Hardin connected with Sergeant Moelchert and his men, and added them to their few soldiers. Ilges transported his men, their horses, and all their equipment across the Missouri River and followed the tracks of the fleeing tribe with what speed he could as he moved up Cow Creek.

Some ten miles farther upriver, the wagoners with the bull train and the passengers from the *Fontenelle* were traveling at the slow pace of oxen in rough country when they saw Indian riders approaching on the trail behind. After they had endured an uneventful day of being shadowed, a teamster was shot and the wagoners ran for cover in the woods. The shooting may have occurred just as Ilges's men and the Nez Perce caught sight of each other. A party of seventy-five warriors attacked down the trail, breaking into smaller groups as they advanced. Ilges's men and the warriors exchanged gunfire for two hours, until Ilges prudently withdrew back down the canyon after one of the volunteers in his company was killed.[30] Ilges knew he could be easily flanked by the larger force.[31]

The Nez Perce made their way farther up Cow Creek Canyon as the firing diminished. They had traveled nearly one hundred miles since leaving Yellowstone National Park. They would have to cross the Yellowstone River again. And Colonel Sturgis, despite being rebuffed at the canyon, would attempt to rein them in.

11

The Bear Paw Battle

Colonel Nelson A. Miles had a problem. Actually, he had a slew of problems. He did not lack for confidence, and his track record as an officer certainly disposed him to be certain of his ability to outfight and overcome his enemies. From the Civil War to the battles against Geronimo and cleaning up the mess that Colonel Custer had left the previous year, Miles had been the soldier who could get things done for his superiors. Despite his faith in his abilities, the problems that vexed him were logistical, professional, and personal.

Miles seemed to be the epitome of a self-made military officer. He had advanced in rank through the Civil War by leading volunteers in battle, rising to the role of a leader and tactician. But he was an unlikely candidate to become general, having not attended West Point. Much of his knowledge of tactics and strategy was gleaned from studying classical military history. He had managed to distinguish himself from Antietam to Appomattox: wounded four times, cited for gallantry, and awarded the Medal of Honor after his actions at Chancellorsville. Brevetted as high as brigadier general during the war, he was finally rewarded with a commission as a colonel in the regular army in 1866.

Professionally, he had done everything he could to make sure his superiors recognized his contributions in the campaigns he had fought. Relentlessly self-promoting, he was tireless in his pursuit of recognition. He had fought hard to achieve recognition as a warrior, rising from common store clerk in Boston to a general. And he had strategically married the niece of William T. Sherman. But success in battle was how he had been promoted in the past and he had to advance by merit again. Now he feared that fortune might not favor him in his desire to lead his men in the pursuit and defeat of the Nez Perce. With the confusion of commands and the involvement of so many other commanders given opportunities in the fight, he must have wondered if he would get his chance. And his position in the midst of Sioux country was one that the army wanted to maintain if possible, rather than pull him out of position. The situation with Sitting Bull was fluid. If the Sioux chief came raiding from the north in Canada, Miles would be the commander to deal with the threat.

He had orders to be prepared and ready to move to join the fight against the Nez Perce, but he personally had not joined the contest proper. A highly competitive man, Miles viewed every battle as a personal and professional challenge that he must overcome. His first problem was that it looked like he might be left out of the fight entirely.

He had correctly determined, as events proved, that the Nez Perce would strike for the Judith basin. Acting on his intuition, on August 10 he had dispatched Colonel Sturgis of the 7th Cavalry with six companies to contain the Judith Gap. At the same time, he had tasked Lieutenant Doane of the 2nd Cavalry, with Company E of the 7th, and his Crow scouts, to cover the approaches between the Musselshell River and the Missouri.[1]

He was more than a little frustrated with Sturgis for being drawn out of position and later missing his opportunity at Canyon Creek. He had urged Sturgis on August 27, "I would prefer that you strike the Nez Perces a severe blow if possible before sending any word to them to surrender."[2] Sturgis had discovered that bottling up the Nez Perce was like trying to contain mercury: they had simply slipped away again. This development did not reflect well upon the regiment, and it created Miles's second problem: how could he use this squandered opportunity to his advantage?

So Miles was relieved and intrigued when he received General Howard's dispatch on the evening of September 17. Miles was in his camp near the mouth of the Tongue River in southeast Montana, located halfway between the Powder and Bighorn rivers. All three waterways were tributaries of the Yellowstone River. The post he was at, called the Tongue River Cantonment, was strategically and purposefully located. He had built it himself after the Sioux defeat of Custer in 1876.[3] Howard had sent the message on the twelfth from the Clarks Fork, but the terrain was difficult and dangerous, forcing the dispatch riders to carefully pick their way between commands in order to avoid the Nez Perce scouts.

Miles's forces then included three troops of the 7th Cavalry, three of the 2nd Cavalry, and six mounted companies of the 5th Infantry accompanied by elements of the 1st Infantry.[4] The command possessed two field pieces, a 12-pound Napoleon cannon and a 1.65-inch Hotchkiss breech-loader.[5] Miles had 383 men at his command, their morale was good, and their horses were reasonably fresh.

Howard's dispatch informed Miles that the Nez Perce had eluded the US forces to the north of them by escaping western Montana through the Clarks Fork Pass and were moving toward the Canadian border. Howard laid out the situation for Miles:

> Colonel: While Colonel Sturgis was scouting toward Stinking Water the Indians and my force in close pursuit passed his right, and they, after a short detour, turned to Clarke's [Clarks] Fork and by forced marches avoided Sturgis completely.
>
> I have sent Sturgis with Major Sanford, First Cavalry, and Lieutenant Otis, Fourth Artillery, with howitzer battery, in fast pursuit, and myself following as rapidly as possible with the remainder of my own immediate command. The Indians are reported going down Clarke's [Clarks] Fork and straight toward the Musselshell . . . and make all haste to join a band of hostile Sioux. . . . I earnestly request you to make every effort in your power to prevent the escape of this hostile band, and at least to hold them in check until I can overtake them. Please send me return couriers with information of your and the hostiles' whereabouts, your intended movements, and any other information I ought to know.[6]

Miles was already champing at the bit, and Howard had released him from his concerns about the threat to the north from Sitting Bull. He would keep the Nez Perce from linking up with the Sioux at all costs.

Miles knew he had to get the best scouts in the world if he were to have any chance against the Nez Perce warriors. He began to gather men he had known and who had worked with him before. Luther S. "Yellowstone" Kelly was one of those men. Kelly had received his nickname after exploring the Yellowstone basin drainage in 1870. He was one of the first white men to venture throughout the reaches of the Yellowstone and its tributaries. Miles wanted to find white men who could live like Indians and ride all day without complaint. The men he was looking for needed to be able to speak multiple Indian dialects; French would be helpful also. They should be able to use Indian sign language to make themselves understood. And they needed to know the country. Kelly, Miles's chief of scouts, fit the bill perfectly, and Miles would call him into the chase and give him an assignment: find Louis Shambow.

Shambow was a roustabout, a freight-wagon driver, and a cowboy. He spoke perfect French, and he knew six or seven native dialects. He was also the best natural scout Miles had ever met. Miles dispatched troopers to go collect Kelly at the Carroll Landing, another army river depot on the Missouri River, where he had been sent to see to the protection of supplies stored there. Kelly was to find Shambow and proceed to the mouth of the Musselshell River to rendezvous with Miles.

Miles's command set out on the morning of the eighteenth, hard on the trail of the Nez Perce. Miles had at his disposal some newspaper stories, official reports, and good knowledge of the terrain. He had five companies of tested infantry and two troops of cavalry. He moved George L. Tyler's 2nd Cavalry across the Missouri by the steamer *Fontanelle* in order to rendezvous with General Terry and his escort farther north.

Miles's column reached the Missouri River, close by the mouth of the Musselshell River, and received word on the morning of the twenty-fifth that the Nez Perce had crossed the Musselshell at Cow Island two days earlier, moving north after having destroyed the depot there and skirmishing with Major Ilges. Miles crossed to the far bank of the Musselshell River, intending to move along the southern bank of the Missouri toward the Judith basin, which straddled the exact center of Montana. He hoped he could intercept the tribe and prevent its moving any farther north toward Canada.

Near the Carroll Landing, Kelly and Shambow joined Miles, and he ordered them to scout ahead for any sign of the Nez Perce. Kelly and Shambow ranged ahead, working in two separate groups, each with their own group of Cheyenne scouts. The independent Shambow had held out for four times the normal scout salary. Miles found a way to pay him, and he expected results.

Nelson A. Miles as a breveted general during the Civil War. He held a rank of colonel during the Nez Perce War. (*Library of Congress*)

By dispatch, Colonel Sturgis suggested to Miles that he would reduce the speed of his own advance in order to slow down the Nez Perce and not risk alerting the tribe or causing them to cover ground even faster. Sturgis wanted to give Miles a chance to head off the Nez Perce. If Sturgis pushed too close on their heels, the tribe might disappear again, and Miles would never catch them.

Also on September 25, Howard was met on the trail by a dispatch rider from Fort Benton and learned that the Nez Perce had forded the Missouri at Cow Creek and skirmished with the army detachment there, taking many supplies. Howard decided to resume a quicker pace and moved his men by riverboat to Cow Island to pick up the trail.

On the twenty-sixth, Miles began chasing his enemy in earnest across the Missouri River as the fleeing Indians continued their journey north toward Canada. Miles advanced rapidly, leaving his supply train far to the rear, and this was the logistics problem he faced. He had outpaced his supply lines and pushed his men as hard as possible, while trying to find the perfect pace so that their horses would not give out as they drove them across the vast plains. Miles was gambling that he and his men would be able to move fast enough to intercept the Nez Perce and pin them in a place where his supplies could then catch up to his fast-moving cavalry. He also suspected that Howard would be eager to shadow him, using him like a hunting dog to locate the prize and then sweep in to claim the victory. That outcome he would not allow.

His men were constantly cold, and they had as little shelter as the Indians they shadowed because their tents, heavy coats, canvases, and blankets were many miles to the rear with the supply trains. His men had thin clothing and few of the comforts that would protect them from the increasingly cold days and bitter nights. Their rations were meager and had to be made to last until the supplies caught up with them. Still Miles drove his men relentlessly through grueling, eighteen-hour days.

Miles sent out his scouts—Dakota, Cheyenne, trappers, and men of the Great Plains and mountains—to all points of the compass with one purpose: to determine the direction and pace of the fleeing tribe. The Indian scouts were eager to capture whatever glory they could, but the real prize for them would be the Nez Perce horses. Night was short enough after the impossibly long days of riding, but sleeping was even harder because the men were constantly shivering to keep warm. Miles felt it himself. He needed the men to be as sharp as possible. He needed his scouts to do the impossible. He needed them to find the trail of the elusive Nez Perce in this vast wilderness.

Miles pushed his column behind the Little Rockies, which helped screen his forces from the trail where his scouts indicated the Nez Perce were moving. His men would be hidden by the mountains until his cavalry burst around the upper lip of the mountain range beyond which he assumed the Nez Perce would be found. He pursued his

A US Army column marching in pursuit of the Nez Perce. (*National Archives*)

enemies across the Bear Paw Mountains, arriving on the evening of the twenty-ninth on the other side of the Missouri Plateau in north-central Montana Territory.

Meanwhile, three significant events took place within the Nez Perce tribe. The first was that Looking Glass had regained enough influence within the tribe to oppose Lean Elk's efforts to keep moving at the exhausting pace he had been setting in order to safely reach their safe haven in Canada. Looking Glass argued with Lean Elk that the people were exhausted; the pace he was setting was too hard on the old and wounded. Here was a place, he argued, where the people could rest, while meat and robes could be obtained from the abundant buffalo herds nearby. After much discussion, Lean Elk finally agreed, but he insisted that the camp be placed near but below the high bluffs and in the Snake Creek's wash.

Snake Creek was so named because it was sinuous and wound back upon itself as it ran across the prairie. Lean Elk and Looking Glass found this a suitable place for their compromise of a few days' rest. The tribe's shelters were then built twenty to thirty feet below the level of the prairie and inside the deep banks that the river had cut. Their camp would not be seen easily from any point on the prairie above the cut banks. The horses were put to pasture just across the creek from their lodges. Their campsite was the most sheltered spot they found, with several small, elevated hills above the cut banks from which they could see trouble coming and defend themselves if necessary.[7]

For several days the people hunted and warmed themselves as best they could. There was plentiful fuel for fires in the form of dried buffalo dung. It burned hot and made little smoke. On the second day in their shelter, the weather began to change, and the gentle rain soon turned to a bitter torrent of sleet, and then snow. Their shelters were the rough furs and robes they had freshly produced from their hunting. After fight and flight, none of their lodge materials had survived along the journey. Their moccasins were worn out, and their clothing was also thin and in disrepair. Everyone began to worry about the coming winter. They knew they had to press on as soon as possible.[8] As they slept, they had no idea that Miles's scouts had discovered their trail the day before, and that the cavalry was moving around the northern end of the Bear Paw Mountains in an attempt to cut them off. It was September 29.

In the morning, the warrior Wottolen awoke after a dream that he believed was a prophetic vision. Wottolen was known to be prescient, so when he ran through the camp telling the people that he had foreseen the soldiers upon them at the place they were camped, he found willing listeners. He said they must all flee immediately to Canada. Many people were distressed by Wottolen's prediction of danger and hurried in their preparations.[9] A frigid rain pelted them overnight and turned to sleet and light snow by the morning. Everyone knew they would have to move on before the full weight of winter was unleashed upon them.

A view of the Bear Paw Mountain landscape. (*Washington State University Library, MASC*)

In the early dawn of September 30, Lieutenant Marion Maus and his scouts, including "Yellowstone" Kelly, explored the edges of the Bear Paw Mountains and the plains beyond, looking for any signs of the Nez Perce. Maus and Kelly were moving to the south around the lower edge of the mountain range. They had made their camp in the lower reaches the previous night. Meanwhile, Shambow and his ten Cheyenne scouts to the northwest believed they picked up the trail of the Nee-Mee-Poo. They followed the tantalizing hints of tracks and found disturbed ground. Shambow immediately sent a Cheyenne scout back to Miles with news of their discovery. Not long after that, the Indian scouts and Shambow lay on a ridge and gazed upon the plain. They could not yet see the village, but the horse herd beyond was visible.[10]

The scouts soon located the camp from the faint smoke rising from early morning fires and immediately sent word to Miles. After a short time checking to make sure they had not been detected, Shambow and his scouts rode quickly back to Miles to give him the location he needed.

The camp was set deep in a crescent-shaped wash in a deeply cut section of Snake Creek. If not for the smoke from the fires, it would have been invisible to an observer on the prairie. The camp was bisected by deep coulees that ran down to the creek.

The 5th Infantry took the lead, followed by the 2nd and 7th regiments, with foot soldiers of the 5th Infantry bringing up the rear as the men moved into position to attack.

The Nez Perce had only a few minutes warning that the army was upon them.

Chief Joseph and his oldest daughter, Noise of Running Feet, who must have been in her late teens, were preparing the horses across the creek when they heard and saw the Nez Perce outriders who scouted around the camp returning at high speed and signaling that soldiers were indeed coming. Joseph put his daughter on a strong horse, and with a spare mount on a lead, he told her to run for the border and not look back. She rode to an area where one hundred horses were already packed and women had been preparing the horses to move. She joined women and their children on horseback, riding hard from the oncoming soldiers. At least sixty warriors rode along to escort them. Joseph watched his daughter get away with the others, then he ran back to help organize the people.

Miles knew that the Canadian border was forty miles away, only a one-day march for the tribe. To carry out the attack, he ordered the 5th Infantry, led by Captain Simon Snyder, and the two battalions of the 7th Cavalry under Captain Owen Hale to make the initial attack on the southern exposure of the camp. Hale complained, "My God! Have I got to be killed this cold morning?"[11]

Snyder was supported by Lieutenant Maus and his scouts. He directed Captain Tyler and his battalion of the 2nd Cavalry to sweep behind the camp and capture the livestock and horses while also attacking from the rear.

Tyler rode wide to the left of the camp with his cavalry and forded Snake Creek where the cut bank leveled out and was not so deep.[12] Nearly one thousand horses were milling on the plain, now cut off from the village. In previous engagements, the cavalry was not able to capture a significant enough number of horses to eliminate the tribe's mobility.

The Nez Perce saw the dash of the cavalry to get to their horses. It would be suicide to run out onto the open ground to oppose them. A group of perhaps sixty warriors who had been able to get to some of the animals that were already loaded with packs, as well as some women and children from the tribe, dashed off toward the Canadian border. A detachment of Tyler's cavalry, led by Lieutenant Edward McClernand, pursued them. The remaining warriors took up their places in rifle pits and coulees, behind whatever cover they could find. The warriors' families sought shelter farther down the creek. The warriors grimly continued to dig in. When they saw that their horses were unattainable and taken by the cavalry, they knew in their warrior souls that their freedom was lost.

As Tyler swept around and began to drive the horses away, he knew they had succeeded in this essential part of their strategy. The fast-moving cavalry detachment would take most of the horses and mules away from the camp while the majority of the cavalry attacked and engaged the defending warriors. A mounted Nez Perce warrior with mobility, speed, and a perfect sense of where to attack was worth a squad of cavalry troopers. Dismounted, he was still a remarkable fighter and accurate marksman, but his most significant weapon had been taken from him. Miles had learned from Howard's experience at the Battle of the Clearwater that the Nez Perce warrior had little stomach for entrenched warfare.

The defense was strong, but the ground was fiercely contested, and men from both sides sought cover in the gulleys and the fighting places they had prepared earlier as a precaution. The initial attack involved cavalry and infantry driving for the heart of the camp. The fighting broke out at once; it was hard and at close range. Lean Elk was killed from friendly fire in the first rush of cavalry, soon followed by Lone Bird and Pile of Clouds. Other warriors fell during the day. In the confusion, Husishusis Kute accidentally shot several Nez Perce warriors thinking they were Cheyenne or Dakota. Two Moons was anguished when he saw a Cheyenne run down and kill a Nez Perce woman.

Many people of the tribe had been caught out in the open as the soldiers charged.

When the attack came, warrior Husis Owyeen (Shot in Head) was caught in a no-man's-land outside the camp preparing the horses to move. "Then the crack of guns filled the air. Everybody was outside, running here, there, everywhere," he recalled later. He witnessed the same incident Two Moons had as the Cheyenne on horseback chased the woman down. He could do nothing to help her.

"I untied my horse. He leaped up and ran away from me. It was the noise of the guns that scared him. Horses running in every direction. Women, old men, and young men were trying to capture saddle horses. The trying was in vain."[13]

Shot in the Head finally mounted and, with several other men, rode through the hail of bullets slicing the air and reached safety outside the lines of troops surrounding them. As darkness enveloped the surrounded camp, "night grew colder and I . . . remained out from the corral of soldiers guarding the camp. No cloth to cover my body, no moccasins on my feet, and the snow beginning to fall."[14] He worried about his wife, Penahwenomi, inside the camp.

Penahwenomi had just returned to the camp from the horse herd when the soldiers attacked. She was standing shivering, warming her feet by the fire, behind a canvas that broke the cold wind a bit. She heard Indian scouts calling

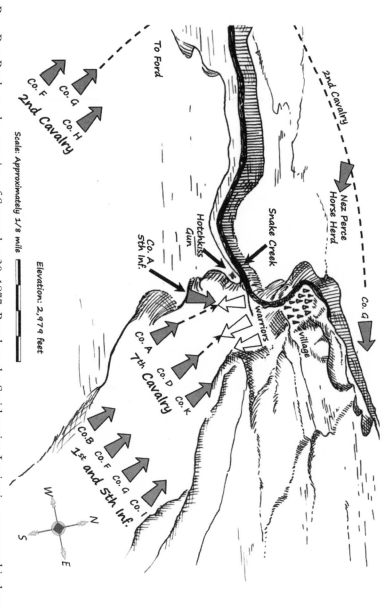

The Bear Paw Battle on the morning of September 30, 1877. Based on the Smithsonian Institution topographical map of the battlefield. (*Author*)

from a nearby bluff. "Soldiers!" they called, "soldiers coming." The scouts had come running into the camp breathless, saying that they had just barely escaped being killed. Her mother told her to go out to see if it was true that the soldiers had come. She stepped out of the canvas shelter. Far up the rising slope to her front she saw the enemies coming, and she was afraid. She heard people calling to her to save the horses. Still in bare feet, with only a thin shawl over her shoulders, she ran swiftly for the horses. The soldiers were nearly upon her. She grabbed a passing horse and swung up, riding ahead of the attack along with some others who had also been able to find horses.[15] They outran the Cheyenne who were trying to catch them and the soldiers behind. She worried about her mother, her sister, and her husband.[16]

While the few scatted individuals and groups broke away from the camp, Captain Tyler's sweep to the left with the 2nd Cavalry opened up the southern end of the camp to an assault by the three battalions of the 7th Cavalry, supported by Company A of the 5th Infantry.[17] Company A, under Captain Miles Moylan, on the left, received the order to charge and passed it along the line. Company D, under Captain Edward Godfrey, rode up the center. Company K, under Captain Owen Hale and Lieutenant J. W. Biddle, rode in on the right. The charge brought Companies A and D to the edge of the cut bank, but they found the bank too steep to negotiate. The warriors rose from excellent positions to deliver enfilading fire and poured it mercilessly into the stalled cavalry. Seeing this, Hale turned slightly to the right and noticed some shallower ground and the unusual coulees ahead. Moylan motioned for Godfrey to follow him. Company D was also taking severe fire from the coulees, and Godfrey was unhorsed and nearly killed. Lieutenant Edwin P. Eckerson withdrew the men several hundred yards until Godfrey stopped the movement.

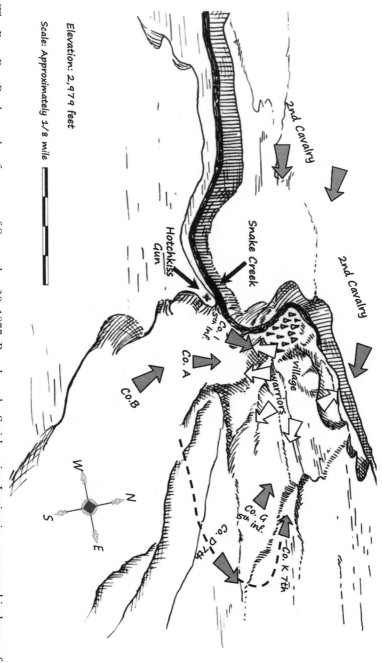

The Bear Paw Battle on the afternoon of September 30, 1877. Based on the Smithsonian Institution topographical map of the battlefield. (*Author*)

Elevation: 2,979 feet

Scale: Approximately 1/8 mile

2nd Cavalry

2nd Cavalry

Hotchkiss Gun

Snake Creek

Co. I 7th Inf.

village

warriors

Co. A

Co. B

Co. G 5th Inf.

Co. D 7th

Co. K 7th

W

N

S

E

Company K was involved in hand-to-hand combat over the high ground of the bluffs above the camps. A murderous fire crisscrossed through the troops as Hale tried to form a line rather than continuing the charge. After Godfrey and Moylan both became casualties in the field hospital, Lieutenant George W. Baird was sent with Miles's orders for Hale. When he arrived at the line of Hale's command, he found the captain and Lieutenant Biddle lying dead next to each other. Biddle had just joined the army in May 1877. It was his only battle.

Miles ordered Company G of the 5th Infantry to advance along the terrain to a place where their counterfire would be more effective. The bugler was ordered to sound the movement, but he replied that he had been shot and lacked the strength to blow the horn. A sergeant moved the men along in a crawl to stay below the bullets, and he urged the men who were not moving to join them, but they would never be able to obey his orders: they had already been killed. The attack soon lost momentum because of the deadly accuracy of the Indian fighters.

Louis Shambow used his dead horse as cover from the hail of bullets. Eventually he found shelter behind a rock formation along with "Yellowstone" Kelly and Corporal John Haddo. The men gamely tried to fire on the Nez Perce marksmen, but it proved an uneven duel, with the corporal soon joining many of his comrades in death. Shambow would later state: "Those Nez Perce were the best shots I ever saw. I would put a small stone on the top of my rock and they would get it every time."[18]

Company A of the 5th Infantry slugged it out with the warriors at the cut bank using more aggressive rifle work, and both the angle and the height now exposed the warriors defending the camp to a hail of deadly fire. The fusillade continued for some time. The troopers thought that the enfilading fire had greater effect than the initial charges by soldiers.

By nighttime, the soldiers had gained positions on the high bluff. Through the night, the warriors scraped their rifle pits deeper with their knives and whatever implements they could find. The soldiers were entrenching also. Captain Henry Romeyn of the 5th Infantry noted the layout of the defenses:

> The camp was located on a small stream called Snake Creek, as it proved an excellent position for defense in a kidney-shaped depression covering about six acres of ground, along the western side of which the stream ran in a tortuous course, while through it, from the steep bluffs forming its eastern and southern sides, ran "coulees" from two to six feet in depth and fringed with enough sage brush to hide the heads of their occupants. Here the Nez Perce chieftain had pitched his camp and here he now made his last stand for battle.[19]

Unknown to Miles, during the night of September 30, the Nez Perce sent six warriors with a message for Sitting Bull to come and help them. Miles's strategy of surprise and containment had successfully trapped most of the Indians in the village. His objective to remove their mobility had been achieved through the capture of most of their horses. He had succeeded in one area where Gibbon could not at Big Hole: he had captured the horse herd. But a forgotten lesson from the struggle at Big Hole was that the Nez Perce could re-form, even if they were surprised. They did not panic. The warriors would form an impenetrable and deadly gun line. Miles's soldiers would suffer horrendous casualties in another direct attack. Miles's attack had produced many casualties among his own forces in the initial assault.

The eastern side of the camp was overlooked by a bluff twenty to thirty feet high. On the southern side there was a perpendicular bluff with excellent cover. When the soldiers were within two hundred yards of the Indian camp, the warriors began a devastating enfilading fire on the advancing troops. Miles observed that the southern side of the camp had given the enemy a stronger position to defend than he had thought. Miles directed his artillery officer to wheel the Hotchkiss gun into position on a spur that overlooked the highly fortified southern face of the camp. The crews manning the Hotchkiss gun were being killed at an alarming rate.

Miles found he had seventy men killed or wounded, including all of the first sergeants. He had set up a field hospital, but real medical care for the wounded was days away. Many men suffered terrible head wounds until it became clear to them that they could not peer over their cover at the enemy without an immediate and accurate response in the form of a well-aimed bullet. Lieutenant Baird, Miles's adjutant, had his arm shattered and an ear shot off.

Due to the casualties, Miles was forced to reconsider his strategy. His men were wary of any direct action against the Nez Perce positions because they had sustained casualties at one thousand yards from Nez Perce marksmen. Miles intended to finish the war once and for all, and he left his options open, including giving the Nez Perce a chance to surrender. He switched his tactical plan from attack to siege by ringing the camp with soldiers and maintaining fire and artillery to bring the tribe to capitulation. Miles was also nervous about having his flank exposed to Sitting Bull should he sweep down from Canada. He decided to begin shelling the Nez Perce camp. Although his Hotchkiss gun was portable, he was forced to use it as a mortar, because the barrel could not be depressed sufficiently to fire a straight trajectory into the camp. By October 1, the much bigger 12-pound Napoleon cannon had arrived, and he began shelling the camp in earnest. At first the shells ranged too far. It was necessary to excavate and bury the

The skirmish line commanded by Nelson Miles exchanging fire with the Nez Perce. (*Library of Congress*)

trunion so the elevated barrel could shell the camp. The exploding shells rained death and terror on the Nez Perce.

Miles's men were now entrenched in the positions they had taken on the thirtieth, and their own freedom of movement was nearly as restricted as that of those they had ringed in the camp. Miles knew he had to do something to break the stalemate. He had been taking steady casualties each day of the battle. His men's morale was low. It was clear to him that their hearts were not in the fight and they were exhausted. He worried that the Nez Perce would try an attack or breakout that his worn-out men might not be able to withstand.

A Chinook Indian with a white flag took a message of parley from Miles. He shouted in the Chinook language, which was somewhat known to the Nez Perce, that Miles wanted to meet with Joseph.

Miles insisted that the Nez Perce surrender their arms, which was a significant barrier to continuing the talks. Joseph insisted that the people would need to keep at least half of their rifles to shoot game in order to sustain themselves and provide for the tribe. Equally likely, Joseph probably suspected that the situation with the army could become unpredictable regardless of whatever agreement was struck, but a tribe with some rifles would not be ignored or abused. Disarmed, they might be overwhelmed, perhaps even killed. But Miles remained intractable and refused to consider Joseph's counteroffer.

Joseph alluded to the fact that the Lakota were coming and Sitting Bull could be upon them at any time.[20]

Miles would not consider any further discussion until his demands were met. The parley ended as Joseph and his men began to walk back from the soldiers' camp to their own lines. Suddenly, Miles dispatched several men to seize and hold Joseph without explanation. Miles needed to force Joseph to surrender in order to forestall Howard from capturing the victory that was almost in his grasp. Miles wrote later in his report:

> On the morning of October 1, I opened communication with the Nez Perces and Chief Joseph and several of his warriors came out under a flag of truce. They showed a willingness to surrender and brought up part of their arms (11 rifles and carbines), but as I believe, became suspicious from some remarks that were made in English in their hearing and those in camp hesitated to come forward and lay down their arms.
>
> While Joseph remained in our camp, I directed Lieut. L. H. Jerome, Second Cavalry, to ascertain what was being done in the Indian village and [Jerome] was detained (but not harmed) until Joseph returned to his camp, in the afternoon of the 2nd.[21]

Yellow Bull, who was a close personal friend of Joseph's, was enraged that Miles had detained Joseph under a flag of truce. He ordered Wottolen to capture Lieutenant Jerome, who was reconnoitering the camp. On October 2, Jerome was exchanged for Joseph. Jerome's lack of caution had cost Miles his attempt to force a surrender by holding Joseph hostage, but Jerome was able to report on the numbers and condition of people still in the camp.

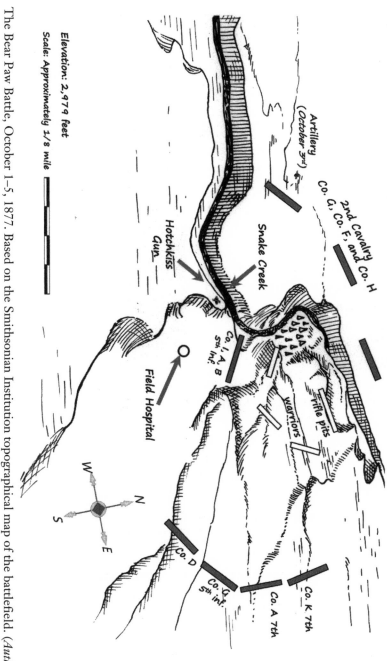

Elevation: 2,979 feet

Scale: Approximately 1/8 mile

Artillery
(October 3rd)

2nd Cavalry
Co. G, Co. F, and Co. H

Hotchkiss
Gun

Snake Creek

Co. I, A, B
5th Inf.

Field Hospital

Warriors

Rifle Pits

Co. D

Co. G
5th Inf.

Co. A 7th

Co. K 7th

W   N
S   E

The Bear Paw Battle, October 1–5, 1877. Based on the Smithsonian Institution topographical map of the battlefield. (*Author*)

The Nez Perce debated between surrendering, continuing to fight, or retreating. Joseph refused to attempt a breakout because it would mean leaving the wounded, the sick, and the elderly. Artillery fire continued through October 4, killing some children and elderly women, and the Nez Perce resolve began to wane. Ollokot died defending the edge of the camp with his rifle. Hopes were fading that the six men sent to Sitting Bull would bring the relief the Nez Perce needed to break free for the border. In fact, the warriors never made it beyond the "medicine line" to Sitting Bull. Among the tribes of the area, the "medicine line" was the Canadian border, so named because it magically stopped US troops at its edge. In the unfamiliar landscape, the warriors wandered into an Assiniboine camp and were all killed.[22] With them died the last hope of the people besieged on the battlefield that help would be coming from Sitting Bull.

Absorbed in watching the siege, Miles was surprised when a familiar figure appeared from the darkness and shook his hand. General Howard, with a small group of men, had completed his journey to meet up with Miles. Miles had sent a message asking him to hasten his march. Howard reassured Miles that he did not intend to assume command. Later that evening, Howard suggested using two of the Nez Perce scouts he had with him to urge the Nez Perce to give up the fight. Miles agreed.

In the early morning of October 5, those scouts, Captain John and Captain George, called out to the Nez Perce camp. They found the people weary of the long journey, the sacrifices and fighting, the lost loved ones, and missing their homeland.[23] Miles ceased his shelling.

In the no-man's-land between the camps, Joseph, Miles, Howard, and their interpreters began to work out the final details of a surrender. They were agreed upon by midafternoon, and White Bird, who had not attended the meeting,

A *Harper's Magazine* illustration showing a Nez Perce rifle pit being used as a refuge for women and children during the battle. (*Library of Congress*)

concurred, saying, "What Joseph does is all right; I have nothing to say."[24]

Howard badly wanted Joseph to surrender to him personally. It would vindicate him and his efforts in wrapping up the Nez Perce problem with his superiors and would represent the crowning achievement in his career. Howard tried to allay Joseph's fears and promised to personally take him to the reservation. Here began the subtle conflict between two unabashed careerists, with Howard's aide-de-camp, Lieutenant Charles E. S. Wood, in the middle. The controversy would rage throughout the commands about who had subdued Joseph and the Nez Perce, and it even played itself out in the popular press.

It was understood by the tribe that Joseph's capitulation did not bind Looking Glass and White Bird. The feeling among the other tribal bands was that Joseph did have the right to surrender the Wallowa bands, but not the Lamtama or the Alpowai. And he certainly did not speak for the Palouse band. Looking Glass was considering passing through the lines around the Crows and Gros Ventres who were watching the perimeter. He and some of his people had decided that White Bird was right. Still, he hoped for the Sioux to arrive and save them. He joined his brother Tookelikcema in a high rifle pit facing the south. Looking Glass stood up to look, thinking an Indian he saw ahead was dressed like a Sioux warrior. The distant Indian fired a shot, and it struck Looking Glass in the forehead. The Indian who had shot him was not a Sioux, but a member of one of the tribes allied with Miles. Looking Glass fell dead at his brother's feet. He was the last Nez Perce man to be killed in the Bear Paw battle.[25]

The treaty Nez Perce scouts continued to shuttle messages between the two sides. Once Joseph was confident his people would not be harmed, he sent his last message to the commanders through the scouts. Ad Chapman translated his message, which Lieutenant Wood wrote down for posterity:[26]

> Tell General Howard I know his heart. What he told me before I have in my heart. I am tired of fighting. Our chiefs are killed. Looking Glass is dead.
>
> Tu-hul-hul-sote [Toohoolhoolzote] is dead. The old men are all dead. It is the young men who say yes or no. He who led on the young men is dead [Ollokot]. It is cold and we have no blankets. The little children are freezing to death. My people, some of them, have run away to the hills, and have no blankets, no food; no one knows where they are—perhaps freezing to death. I want to have time to look for my children and see how many of them I can find. Maybe I shall find them among the dead. Here me, my chiefs. I am tired; my heart is sick and sad. From where the sun now stands I will fight no more forever.[27]

Somewhere on the bluff above the southern end of the camp, Joseph met Miles and Howard and presented his rifle in surrender to Miles. The Nez Perce War was over.

When the battle of Bear Paw Mountain was finally over, twenty-one troops had been killed and fifty wounded. The Nez Perce had twenty-six killed (including two women and a child) and forty-six wounded.

After the surrender, Ollokot's widow, Wetatonmi, expressed her sorrow and inconsolable grief for her husband, the loss of her way of life, and the uncertainty of exile to the reservation:

> It was lonesome, the leaving. Husband dead, friends buried or held prisoners. I felt that I was leaving all that I had but I did not cry. You know how you feel when you lose kindred and friends through sickness and death. You do not care if you die. With us it was worse. Strong men, well women, and little children killed and buried. They had not done wrong to be so killed. We had only asked to be left in our own homes, the homes of our ancestors. Our going was with heavy hearts, broken spirits. . . . All lost, we walked silently into the wintry night.[28]

Howard's men had literally worn out the leather soles of their shoes chasing the Nez Perce. Howard estimated how far they had all come:

> From the beginning of the Indian pursuit across the Lolo trail, until their embarkation on the Missouri River for the homeward journey, including all halts and stoppages, from July 27th to October 10th, my command marched one thousand three hundred and twenty-one miles in seventy-five days. Joseph, the Indian, taking with him his men, women, and chil-

dren, traversed even greater distances, for he had to make many a loop in his skein, many a deviation into a tangled thicket, to avoid or deceive his enemy. So that whatever side of the picture we examine we find there evidence of wonderful energy, and prolonged endurance.[29]

Two very different journeys began from this point in time. Both were difficult and ended in lands that were utterly alien. The captured who laid down their arms faced an arduous journey in inhumane conditions to the Indian Territory and extended exile from their traditional homelands. Joseph would continue to be singled out by the government and made a permanent exile, first in Oklahoma and then in Washington. In his old age, Joseph was able to briefly set foot in Idaho in order to give speeches. Those who escaped the battlefield faced a desperate flight to exile and freedom in British Canada.[30]

12

White Bird's Freedom

The Nez Perce who had left days earlier to get assistance from the Sioux were the first to reach Sitting Bull's camp. Among them was Half Moon, a man named Left Hand, and another named Wellahawit. But the warriors encountered communication problems because they did not share a common language with the Sioux and had to rely on sign language and pantomime. When signing Snake Creek as the position where the battle was taking place, the sign for the river was incorrectly given or received, and the Lakota believed that the Nez Perce were fighting along the Missouri River. The Lakota were anguished because that was simply too far to go with a force of warriors to rescue the tribe.

Shot in Head's wife, Penahwenomi, and her band had been buffeted by the snowstorm. Their experience was typical: bone-tired and freezing, they shuffled and rode through the piling snow, completely disoriented. "We had no blankets when we escaped," she said later. "Stormy and snowing. No stars, no sun, we could not know which way to go. Hungry, half-naked and freezing, we wandered in our riding until the friendly Chippewas were reached. There we were given clothing and food, and some matches before going on to the Sioux camp." She allowed herself to believe that they might make it.[1]

While Joseph was surrendering to Miles and Howard, Wottolen, one of White Bird's respected Lamtama warriors; his son, Black Eagle; and some forty others, including women and children, trudged into the darkness on foot in the snow on their way to find Sitting Bull. Wottolen later remembered:

> Chief White Bird did not surrender. I belonged to his band. We left in the night and travelled afoot to Sitting Bull's camp across the Canadian border. Women and a few children were with us, and some wounded. Half naked, it was a hard journey of several suns. But we escaped the bondage that was for Joseph and his people. They were blinded by the life promises of . . . Miles.[2]

White Bird had gathered the Lamtama and passed through the perimeter before the soldiers or Bannocks could stop them. Looking Glass's brother, Tookelikcema, was with him. Both men had secreted some of their people out earlier.

Peo Peo Tholekt recalled, "When Chief Joseph came from talking with the soldiers, he asked for Chief White Bird who was already gone. This was after many had given up their guns and night darkness covered all." Not only was it dark, but the smatterings of snowflakes that had fallen in the early evening now turned into a full-fledged blizzard.[3] The soldiers had settled down in their shelters; they could tell that the end of the fight was near. They had no reason to believe anyone would try to sneak past them.

The soldiers had a huge perimeter to guard, and many of their Cheyenne allies were out trying to recover stray Nez Perce horses. It must have been relatively easy for the chiefs to move small groups along the coulees and streambed and out of the camp.

"It was alright for Chief Peo-Peo-Hi-Hi [White Bird] to go out from that battlefield," Yellow Wolf said later. "We did not think it good to become prisoners when we could escape. I, of Chief Joseph's band, left in the breaking of day the next morning."[4]

While the blizzard continued, Joseph knew that people were slowly leaving the camp in small groups. It is plausible that he may have stalled for time, holding out in lengthy parlay with Miles and Howard, which would allow White Bird and others to flee. Joseph may have surrendered knowing that he was actually helping White Bird and others to escape. He would have known that of all the bands, the Salmon River Lamtama faced the greatest danger of punishment. White Bird clearly preferred death before surrender on principle.

Many disconnected clans, families, and individuals moved without surety that they knew where they were going in the whiteout conditions of the blizzard. One such group included Peo Peo Tholekt, Koo-sou-yeen, and James William. Along with their followers, they crossed the prairie on foot with little cover. Ollokot's widow was among them. They had some blankets and provisions, but the cold and shock of the battle still took their toll on the refugee band.

Although the snow was bitter cold and hard to endure, it helped those who made their way out of the camp by making the visibility poor for the soldiers at the pickets who had the camp cordoned off.

Shot in Head's wife was traveling with ten other women, their children, and a few men who had fled at the outset of the battle. They were all riding bareback; they had few robes and blankets, as they had been caught unprepared to flee the camp. They could hear the gunfire as they rode into the darkness on the first night. Joseph's older wife and daughter were among them. As they traveled, their group became larger and more ragged as they encountered people who had fled the camp nearly naked and were on the verge of freezing to death. When they stopped, their camp was cold and dark. Fires were too risky with the Cheyenne and Gros Ventres chasing them. The women cried as the gunfire continued throughout the night. The next day, as they traveled over the flat, featureless prairie, they could hear only the booming of the big gun being used in the siege. There was no food for anyone. It began to snow, and many, including Shot in Head's wife, were barefoot. On the fifth day, they managed to kill a buffalo and chanced making a fire. Their thirst was terrible, and it was hard to eat with parched throats. Some Chippewa discovered their plight and shared food and their robes and moccasins.

Believing the Lakota were coming, Shot in Head had once again fought his way out of the camp on horseback. Freezing in the cold and almost naked in only his breechcloth, he put on the clothing of a soldier he had just shot. Then he turned his mount and went north to find Sitting Bull's people and his wife.

Yellow Wolf waited another day to try to leave the camp, making his intention to leave known to Joseph, his uncle. Yellow Wolf's mother had escaped on the day of the attack along with Joseph's daughter. Joseph implored his nephew to go find them and bring them back. Yellow Wolf agreed and said goodbye. Around his shoulders he wrapped a bulky robe, under which he was wearing leggings and a shirt. He was thus able to smuggle his carbine through the soldier's pickets by sliding it under his leggings. He walked out past some army guards who seemed unconcerned that the young warrior was leaving the battlefield.

Not all the Nez Perce left the greater area of the camp. Some, like Shot in Head's wife and Joseph's daughter, stayed in the general vicinity of the camp with her group. They spent their time hiding with little to eat while they awaited the outcome of the battle.

For each group of travelers, one day flowed into another without any change in the weather or their mute exhaustion. The only thing that kept their legs moving was the thought that they had friends and perhaps a safe haven beyond the horizon in Canada, with the Lakota.

Many groups kept moving to the north, finding others as they went, old friends, sometimes family. In *Nez Perce Summer 1877*, Jerome Greene notes that a mounted policeman near the Lakota camp saw a group of as many as fifty people entering Sitting Bull's camp.[5]

The danger had increased for the refugees: Miles had dispatched all of his scouts with offers of rewards for their capture. His Assiniboine and Gros Ventre Indians were also promised rewards, and bounties. He mobilized three detachments for the purpose of capturing or killing White Bird and his people before they could get into Canada.

With Miles's men scouting and unfriendly Indians in the area, the stakes were high for the shadowy figures leaning into the bitter wind. They couldn't know for sure if the indistinct figure ahead was a lost family member, one of Louis Shambow's Cheyenne scouts, or a friendly Sioux. Some encounters in the storm were deadly. Miles's net did catch some of the Nez Perce, with terrible consequences.[6]

The Indians who were out hunting during the army's initial attack on the camp and were seen by Shambow and his Cheyenne probably fled. Greene suggests that they may not have been able to return to the camp and so ventured on to Canada. These were some of the first envoys to Sitting Bull's camp, when the communications between the two tribes was initially poor.[7] However, at least three men (besides Shot in Head) who had been outside the camp made it back through the lines to help defend their people.[8]

Yellow Wolf came upon shadowy figures ahead in the snow, and even he, formidable as he was, cautiously made his way toward them, listening and ready to run or fight. He was worried they were Cheyenne, but he soon discovered that they were Nez Perce fleeing the camp into the storm, like himself. The young warrior and his wretched group staggered on through the blizzard without clothing or shelter.

Elsewhere on the cold prairie, Black Eagle was trying to determine the best way ahead as the storms limited his view of the horizon with swirling snow and cutting sleet. With grey clouds above and endless prairie all around him, he had no way of knowing if he was leading his group of refugees to freedom or death.

On the fourth day of traveling over the border and into Canada, one of the fatigued group of refugees approached Sitting Bull's camp. Someone conversant with the Lakota language related to the Sioux outriders the desperate battle they had left and gave the location correctly, on Snake Creek by the Bear Paw Mountains. Sitting Bull's camp was suddenly aroused with the sounds of hoof beats and war cries as Lakota warriors mounted their horses. Sitting Bull himself rode out with one thousand warriors. The storm had abated, Snake Creek was not far for men on horses, and they knew the place well. They would ride to the rescue of the besieged Nez Perce.

After their communications problems had been resolved, Peo Peo Tholekt joined the warriors as they rode out onto the plains to the relief of the Nez Perce, "When coming with the Sioux to help fight the soldiers I met Chief White Bird and some of his people afoot, hunting for the Great Sioux Camp across the Canadian border."[9] White Bird had brought ninety men and two hundred women and

White Bird, left, Joseph's daughter, and No Hunter photographed in
Canada soon after their arrival. (*George Kush Collection*)

children out of the camp, across the snowbound prairie, to
the north and across the border into Canada. White Bird's
family was with him, including his wife, Heyume Teyatkikt.
Only six Lamtama had surrendered with Joseph.

Peo Peo Tholekt related that the overwhelming majority of people from White Bird's band had chosen the dangerous option of Canada and had run the gauntlet of hostile soldiers and Indians to get there. It is possible that their
motivation was as much fear of punitive action against their
band for the killings on the Salmon River as it was White
Bird's unwillingness to surrender. In any event, the strategy
or the happenstance of departing the camp in small groups
proved effective in getting through the army and Indian
cordon around their camp.

White Bird recognized the great Chief Sitting Bull
astride a fine grey horse. Sitting Bull asked White Bird of
the news from the fight and of the fate of Joseph. White
Bird had to tell him that Joseph had surrendered his band.

He recounted the dead that he knew of from the final battle and that the fighting was long since over. Only the stragglers making their way to the Lakota had escaped; they were scattered and would need help from Sitting Bull. He promised to do everything he could to find and help them.

Profoundly saddened, Sitting Bull got down from his horse and his warriors followed. He raised his hands and began a wailing lamentation for the many deaths and to celebrate the bravery of the Nez Perce. His warriors and the Lamtama joined in. Eventually, horses were brought for White Bird's people, and they rode safely tucked among the ranks of a thousand Sioux warriors. They rode north beneath the unfamiliar Canadian skies into the vastness of those foreign plains.

Appendix: Poet Warriors

In a conflict of such scope and tragedy as the Nez Perce War, it is fitting that many of the written and spoken words that record and define the event are so profound and beautiful. From rhetoric and poetry to reports, the people involved infused their writing with the experiences they were living. The poetic record of the experience speaks passionately to us across the years.

Colonel J. W. Redington

J. W. Redington was a war correspondent, writer, courier, and army scout, and he left a small body of work that documented his times and adventures. Redington was a scout for General Oliver Otis Howard and served the army in later duty. He eventually edited the *Heppner Gazette* in Oregon. He published a book on his exploits, *Scouting in Montana in the 1870's*. In the 1930s, he carried on a correspondence from his bed in the National Military Home with L. V. McWhorter regarding his Nez Perce campaign experiences. His humor and dramatic style were maintained in all the letters. In the following excerpt, Redington tells the story of a young man killed in the Camas Meadows fight. While writing in the romantic style of the period, he expresses a great deal in his short tribute. This little piece of prose helped lay the rails that cowboy poetry has run on ever since.

Story of Bugler Brooks

Brief was the service read by Colonel Mason, touching the remarks by General Howard, heavy the hearts of those who stood by. And as the little mound was rounded up and the farewell volleys rang out on the evening air, the setting sun slanted its shadowing shafts against the soaring summits of the Snake River sentries, the Three Tetons, the wondrous western clouds took on their fairy forms and tints of rose and amber and purple, the stars let down their hanging lamps, and the rising autumn moon saw soldiers resuming their stern realities of wicked war, with trumpeter Sembower sounding the calls.[1]

LIEUTENANT CHARLES ERSKINE SCOTT WOOD

C. E. S. Wood was a professional poet in later life. As a young man he served in the Nez Perce War as General Howard's aide-de-camp. After a military career in which he achieved the rank of colonel, he became a supporter of the Nez Perce tribe during his civilian legal career. His son would often visit Chief Joseph at Nespelum and stay there for extended visits. This excerpt from *The Poet in the Desert* expresses Wood's wistful desire to understand his "brown brothers."

> XLIX
> I have lived with my brown brothers
> Of the wilderness
> And found them a mystery.
> The cunning of the swift-starting trout
> A mystery, also;
> The wisdom of voyaging birds;
> The gophers' winter-sleep;
> The knowledge of the bees.
> All a mystery.
> I have lain out with the brown men
> And know they are favored.
> Nature whispered to them their secrets,
> But passed me by.
> They instructed my civilization.

Stately and full of wisdom
Was Hin-mah-too-yah-Laht-Kt:
Thunder rolling in the mountains;
Joseph, Chief of the Nez Perces;
Who, in five battles from the Clearwater
To Bear Paw Mountains,
Made bloody protest against Perfidy and Power.
Ah-laht-ma-kahlt [Ollokot], his brother,
Who led the young men in battle;
Tsootlem-mox-mox, Yellow Bull;
Cunning White Bird, a brown Odysseus,
And indomitable Too-hul-hul-soot,
High Priest, dignified; unafraid; inspired;
Standing half-naked in the Council Teepee,
Insisting in low musical gutturals,
With graceful gesture,
"The Earth is our Mother,
"From her we come;
"To her we return.
"She belongs to all.
"She has gathered into her bosom
"The bones of our ancestors.
"Their spirits will fight with us
"When we battle for our home
"Which is ours from the beginning. . . .

L
Just over there where yon purple peak,
Like a great amethyst, gems the brow of the Desert,
I sprawled flat in the bunch-grass, a target
For the just bullets of my brown brothers betrayed.
I was a soldier, and at command,
Had gone out to kill and be killed.
This was not majestic.
The little gray gophers

Sat erect and laughed at me.
In that silent hour before the dawn,
When Nature drowses for a moment,
We swept like fire over the smoke-browned teepees;
Their conical tops peering above the willows.
We frightened the air with the crackle of rifles,
Women's shrieks, children's screams,
Shrill yells of savages;
Curses of Christians.
The rifles chuckled continually.
A poor people who asked nothing but freedom,
Butchered in the dark.
The dawn would not linger,
Nor the slow-advancing day refuse to come.
The larks salute the morn
As if there had been no murder.
In the accusing light of the remorseless Sun
It was not good o see brown boys and girls
Scattered about the grass in Death's repose;
On their sides, in reckless weariness.

CHIEF JOSEPH

Chief Joseph was taken into exile in Kansas and later
Oklahoma with those people who surrendered at the Bear
Paw battle. After years in the Indian Territory reservation
in Oklahoma, he was allowed to return to the Northwest
on May 22, 1885. Of the surviving 268 Nez Perce Indians,
118 were able to travel to Lapwai, Idaho. Joseph and the
others were sent to the Colville Indian Reservation in
Washington, where they would live in exile.

Joseph spoke in 1879 before a group of cabinet members
of the Rutherford B. Hayes administration about the plight
of his people and their wish to return to their land. He was
accompanied by Chief Yellow Bull, and Arthur Chapman as
his interpreter.[2]

I have shaken hands with a great many friends, but there are some things I want to know which no one seems able to explain. I cannot understand how the Government sends a man out to fight us, as it did General Miles, and then breaks his word. Such a Government has something wrong about it . . . I do not understand why nothing is done for my people. I have heard talk and talk but nothing is done. Good words do not last long until they amount to something. Words do not pay for my dead people. They do not pay for my country, now overrun by white men. They do not protect my father's grave. They do not pay for my horses and cattle.

Good words do not give me back my children. Good words will not make good the promise of your war chief, General Miles. Good words will not give my people good health and stop them from dying. Good words will not get my people a home where they can live in peace and take care of themselves.

I am tired of talk that comes to nothing. It makes my heart sick when I remember all the broken promises. There has been too much talking by men who had no right to talk. Too many misinterpretations have been made; too many misunderstandings have come up between the white men about the Indians.

If the white man wants to live in peace with the Indian he can live in peace. There need be no trouble. Treat all men alike. Give them the same law. Give them all an even chance to live and grow. . . .

Let me be a free man, free to travel, free to stop, free to work, free to trade where I choose, free to choose my own teachers, free to follow the religion of my fathers, free to talk, think and act for myself— and I will obey every law or submit to the penalty.

Whenever the white man treats the Indian as they treat each other then we shall have no more wars. We shall be all alike—brothers of one father and mother, with one sky above us and one country around us and one government for all. Then the Great Spirit Chief who rules above will smile upon this land and send rain to wash out the bloody spots made by brothers' hands upon the face of the earth. For this time the Indian race is waiting and praying. I hope no more groans of wounded men and women will ever go to the ear of the Great Spirit Chief above, and that all people may be one people.[3]

YELLOW WOLF

Yellow Wolf was a warrior of the Wallowa band and confident in the way that only young men can be. He saw, fought in, and left a record of most of the actions of the war. As a result, Yellow Wolf became one of the great firsthand Indian sources on the Nez Perce War. With Wottolen and a few others, he left a cogent record of their side of the conflict. With a warrior's pride, which stayed firmly intact in his declining years, he told L. V. McWhorter what he thought about claims by General Howard that the Nez Perce had been defeated at the Battle of the Clearwater, and as he refuted the claim, his argument managed to succinctly summarize the entire war.

> But we were not whipped! Had we been whipped, we could not have escaped from there with our lives.
> We could not have stopped General Howard at the Kamiah Crossing.
> We were not scared at that crossing.
> We then waited into the third sun for Howard to cross and give us war.
> He would not cross. It was then we started over the Lolo Trail.
> Had we been whipped we could not have passed the Lolo barricade.

We could not have beaten General Gibbon at Big Hole.
We could not have captured two hundred and fifty good horses at Horse Prairie.
We could not have captured General Howard's pack mules at Camas Meadows.
We could not have held off the new army at Canyon Creek.
We could not have captured the big supplies at Missouri River Crossing.
We could not have stood against General Miles during four days.[4]

UNKNOWN NEZ PERCE WARRIOR

The following song was written by an unknown Nez Perce warrior as a poignant memorial of Rainbow and his warrior friend Pahkatos who died during the Battle of the Big Hole. The poem appeared in L. V. McWhorter's *Hear Me, My Chiefs!* and also in Merrill D. Beal's *"I Will Fight No More Forever."* Although brief, it imparts the essence of a pact between two warriors to fight and die on the same day as their fathers had done.

Sad Brothers, Weeping Sisters, Farewell!
Gone is the Rain-bow, my War-time brother,
Bravest in Battle, kindliest in Peace.
Falling where the fighting raged,
Why was I not there?

By compact, both our fathers died in war,
And likewise this day their sons.
Changed as water is my warrior-power,
And I, "Pah-ka-tos," now yearns for death.

From the Night-trail my "war-mate" calls me,
And I answer, "YES!"

Tis well. Better this than bondage;
For the oppressor's hand is iron.

I go, again not to return.

Sad Brothers, Weeping Sisters, Farewell![5]

Notes

Chapter One: The Grant Peace Policy

1. Francis Haines took time to describe the expanse of the drainage of the Snake, Salmon, and Clearwater rivers, and the Columbia Plateau to the Bitterroot Mountains, as "a land well suited to the needs of man, red or white." Haines, *The Nez Perces*, 7.

2. Chiefs Looking Glass, Old Joseph, and Lawyer (Hallalhotsoot) signed the 1855 treaty.

3. Elias D. Pierce made significant gold finds in the fall of 1860. The following spring, the mining town of Pierce was established despite a US Army detachment that was detailed to evict the miners from the Nez Perce lands. In fact, the gold area was widely known as the Nez Perce Mines. "News from the Nez Perce Mines," *Idaho Yesterdays* 3 (Fall 1959), 19-29.

4. *The War of the Rebellion*, series 1, vol. 34, part 3, 531-532, and series 1, vol. 34, part 4, 151.

5. Hays, *A Race at Bay*, 242.

6. McFeely, *Grant*, 308-309.

7. Ibid., 305.

8. Clum did what he could to put Grant's plans into action with the Wallowa experiment. Greene, *Nez Perce Summer 1877*, 456.

9. The office of the commissioner of Indian affairs had a revolving door, with five men holding the position from 1871 to 1873: Ely S. Parker (1871), H. R. Clum (acting, 1871), Francis A. Walker, (1871–1872), Clum (acting, 1872–1873), and Edward Parmelee Smith (1873-1875), a Congregational minister. McFeely, *Grant*, 315.

10. *Indian Affairs: Laws and Treaties*.

11. In the view of the many Indian bands of the area, the Chief Lawyer lacked the standing and legitimacy to represent them. They considered the signing of the 1863 treaty null and void because he had no authority to sign away their land. Greene, *Nez Perce Summer*, 10-11.

Chapter Two: Showing the Rifle

1. Highberger, *The Death of Wind Blowing*, 11.

2. Alexander Findley later explained, "I cocked my gun and held it ready, waiting to see the result of the scuffle over the gun of McNall. . . . I had not decided to shoot when I heard the report of my gun. I was not conscious of pulling the trigger." Highberger, *Death of Wind Blowing*, 13.

3. When he assumed command, Howard had a staff of fourteen and a strength of 1,116 men spread among four states and territories and twelve forts. *The Washington National Guard in the Philippine Insurrection*, vol. 4, 8.

4. At that time, the US Army was the enforcement arm of the various executive agencies associated with Indian welfare, sometimes as advocate, sometimes in a punitive role. Howard was well within his domain by insisting on justice.

5. Two men, Gerald Cochran and Al King, vowed to kill and scalp Joseph. Highberger, *Death of Wind Blowing*, 25.

6. Forse knew that the entire chain of command up to General McDowell was watching the outcome carefully.

7. Highberger, *Death of Wind Blowing*, 28.

8. Josephy Jr., *The Nez Perce Indians and the Opening of the Northwest*, 473-475.

9. In Howard's view, this meant Christianizing, while schooling the children and teaching the men trades, on a reservation. Josephy, *Nez Perce Indians*, 475.

10. Highberger, *Death of Wind Blowing*, 19. For the complete legal evaluation by Major Wood, see Brown, *The Flight of the Nez Perce*, 37.

11. Greene, *Nez Perce Summer*, 22.

12. Howard was also in correspondence with an influential minister in Portland, Reverend A. L. Lindsley, who was cut from the same cloth as Howard. While he preached for the welfare of the Indians, his solution was to move them out of Oregon. Like Howard, he had a private sympathy and believed in the Nez Perce land rights, but lacked the character to advocate for them in public. Josephy, *Nez Perce Indians*, 473, and Lavender, *Let Me Be Free*, 210-211.

13. Josephy, *Nez Perce Indians*, 475-476.

14. L. V. McWhorter, Unused Chap. 17 for Possible Use, box 11, folder 75, McWhorter Collection, Washington State University. Also see Brown, *Flight of the Nez Perce*, 70.

15. Howard lost an arm; Jackson would die of a similar wound in his final action at Chancellorsville.

16. Underwood and Buel, eds., *Battles and Leaders of the Civil War*, vol. 3, 287-289.

17. Secretary of War William Belknap accused Howard of improper conduct in his administration of the Freedmen's Bureau, which resulted in Howard's return to military service. McFeely, *Grant*, 438.

18. Jessup and Coakley, *A Guide to the Study and Use of Military History*, 203.

19. "In 1876, after an Indian had been killed by a white man in a dispute concerning some stock, I entreated the President to send a good commission with sufficient power to settle these Nez Perce difficulties. At last the Commission came and held its session in Lapwai in November, 1876. No better men could have been selected for that purpose." Howard, *My Life and Experiences among Our Hostile Indians*, 243.

20. The commission was created over the objections of Secretary of War J. D. Cameron. Brown, *Flight of the Nez Perce*, 71.

21. Responding to L. V. McWhorter's inquiry of May 14, 1929, retired Colonel Henry Clay Wood wrote, "The whole Nez Perce trouble arose from the stupid assumption by a Commission of politicians that majority rule prevailed or should be made to prevail among the Indians. So, as the number of chiefs signing the new treaty was greater than the number refusing to sign, they held that these minority chiefs were bound by the signatures of the majority. In fact this idea never entered the head of any chief. Majority rule is unknown to them. Each band is autonomous, and acts for itself, and the chiefs signatory to the treaty never imagined that they were acting for or binding any but themselves; each for his own band. Well, the whole thing from the beginning was a stupid bit of injustice." McWhorter, Unused Chap. 17 for Possible Use, McWhorter Collection, Washington State University.

22. Report of the Secretary of the Interior, 1876, no. 1, 394.

23. General Howard had suggested US District Judge M. P. Deady, R. R. Thompson, General Joel Palmer, J. W. Nesmith, Indian agent John B. Monteith, and himself. He did not suggest Major Wood, who had filed his report from his visit to the Wallowa Valley.

24. Primogeniture, the right of inheritance of the first son, was as much a factor in tribal polity as it was for kings in Europe. Most of the influential leaders had fathers who preceded them as chief. It was common enough practice that multiple generations of men would hold the position of chief, possibly with the same name. The name Joseph was given to Old Joseph, the elder, by the Christians; the young Joseph inherited the mantle and the name. According to Black Eagle, an early tribal historian, no nontreaty Indians had white names at the time of the war unless they were given nicknames by whites. McWhorter, *Yellow Wolf*, 306.

25. Brown, *Flight of the Nez Perce*, 83.

26. In frustration, Howard referred to Toohoolhoolzote as a "growler of growlers" and later as a "cross-grained growler." Howard, *Nez Perce Joseph*, 30, 64.

27. Howard and McGrath, *War Chief Joseph*, 87.

28. Ibid., 88.

29. It is interesting to note that a report by the commissioner of education with the Department of the Interior noted that the Pacific Coast tribes "heretofore have not shown much interest in schools." Report of the Secretary of the Interior, 1872-73. We must wonder if it was education, or the cultural accommodation the government required, that was the obstacle.

30. "They held that their dead would arise and sweep the white race from the earth. Joseph said that the blood of one of his people who had been slain in a feud, by a white man, would call the dust of their fathers back to life, to people the land in protest of this great wrong." Report of the Commissioner of Indian Affairs, 397-728.

31. The basic traditional belief of the Nez Perce regarding creation and the origin of man was that the world and all of its life was created by Wha-me-me-ow-we: the Man Above or Supreme Chief. McWhorter, Dreamer Cult, box 8, folder 44, McWhorter Collection, Washington State University.

32. Ibid.

33. Monteith was allowed to comment for the report on how to deal with the nonreservation Indians, and what he had to say was chilling: "The two brothers Joseph have about sixty horses each. The band has about two thousand horses and about one hundred and fifty head of cattle. They are armed with breech-loading rifles, Henry, Spencer, and United States carbines. They could not raise over sixty to sixty-five fighting men. The better course is to put them on the reservation by force, before any further trouble with the whites, as when another collision occurs, then a fight is inevitable. Nothing can be done with the other non-treaty Indians until Joseph is disposed of, and nothing could be done . . . until this non-treaty question is settled." Board of Indian Commissioners, Eighth Annual Report of the Board of Indian Commissioners for the Year 1876, 1877, 41.

34. Brown, *Flight of the Nez Perce*, 75. See also Haines, "The Nez Perce Tribe Versus the United States," 20-23.

35. *Washington National Guard*, 18.

36. Howard, *Nez Perce Joseph*, 29.

37. Ollokot told Joseph, "Government wants all Indians put in one place." Josephy, *Nez Perce Indians*, 496.

38. The Indian agent wanted the Dreamers moved to a reservation as well. Having a group of nonreservation Indians so near to Walla Walla was dangerous because they could stir up trouble with the Walla Walla Indians and were too close to the nontreaty Dreamers in Idaho. Ruby and Brown, *Dreamer-Prophets of the Columbia Plateau*, 74.

39. Josephy, *Nez Perce Indians*, 496. Smohalla remained defiantly in place. Howard later dispatched troops to see if the Dreamers had joined the rebellious tribe. The detachment found them still at Wallula in late July.

40. Ibid., 498-499. Monteith had dispatched James Reuben with others to urge the Wallowa band to comply.

41. Nerburn, *Chief Joseph and the Flight of the Nez Perce*, 74.

42. The nontreaty Palouse were in the same situation as the Nez Perce: they had refused to go to the government reservation at Yakima. Monteith had wanted to move the Palouse there, but by 1881, the Yakima Indian agent, Reverend James Wilbur, complained that thousands of Palouse Indians "still occupied their original lands." Wilbur was a Protestant minister and opposed the Dreamer faith. George Hunter, who would play an early role in opposing the Nez Perce, became an advocate for the Palouse tribe, and he wrote every party involved to fight off the attempt to move the Palouse. He found himself contesting with the ever-vigilant Monteith as well. The agent sought to exploit the Nez Perce War as an excuse to displace the Palouse bands to reservations. Hunter showed a cunning legal mind as he argued successfully that the Palouse were not part of the Nez Perce treaty of 1863 and also possessed additional protections not available to the Nez Perce. Eventually, he managed to get General Howard to assist him in filing land claims for all members of the tribe, and Howard asked Hunter to act as an advocate because they had no "agency." In return for his protection and long friendship, Hunter was invited by Chief Big Thunder to join the tribe as a chief. Trafzer and Scheuerman, *Renegade Tribe*, 128-129.

43. Nerburn, *Chief Joseph*, 80.

44. Howard, *Nez Perce Joseph*, 45.

45. Lieutenant William Parnell wrote that during the meetings, "defiant words fell from the lips of the Indians, more particularly from those of White Bird who was the worst devil of the lot." His description and memory were no doubt colored by the desperate hours of his fighting

retreat at White Bird Canyon. Highberger, *The Soldiers' Side of the Nez Perce War*, 14. See also Howard, *Nez Perce Joseph*, 65.

46. Greene, *Nez Perce Summer*, 21-22.

47. Ibid., 22.

48. Howard, *Nez Perce Joseph*, 69.

49. McDermott, *Forlorn Hope*, 45.

50. Parnell spoke up for the young man, and he was put back on duty. "The Battle of White Bird Canyon," Historynet.com.

51. *Washington National Guard*, 11.

CHAPTER THREE: THE BATTLE AT WHITE BIRD CANYON

1. Lamtama was the name of the band; its village name, and the name of the creek along which the village lay, was Lamata.

2. McWhorter, *Hear Me*, 190.

3. Greene, *Nez Perce Summer*, 30.

4. Another account tells of the young men (minus Swan Necklace, who had their horses) entering the house and killing Devine with his own gun. McWhorter, *Hear Me*, 192.

5. It is worth observing that it is uncertain where, when, or how Jeanette Manuel died. The accounts are radically different, even when they are from reliable primary sources. For instance, George Hunter, in *Reminiscences of an Old Timer*, claimed to have buried what little remained of settlers from the burned cabins during the same scouting mission that resulted in finding Jack Manuel alive. There are conflicting accounts in the tribe's oral tradition that deal with Jeanette Manuel's abduction from the site of her home. In the ashes of the cabin there was little or no physical evidence that could be used to identify her body. She just disappeared during the events that transpired.

6. McWhorter, *Hear Me*, 216-217.

7. Chapman's nickname, "Ad," was short for "admiral," because he had at one time piloted a ferry over the Salmon River. "The Battle of White Bird Canyon," Historynet.com.

8. Letter from J. G. Rowton to L. V. McWhorter from Kooskia, ID, September 10, 1930, McWhorter Collection, box 6, folder 27, Washington State University.

9. Wot-tó-len. [Chief] Lawyer. [Chief] White Bird, box 9, folder 53, McWhorter Collection, Washington State University.

10. Howard, *Nez Perce Joseph*, 99.

11. Custer was actually the executive officer and junior in rank to Colonel Samuel Sturgis, commander of the 7th Regiment of US Cavalry. He either pulled strings or took advantage of Sturgis's being

transferred to detached duty. In either case, he fatefully took acting command of the regiment with Sturgis gone.

12. Today the city of White Bird sits not far from the site of the Indian village at the base of White Bird Canyon.

13. Francis Haines notes that the Nez Perce were unique among Indian tribes who adopted the horse because "they went a step beyond any other tribe in that they practiced the principles of selective breeding of horses even before the first white man reached their country." And he states that the horse changed their culture forever. Haines, "Nez Perce Horses," 8-9.

14. Highberger, *Soldiers' Side*, 17.

15. Yellow Wolf later carried a Winchester carbine, model 66/44. At the battle of White Bird Canyon, he did not have his rifle. In the first battle, he was armed with a bow and arrow and soon took a weapon from a soldier he killed. McWhorter, *Yellow Wolf*, 56.

16. Yellow Wolf saw a single warrior named Five Fogs (Pahka Pahtahank) fighting alone against a line of infantry soldiers with only a bow and arrows. McWhorter, *Yellow Wolf*, 119.

17. Laughy, *In Pursuit of the Nez Perces*, 45.

18. Highberger, *Soldiers' Side*, 19.

19. Ibid.

20. It was Two Moons who broke the news to the returning Joseph and Ollokot of Wahlitas and his Salmon River rampage. McWhorter, *Yellow Wolf*, 44.

21. The lack of bugles to coordinate the troops certainly contributed to the collapse of the command and the rout that developed. Yellow Wolf named Fire Body (Otstotpoo) as the man who made the shot that killed bugler John Jones.

22. Idaho Military Historical Society, "The Battle of White Bird Cañon," 5.

23. McWhorter, *Yellow Wolf*, 57.

24. Tchakmakian, *The Great Retreat*, 59.

25. McWhorter, *Yellow Wolf*, 60.

26. In his account of the battle, McCarthy did not mention riding with another soldier. Idaho Military Historical Society, "The Battle of White Bird Cañon," 5.

27. Ibid., 6.

28. Ibid.

29. Highberger, *Soldiers' Side*, 22.

30. Ibid., 21-22.

CHAPTER FOUR: THE FIGHT FOR THE PRAIRIE

1. Jessup and Coakley, *A Guide to the Study and Use of Military History*, 204.

2. During the court of inquiry regarding Perry's leadership, Perry did not mention Theller's making two stands as a rear guard or that he had been wounded twice. Frank D. Powers, who was at the scene, said Theller explained quietly and calmly to his men what they were about to do. Painter, *White Bird*, 44.

3. Farwell, *The Encyclopedia of Nineteenth-Century Land Warfare*, 237.

4. Howard wasn't counting Mrs. Manuel and her baby. Painter, *White Bird*, 52.

5. Denison, *Lyman's History of Old Walla Walla County*, 28-29.

6. Beal, *"I Will Fight No More Forever,"* 62.

7. Hunter, *Reminiscences of an Old Timer*, 360-361.

8. Senate Executive Document no. 257, *Claims of the Nez Perce Indians*, 20-21.

9. Howard, *Nez Perce Joseph*, 150-151.

10. Haines, *The Nez Perces*, 265. Five Wounds and Rainbow fought as a team and led in the attack. Elite warriors, they were bound by oaths between their fathers to follow each other into death on the battlefield.

11. McWhorter, *Yellow Wolf*, 72.

12. J. W. Redington to L. V. McWhorter, March 8, 1932, Cage 55, Box 10, Folder 59, "Scout Blewett Correspondence 1908-1943," McWhorter Collection, Washington State University.

13. Bennett, *We'll All Go Home in the Spring*, 341.

14. Pfau, "The Nez Perce Flight to Canada: An Analysis of the Nez Perce-US Cavalry Conflicts," 14.

15. Ibid., 42.

CHAPTER FIVE: CITIZEN SOLDIERS

1. Wilmot, manuscript, *Narratives of the Nez Perce War*, 7.

2. Painter, *White Bird*, 60.

3. Ibid.

4. Ankeny, *The West as I Knew It*, 51.

5. Wilson, "Campaign Against the Nez Perce Indians: The Year 1877," 5.

6. Wilson, *Hawks and Doves in the Nez Perce War of 1877*, 7.

7. Lew Wilmot wrote that the cavalry advanced to within two hundred yards of the volunteers. While Shearer rode into the depression where they had sheltered as described, Wilmot claimed the time was between 3 and 4 in the afternoon. Wilmot, *Narratives of the Nez Perce War*, 9.

8. It is clear from the primary sources that much larger groups of warriors were involved than is commonly thought. The independent sighting by men with binoculars and the estimate by Wilmot of 170 warriors matches closely with Whipple's estimate of the previous day. Eugene T. Wilson claimed there were estimated to be "warriors, numbering 125 mounted men." Wilson, *Hawks and Doves*, 7.

9. It seems likely that Yellow Wolf's party is not the same one that fought the soldiers in the fortified post at Cottonwood House on the fourth and fifth. Whipple engaged a large force on the same day Lieutenant Rains was killed. Yellow Wolf says nothing about attacking Cottonwood House. Perry and other analysts have believed the attacks on Cottonwood House were a deliberate stratagem. It is likely that larger groups of Indians were operating in the area, at the very least to put themselves between the families and livestock and the soldiers as they fled across the prairie in a maneuver very much like the one that would be used at Canyon Creek later. Highberger, *Soldiers' Side*, 39.

10. Hunter, *Reminiscences*, 302. Needle guns had a prepared powder charge and ball inside a cylindrical paper cartridge. The gun worked by inserting a needle inside the cartridge and generating a spark to fire the round.

11. Wilson, "Campaign Against the Nez Perce."

12. Hunter wrote that he had forty-five men from Dayton, while McConville had fifteen men from Mount Idaho. Mixed in were some Pataha Rangers from Washington. Together, Hunter and McConville named them the 1st Regiment of Idaho and Washington Volunteers. Hunter, *Reminiscences of an Old Timer*, 339.

13. Craig was an early mountain man and trapper who took a Nez Perce wife and lived among the tribe starting in the 1840s. His name was attached to many landmarks in the area. Baird, *In Nez Perce Country*, 119.

14. Greene, *Nez Perce Summer*, 74.

15. Ibid.

16. Wilmot, *Narratives of the Nez Perce War*, 25.

17. Wilmot claimed that the Indians were firing at a distance of one thousand yards. Ibid.

18. Still later, it was called "Mount Misery."

19. McWhorter, *Yellow Wolf*, 79.

20. *Claims of the Nez Perce Indians*, 34.

21. Some of this was due to the misadventures of an earlier group of Pataha Rangers and twenty volunteers under J.W. Elliot. See Brown, *Flight of the Nez Perce*, 57, 150.

22. Ibid.

Chapter Six: The Battle of the Clearwater

1. Potucek, *Idaho's Historic Trails*, 125-127.
2. Haines, *Nez Perces*, 273.
3. Greene, *Nez Perce Summer*, 93.
4. Ibid., 96.
5. McWhorter, *Yellow Wolf*, 100.
6. *Claims of the Nez Perce Indians*, 44.
7. Brown, *Flight of the Nez Perce*, 181; Greene, *Nez Perce Summer*, 397.
8. *Claims of the Nez Perce Indians*, 44.
9. McWhorter, *Yellow Wolf*, 98-99.
10. Sergeant Bernard Simpson was wounded in the forehead, and his attempt to lead a company out of "Fort Perry" during the incident of the "brave seventeen" was forgotten.
11. *Claims of the Nez Perce Indians*, 37.

Chapter Seven: Over the Lolo Pass

1. Baird, *Nez Perce Country*, 139.
2. Idaho State Historical Soc., Reference Series, "The Lolo Trail," 1.
3. Potucek, *Idaho's Historic Trails*, 127.
4. *Claims of the Nez Perce Indians*, 10. General Howard sent the telegram from Fort Lapwai, asking for a company of twenty-five treaty Indian scouts. He also commented, "Indians began by murdering a white man in revenge for a murder of his—killing three others at the same time. Since they have begun war upon the people near Mt. Idaho. Captain Perry started with two companies for them. Other troops are being brought forward as fast as possible."
5. L. V. McWhorter, Nez Perce Scouts 1928-1930, n.d., box 11, folder 71, McWhorter Collection, Washington State University,
6. *Claims of the Nez Perce Indians*, 24. On June 29, Assistant Adjutant General John C. Kelton, Military Division of the Pacific, in a dispatch to a Lieutenant Wilson, stipulated that he was to proceed to Fort Hall for the purpose of enlisting twenty Indian scouts and added, "Scouts can mount themselves . . . horses to be paid for eventually by the government."
7. A dozen or more Indian scouts met the expedition at Kamiah, according to Wilson, "Campaign Against the Nez Perce Indians," 5.
8. Testimony of John Cut Nose, *Claims of the Nez Perce Indians*, 84. John Cut Nose, a reservation Indian scout, confirmed that he was present at Weippe with the twenty scouts Howard had enlisted so far, and that three Nez Perce scouts were in the advance in the clearing

when captured. When six more scouts ventured out to find them, the fight began.

9. Wilson, "Campaign Against the Nez Perce Indians," 6.

10. Brown, *Flight of the Nez Perce*, 203.

11. *Claims of the Nez Perce Indians*, 88, 90, 92, 95, 96, 102. Many of the scouts interviewed in Senate Document no. 257 reported that they provided their own horses. Others were provided captured horses, probably from the raid on the village of Looking Glass.

12. In determining the number of scouts at Weippe and who they were, I have consulted multiple sources, including McWhorter, Wilson, the tribal oral tradition, and the US government document *Claims of the Nez Perce Indians*. The sworn testimony of Nez Perce scout Moses Stimilh indicates there were twenty other scouts present at Weippe. Most had been in the fight at the Clearwater River. Others were in the vicinity of Kamiah or dispatched to other duties.

13. McWhorter, Nez Perce Scouts, McWhorter Collection, Washington State University. The accounts of Benjamin Pahatkokoh and John Cut Nose support Abraham Brooks's recollection of the events at Weippe. The army interviewed all the scouts and kept records of their statements in order to finally pay them, in 1890. Six scouts went forward at Chapman's order to check the clearing ahead: James Reuben, John Levi, Abraham Brooks, Captain John, Benjamin Pahatkokoh, and Tamalushimlikt—these men are named in several affidavits. Brooks's account also mentions Paul Kalla. The Congressional Record indicates that John Cut Nose, Hahats Ilp Ilp, Moses Stimilh, Sam Lawyer, and Charlie Tlitlkim were there, but not in the first two groups of scouts in the clearing.

14. Wilson, "Campaign Against the Nez Perce Indians," 8.

15. This was John Levi (Sheared Wolf), not Captain John, as is sometimes noted.

16. Wilson, *Hawks and Doves*, 14.

17. Wilson, "Campaign Against the Nez Perce," 8.

18. *Claims of the Nez Perce Indians*, 10. Benjamin Pahatkokoh said, "We picked up John Levi's body and carried it this way [toward Kamiah] and buried it, and I rode behind Abraham Brooks to hold him on; blood run all over me, and they took him off and carried him on a stretcher."

19. There was a disagreement between the Presbyterian Indians and those of the traditional faith over the burial. It should be noted that oral tradition maintains that Levi was not permanently buried on the trail. He may have been reinterred. Wilson, *Hawks and Doves*, 14.

20. Josephy, *Nez Perce Indians*, 554.

21. Brown, *Flight of the Nez Perce*, 202. There is some uncertainty on the matter of their neutrality, but the story of Red Heart's band is certainly consistent with the normal practice of buffalo hunting in Montana. In either case, his people chose not to align themselves with the patriots and were trying to get to the reservation when arrested.

22. Greene, *Nez Perce Summer*, 100.

23. McWhorter, *Yellow Wolf*, 310.

CHAPTER EIGHT: THE BATTLE OF BIG HOLE

1. *Claims of the Nez Perce Indians*, 40.

2. Brown, *Flight of the Nez Perce*, 208.

3. Ibid., 212-213.

4. The Hardee hats Gibbon's men wore were also adorned with ostrich plumes and looked like the iconic cowboy hat, but with a taller crown.

5. Brown, *Flight of the Nez Perce*, 215. General Sheridan had received approval for construction of the fort from the secretary of war in May of 1877: "$20,000 for the construction of a post near the town of Missoula."

6. Ibid., 215–216. Captain Rawn left on June 9 from Fort Shaw and arrived at Missoula on the nineteenth. Captain Logan arrived a week later. Logan's company would work on construction of the new fort, and Rawn's company would be the garrison force.

7. John Gibbon, *The Artillerist's Manual*.

8. Beal, *"I Will Fight No More Forever,"* 94. The structures Rawn began would eventually become Fort Missoula. Erection of the fort had been planned since 1875.

9. Although General Sherman actively brought about a sea change in the structure, organization, and training of the army, the infantry, engineers, and artillery were far along in that process, while the cavalry lagged behind considerably.

10. Captain Rawn's official report to the Department of the Dakota, Scout Blewett Correspondence 1908-1943, box 6, folder 32, McWhorter Collection, Washington State University.

11. Ibid.

12. *Claims of the Nez Perce Indians*, 51.

13. Howard had complained of problems with transmission and reception of telegrams. And he had not yet begun to follow the Nez Perce over the Lolo Trail. McDowell was evidently overly optimistic about Howard's departure, which would not begin until July 31.

14. Report of the General of the Army, 1877, box 7, folder 35, McWhorter Collection, Washington State University.

15. John Buckhouse describing Fort Fizzle, box 6, folder 32, McWhorter Collection, Washington State University. Young John Buckhouse, who was quartered inside the barricade for four days, described it as a quarter mile long and consisting of rifle pits, trenches, and logs. He may have been referring to the works in its entirety and not just the log stockade. The boy knew that a fight with the warriors would be brutal. He could see how they could fire on the fort from the surrounding elevations. He related that the men expected a fight and did not expect to survive it because "they could have poured bullets down on us from the heights."

16. McWhorter, *Hear Me*, 353.

17. Buckhouse, McWhorter Collection, Washington State University.

18. Ibid. Buckhouse was close enough to Looking Glass to shake hands, and he wrote that Joseph was nowhere evident in the first meeting.

19. Rawn must have reported the dates of the meetings incorrectly. Other sources confirm the parleys (among the volunteers, Buckhouse and Amos Buck confirmed that there were at least two meetings with the Nez Perce), while Yellow Wolf knew of one, and Sergeant Charles N. Loynes mentions only one date in correspondence with L. V. McWhorter, July 28, the day the Nez Perce bypassed the fort.

20. McWhorter, *Yellow Wolf*, 107.

21. Haines, *Battle of the Big Hole*, 15. The Montanans had a wry and self-deprecating sense of humor (and irony) when nicknaming forts. They named their first edifice "Fort Brave," and dubbed the sod fort at Skalkaho "Fort Run," while at Corvallis, their fort was dubbed "Fort Skedaddle."

22. Glassey, *Pacific Northwest Indian Wars*, 217.

23. Lowie, *The Crow Indians*, 327.

24. Brown, *Flight of the Nez Perce*, 232-233.

25. Eliot West correctly identified the telegraph as the technological weapon that the tribe could not have anticipated being their greatest enemy. The ability of General McDowell to deliver instant status reports within his division and to other military departments was crucial in the pursuit of the Nez Perce through Montana. West, *The Last Indian War*, 176.

26. Baird, *In Nez Perce Country*, 199.

27. Greene, *Nez Perce Summer*, 115. "The position was a very strong one," Howard noted, "and it is to be regretted that the Indians could not have been met and driven back on me."

28. Josephy, *Nez Perce Indians*, 589.

29. Painter, *White Bird*, 72.

30. Gibbon had originally ordered Bradley, with his mounted force that advanced on the seventh and eighth, to attack the camp at night and drive away the stock, stampeding the horses if possible. He was sticking to his original plan. Highberger, *Soldiers' Side*, 72. Gibbon, in his report to the secretary of war, noted that Bradley was unable to attack on his foray because "daylight had overtaken him before he had succeeded in reaching the camp of the Indians." Annual Report of the Secretary of War, vol. 1, 502.

31. Howard and McGrath, *War Chief Joseph*, 210.

32. McWhorter, *Hear Me*, 389. The exact circumstances of the death of Wahlitas remain uncertain, although the broad facts are documented through Yellow Wolf. We know the location, that the attack came from the willows, and that he died early in the battle. And that a woman was beside him.

33. Greene, *Nez Perce Summer*, 132.

34. Ibid., 133.

35. McWhorter, *Hear Me*, 383. These long, heroic exhortations are attributed to White Bird in the heat of battle. His remonstrations to his fleeing men were likely briefer—sharp and pointed—conveying essentially the same message.

36. Ibid. It is certain that White Bird stopped the flight of fighting men and organized the counterfire that Gibbon made note of in his record of the battle. Annual Report of the Secretary of War, 503.

37. Utley, *Frontier Regulars*, 316.

38. Beal, *"I Will Fight No More Forever,"* 137.

39. Annual Report of the Secretary of War, 504.

40. McWhorter, *Yellow Wolf*, 128.

41. Ibid., 156-157.

42. Charles Loynes letter to L. V. McWhorter, December 16, 1928, box 8, folder 42, McWhorter Collection, Washington State University.

43. Greene, *Nez Perce Summer*, 364.

44. West, *Last Indian War*, 194. Bound by a warrior's oath, Rainbow and Pahkatos died together—as had their fathers.

45. George Shields describes Wahlitas's rushing to attack late in the battle, but in fact he was killed just outside his lodge early in the fight. Shields, *The Battle of Big Hole*, 53. (Gibbon, a colonel throughout the Nez Perce War, was later promoted to general.)

46. Beal, *"I Will Fight No More Forever,"* 127.

47. McWhorter, *Yellow Wolf*, 131. From the warriors' perspective, the pact they had sealed at the pass with the Montanans had been violated, and their own innocents had died as a result. Yellow Wolf called this a "lie-treaty."

48. *Claims of the Nez Perce Indians*, 67-68.

49. Ibid., 69.

Chapter Nine: The Battle of Camas Meadows

1. Eagle of the Light was an influential Nez Perce Chief who, along with other Nez Perce chiefs like Old Looking Glass, Old Joseph, and Toohoolhoolzote, rejected the treaty of 1863, which he described as bringing more preacher/traders into their land "two in one, one a preacher and the other a trader. And now from the East has spoken and I have heard it. I do not wish another preacher to come and be both trader and preacher in one." Eagle of the Light did not trust Washington Territory Governor Isaac Stevens, and he was sure that Chief Lawyer was making a bad treaty. McWhorter, *Hear Me*, 94.

2. Beal, *"I Will Fight No More Forever,"* 282.

3. Lavender, *Let Me Be Free*, 290.

4. After the desperate fight at Big Hole, the last of the warriors delaying the soldiers moved on to the camp, half a day, or about fifteen miles, away. McWhorter, *Yellow Wolf*, 161.

5. Utley, *Frontier Regulars*, 46.

6. As early as 365 BC, the great Greek strategist Xenophon wrote extensively about the need for rigorous training and practice of cavalry in all kinds of conditions and terrain. He also wrote that a commander should demand continual practice by the soldiers. Xenophon, *Scripta Minora* (Harvard College, 1968), 239-243.

7. Local settlers indicated that as many as one hundred and fifty horses may have been captured in the raids. Brown, *Flight of the Nez Perce*, 276.

8. Mrs. Winters caught up to the party on the road, mounted on a good horse with a revolver belted around her waist. Brown, *Flight of the Nez Perce*, 275-276.

9. Greene, *Nez Perce Summer*, 143.

10. Brown, *Flight of the Nez Perce*, 277.

11. Greene, *Nez Perce Summer*, 143.

12. McWhorter, *Yellow Wolf*, 162.

13. Charles Go Hing later recounted the story of the ill-fated wagon train. Greene, *Nez Perce Summer*, 144.

14. Letter from L. C. Morse to George L. Shoup, Aug. 27, 1877,

Special Collections Department, Eli M. Oboler Library, Idaho State University, Pocatello.

15. About this time, Howard made the acquaintance of adventurer and novice scout J. W. Redington. In *Flight of the Nez Perce*, Brown intimates that Redington may have perpetuated a small fraud on Howard by claiming to represent the press. Redington was penniless, unarmed, and without horse—a condition that Howard remedied.

16. The name "Stinking Water" derived from the high sulfur content in the water, causing a rotten-egg smell.

17. Shoup was a merchant and a businessman who knew how to organize. He began making preparations for the defense of the area and helped organize volunteers.

18. His Nez Perce scouts assured him that the Yellowstone River's Clarks Fork was the tribe's intended route. Beal, *"I Will Fight No More Forever,"* 146.

19. McWhorter, *Hear Me*, 419. Wottolen blamed a warrior named Otsaki for firing prematurely. Had they more time, they might have gotten away with most of the cavalry horses, instead of just the mules. With the Indians' having fresh remounts and Howard having no way to refit with horses, the outcome would have changed considerably.

20. The raiding party of twenty-eight warriors was divided into two groups, one led by Ollokot and Toohoolhoolzote, and another by Teeweeyounah and Espoowyes. According to the Nee-Mee-Poo tradition, the plan may have evolved from a vision of Wottolen's. Many prominent warriors took part, including Peo Peo Tholekt, Two Moons, and Yellow Wolf. Beal, *"I Will Fight No More Forever,"* 155.

21. A limited number of enlisted men were promoted to the officer corps during this time. Although generally more experienced than the officers they served under, they had to overcome a great deal of prejudice. Byler, *Civil-Military Relations on the Frontier and Beyond, 1865-1917*, 52.

22. Jackson had also been in the enlisted ranks. He was awarded the Medal of Honor for his actions at Camas Meadows. Heitman, *Historical Register and Dictionary of the United States Army, from Its Organization, September 29, 1789, to March 2, 1903*, 567.

23. Norwood had just arrived, having escorted General Sherman to the Yellowstone area as part of his tour of forts in the region. Sherman had sent Norwood and his men ahead to help General Howard. Lavender, *Let Me Be Free*, 289.

24. This maneuver is an example of how dismounted cavalry lost a fourth of their men. At this moment, every fourth man in Captain

Norwood's company had taken the reins of two horses in each hand, and, unable to fight, they now moved to the rear to find shelter for the horses. Norwood then had only thirty-five fighting men on the line, as a dozen men led the horses away. Highberger, *Soldiers' Side*, 97.

25. Critics in the military-reform movement of the time, including General Sherman, recognized that cavalry of the period were really nothing more than mounted infantry. Utley, *Frontier Regulars*, 50.

26. Greene, *Nez Perce Summer*, 157.

27. Redington wrote: "When the boy, for he was scarcely more than that, was shot out of his saddle, he tried at once to spring up on to his feet again, but only succeeded in getting to his knees. His horse, a very intelligent animal, went back to his fallen master, nickered, and edged up alongside of him. Brooks caught the stirrup strap and tried to lift himself back into the saddle, but just then death came. The horse whinnied and champed and stood around Brooks, plainly urging him to remount. It was a snap-shot scene that did not last long, but was quite pitiful while it was passing." Highberger, *Soldiers' Side*, 100-101. John W. Redington returned to Salem, Oregon, after his many scouting adventures to be appointed assistant adjutant general of Oregon and lieutenant colonel in the Oregon National Guard. Stewart, "Col. John Watermelon Redington, My Papa," 12-22.

28. An explosive ball struck Clark, according to Sergeant H. J. Davis, who was in the thicket. Highberger, *Soldiers' Side*, 97.

29. Norwood's troops were the only ones close enough to have inflicted any casualties on the warriors, who reportedly sustained six to seven dead in the fight. H. J. Davis could only say that he saw one warrior shot, and Peo Peo Tholekt explicitly denied that any warriors were killed. Greene, *Nez Perce Summer*, 159.

30. McWhorter, *Hear Me*, 423-424.

31. At the location of Norwood's stand, Howard was ten miles from the Nez Perce camp with minor casualties, yet he did not press the attack.

32. Many horses belonging to the Virginia City volunteers were also taken.

33. Sergeant Davis confirmed that few animals were actually recovered, writing that "we recovered thirty mules that had been dropped by the Indians about midway between the camp and the battleground. The others were never retaken, but were worn out and died before the final surrender." Davis, *Battle of Camas Meadows*, 97.

34. There is evidence that Howard was moving fast during this phase of the campaign. Although it is counterintuitive, testimony of officers

contemporaneous with these events confirm that cavalry had problems on the campaign. Colonel William B. Hazen of the 6th Infantry wrote, "After the fourth day's march of a mixed command, the horse does not march faster than the foot soldier, and after the seventh day, the foot soldier begins to outmarch the horse." Utley, *Frontier Regulars*, 50.

35. Gibbon had requested and been granted the additional scouts from Fort Hall. Along with Bainbridge's ten soldiers, as many as seventy scouts rode to Howard's command. Howard and McGrath, *War Chief Joseph*, 232.

36. *Claims of the Nez Perce Indians*, 66.

37. Beal, *"I Will Fight No More Forever,"* 164.

38. Shively and James C. Irwin, an ex-cavalry soldier, became important sources of information for the army, exactly what the Nez Perce feared. L. V. McWhorter, Indian Letters, box 6, folder 26, McWhorter Collection, Washington State University.

39. The group would come to be referred to in the literature as the Radersburg party because they hailed from that town in the Montana Territory. Greene, *Nez Perce Summer*, 181.

40. Yellow Wolf was ranging out on horseback, watching for any of the army's scouts, when he was joined by Henry Tabador, Tiskusia Kowiakowia, Towassis, and Nosnakuhet Mox Mox. McWhorter, *Yellow Wolf*, 172-176.

41. Ibid., 173-74.

42. Josephy, *Nez Perce Indians*, 602.

43. McWhorter, Nez Perce Scouts, McWhorter Collection, Washington State University.

44. Beal, *"I Will Fight No More Forever,"* 173.

45. Greene, *Nez Perce Summer*, 187.

46. Beal, *"I Will Fight No More Forever,"* 175.

47. Redington referred to "Gaht," meaning Scout S. G. Fisher, nominally Redington's boss. Fisher had brought the large party of Bannock Indians from Fort Hall.

48. L. V. McWhorter, box 26, folder 6, McWhorter Collection, Washington State University.

49. Haines, *Nez Perces*, 177.

50. Josephy, *Nez Perce Indians*, 603.

51. Ibid. Weikert was wounded in the shoulder during a brief skirmish. See also Beal, *"I Will Fight No More Forever,"* 179, and Greene, *Nez Perce Summer*, 190.

52. The fourth Earl of Dunraven, Windham Thomas Wyndham-

Quin, held a peerage in Ireland. He was enjoying hunting in the area with his traveling companion, Dr. George Kingsley.

53. Hugh Scott later wrote that the fight and chase began at Henderson's ranch and that no shots were fired by the soldiers, who chased the Indians and stolen horses. Scott and his men recovered nineteen horses that fell out during the chase. Hugh Scott letter to L. V. McWhorter, November 10, 1930, box 12, folder 26, McWhorter Collection, Washington State University.

54. Brown, *Flight of the Nez Perce*, 332.

55. McWhorter, *Yellow Wolf*, 178.

56. Annual Report of the General of the Army, *Report to the Secretary of War*, 1877, 621.

57. *Claims of the Nez Perce Indians*, 68.

58. Report of the General of the Army, 1877, box 7, folder 35, McWhorter Collection, Washington State University.

59. *Claims of the Nez Perce Indians*, 68.

60. Greene, *Nez Perce Summer*, 167.

CHAPTER TEN: THE BATTLE OF CANYON CREEK

1. Greene, *Nez Perce Summer*, 194.

2. Brown, *Flight of the Nez Perce*, 340.

3. West, *The Last Indian War*, 229.

4. William Clark named the Judith River tributary of the Missouri River after the future Mrs. Clark. The gap took its name from the picturesque river that flows though the plain. Fifer and Soderburg, *Along the Trail with Lewis and Clark*, 107.

5. Highberger, *The Soldiers' Side of the Nez Perce War*, 104. Theodore W. Goldin was a trooper in the 7th Cavalry expedition with Colonel Sturgis. The life of Goldin is another fascinating character study from this period. He claimed to have carried the last dispatch from Custer to Major Reno at the Little Big Horn. But none of the officers involved remembered his doing so. He was awarded the Medal of Honor for separate actions at the Little Big Horn. In the case of Canyon Creek, his narrative closely parallels other records.

6. Ibid., 105.

7. Utley, *Frontier Regulars*, 328.

8. Greene, *Nez Perce Summer*, 208.

9. Luther Rector Hare was another survivor of the Little Big Horn. At the time of the massacre, he was in detached service in Major Reno's battalion with his Indian scouts.

10. Greene, *Nez Perce Summer*, 209.

11. Ibid.

12. Beal, *"I Will Fight No More Forever,"* 187.

13. Greene posits that the horses may have been paraded within a few miles of Dead Indian Pass. Greene, *Nez Perce Summer*, 211.

14. The close ravine, with sheer stone walls, later called Dead Indian Gulch, was described by Lieutenant Charles Wood as "the spout of a funnel." The gradient downhill to the Clarks Fork River ran over a thousand vertical feet in just a quarter mile. Brown, *Flight of the Nez Perce*, 351.

15. The soldiers referred to the dangerously steep and narrow trail as the Devil's Doorway. Highberger, *Soldiers' Side*, 111.

16. Ibid., 113.

17. Bell had been on detached duties while serving with Custer's 7th Cavalry the year before and missed the Big Horn Battle. He would later be brevetted a lieutenant colonel for his leadership at Canyon Creek. Hatch, *The Custer Companion*, 80.

18. Beal, *"I Will Fight No More Forever,"* 195.

19. McWhorter, *Yellow Wolf*, 185.

20. Ibid. The warriors were Teeto Hoonod and Swan Necklace.

21. Brady, *Northwestern Fights and Fighters*, 217.

22. McWhorter, *Yellow Wolf*, 187.

23. Ibid., 188.

24. Yellow Wolf believed he had seen three soldiers shot that he believed were killed. Yellow Wolf was referring to Benteen's cavalry who charged into the canyon mouth. McWhorter, *Yellow Wolf*, 186.

25. Brown, *Flight of the Nez Perce*, 363.

26. The Missouri's Nez Perce name was Kappuchy Wallah (Swift River).

27. Fort Benton, about fifty miles from where the work was being done, was the primary trade and shipping point for hundreds of miles.

28. Josephy, *Nez Perce Indians*, 613.

29. Brown, *Flight of the Nez Perce*, 369-370.

30. Most of the firing was at a distance of one thousand yards. Annual Report of the Secretary of War, 557.

31. Beal, *"I Will Fight No More Forever,"* 226.

Chapter Eleven: The Bear Paw Battle

1. For command and control purposes, the companies were combined into two battalions of three companies. Greene, *Nez Perce Summer*, 205-207.

2. Ibid., 208.

3. The cantonment was a temporary post intended to support military operations during the winter of 1876. The army wanted to garrison the area so that troops would be in position to attack the Sioux and Cheyenne tribes from a central point in the Yellowstone basin during the Great Sioux War of 1876-77. It was located in the very heart of the Sioux domain, and larger forts would be built nearby, emanating from the cantonment. Fort Keogh and Fort Custer are notable examples. Utley, *Frontier Regulars*, 289.

4. Miles did not have all of the cavalry that would make his full strength when he set out from his Tongue River camp. He overtook four more companies of cavalry moving north to meet General Terry and escort him to Canada. Utley, *Frontier Regulars*, 320.

5. The Hotchkiss was a rifled gun with spiral grooves down the barrel to improve accuracy. It was extremely popular among the men—light, portable, and reliable. The breech could be opened and loaded quickly from behind. The gun shot a variety of rounds that looked like a large modern bullet. It could shoot three miles and weighed only 362 pounds. The barrel was much lighter than the mountain howitzer. The Hotchkiss gun would be extensively used in the Spanish-American War. Howser, "1.65 Inch Hotchkiss Mountain Gun," Spanish American War Centennial Web site.

6. Annual Report of the General of the Army, 73.

7. Tchakmakian, *Great Retreat*, 106.

8. McWhorter, *Yellow Wolf*, 204.

9. Beal, "*I Will Fight No More Forever*," 227.

10. Greene, *Nez Perce Summer*, 262.

11. Hale, while attending a quick get-together with friends before departing the Tongue River Cantonment in pursuit of the Nez Perce on September 18, had a premonition he would die in the coming battle as he spoke to Alice Baldwin, wife of Miles's adjutant: "His last words to me, as he shook my hand and bade me and the others goodbye, were, 'Pray for me, for I am never coming back!'" Brown, *Flight of the Nez Perce*, 380. For a slightly different source and version, see West, *Last Indian War*, 269.

12. The slope to the ford was well to the left of the modern highway that crosses the creek. It would have been suicide to try to ride down the sheer banks of the creek elsewhere. Beal, "*I Will Fight No More Forever*," 214.

13. McWhorter, *Hear Me*, 482-483.

14. Ibid.

15. Story of Mrs. Shot-in-Head, box 7, folder 38, McWhorter Collection, Washington State University.

16. Ibid. Penahwenomi would never see her mother or sister again; they were sent with other Nez Perce to the Indian Territory in Oklahoma, where they both died.

17. Beal, *"I Will Fight No More Forever,"* 214-215.

18. Ibid., 217.

19. Incident at the Last Battle, Captain Henry Romeyn, 5th US Infantry, vol. 2, box 10, folder 62, McWhorter Collection, Washington State University. See also Romeyn, *The Capture of Chief Joseph and the Nez Perce Indians*, vol. 2, 287.

20. Incident at the Last Battle, McWhorter Collection, Washington State University.

21. Miles described the exchange of Joseph for Jerome in his official report. Annual Report of the Secretary of War, 527-529.

22. Greene, *Nez Perce Summer*, 308.

23. The army recorded the number of Nez Perce who surrendered at the Bear Paw battle as 448. Greene, *Beyond Bear's Paw*, 67.

24. Brown, *Flight of the Nez Perce*, 406.

25. Beal, *"I Will Fight No More Forever,"* 244.

26. The poet in Wood must have admired the pathos and the language of Joseph's message. See his poetry in the Appendix.

27. McLuhan, *Touch the Earth*, 120.

28. McWhorter, *Hear Me*, 510-511.

29. Most conservative estimates of the distances traveled are close to Howard's. Howard, *Nez Perce Joseph*, 274.

30. Major James Morrow Walsh of the Northwest Mounted Police in Canada estimated the Nez Perce refugees to number 290. Part of Walsh's role was to oversee the refugee Sioux already in Canada. Greene, *Beyond Bear's Paw*, 67.

CHAPTER TWELVE: WHITE BIRD'S FREEDOM

1. Story of Mrs. Shot-in-Head, McWhorter Collection, Washington State University.

2. The Lament of Wot-tó-len. Many Wounds, Interpreter, July 1926, box 10, folder 59, McWhorter Collection, Washington State University.

3. All of the oral tradition accounts described the weather as terrible.

4. Fallacies of History, box 8, folder 40, McWhorter Collection, Washington State University. Also see McWhorter, *Yellow Wolf*, 101.

5. Greene, *Nez Perce Summer*, 339.

6. At least two dozen people were killed by the Assiniboine and Gros Ventres as they fled. Greene, *Beyond Bear's Paw*, 61

7. Ibid., 63.

8. Ibid., 54. The three men were Numb Fingers, Yellowhead, and No Fingers.

9. The Lament of Wot-tó-len, McWhorter Collection, Washington State University.

Appendix

1. Highberger, *Soldiers' Side*, 101.

2. Josephy, *Nez Perce Indians*, 639-643.

3. Cozzens, *Eyewitnesses to the Indian Wars, 1865-1890*, 314-315.

4. McWhorter, *Yellow Wolf*, 100-101.

5. Beal, *"I Will Fight No More Forever,"* 316.

Bibliography

Adkison, J. Loyal. "Benedict Family Closely Related to Early Idaho County History." *Idaho County Free Press*, Grangeville, ID, March 27, 1952.

Ankeny, Nesmith. *The West as I Knew It*. Lewiston, ID: R. G. Bailey, 1953.

Bailey, Robert Gresham. *River of No Return*. Lewiston, ID: R. G. Bailey, 1935.

Baird, Lynn and Dennis. *In Nez Perce Country: Accounts of the Bitterroots and the Clearwater after Lewis and Clark*. Moscow, ID: University of Idaho Library, 2003.

Beal, Merrill D. "Idaho's Indian Wars." *Idaho Yesterdays* 5 (Summer 1961).

————. *"I Will Fight No More Forever."* Seattle: University of Washington Press, 1963.

Bennett, Robert. *We'll All Go Home in the Spring: Personal Accounts and Aventures as Told by the Pioneers of the West*. Walla Walla, WA: Pioneer Press Books, 1984.

Bierce, Ambrose. *Ambrose Bierce's Civil War*. Avenel, NJ: Wings Books, 1956.

Board of Indian Commissioners. *Eighth Annual Report of the Board of Indian Commissioners for the Year 1876*. Washington, DC: US Government Printing Office, 1877.

Brady, Cyrus Townsend. *Northwestern Fights and Fighters*. New York: Doubleday, 1907.

Brown, Mark H. *The Flight of the Nez Perce*. New York: Capricorn Books, 1971.

Byler, Charles A. *Civil-Military Relations on the Frontier and Beyond, 1865-1917*. Westport, CT: Greenwood Publishing, 2006.

Claims of the Nez Perce Indians. Senate Executive Document no. 257. 56th Cong., 1st sess. Washington, DC: US Government Printing Office, 1900.

Cozzens, Charles. *Eyewitnesses to the Indian Wars, 1865-1890: The Wars for the Pacific Northwest*. Mechanicsburg, PA: Stackpole Books, 2002.

Dayton Chronicle. "H. M. Boone Died Saturday Night." June 11, 1936.

———. "John Agee and Former Partner Visit for First Time Since 1878." April 7, 1932.

Eastman, Gene and Mollie. *Bitterroot Crossing: Lewis and Clark Across the Lolo Trail.* Northwest Historical Manuscript Series. Moscow, ID: University of Idaho Library, 2002.

Fazio, James R. *Across the Snowy Ranges: The Lewis and Clark Expedition in Idaho and Western Montana.* Moscow, ID: Woodland Press, 2001.

Fifer, Barbara, and Vicky Soderburg. *Along the Trail with Lewis and Clark.* Great Falls, MT: Montana Magazine, 1998.

Fisher, S. G. "Stanton G. Fisher, Chief of Scouts to General Howard." *Montana Historical Society Contributions.* Vol. 2, 1896.

Forczyk, Robert. *Nez Perce 1877: The Last Fight.* Oxford: Osprey, 2011.

Gilbert, Frank. *Historic Sketches of Walla Walla, Whitman, Columbia, Garfield Co's 1882.* Portland, OR: A. G. Walling, 1882.

Glassey, Ray Hoard. *Pacific Northwest Indian Wars.* Portland, OR: Binfords and Mort, 1953.

Greene, Jerome A. *Beyond Bear's Paw: The Nez Perce Indians in Canada.* Norman: University of Oklahoma Press, 2010.

———. *Nez Perce Summer 1877: The U.S. Army and the Nee-Me-Poo Crisis.* Helena: Montana Historical Society Press, 2000.

Haines, Aubrey L. *The Battle of the Big Hole: The Story of the Landmark Battle of the 1877 Nez Perce War.* 2nd Edition. Guilford, CT: Globe Pequot, 2007.

Haines, Francis. "Nez Perce Horses." *Idaho Yesterdays* 4 (Spring 1960).

———. *The Nez Perces: Tribesmen of the Columbia Plateau.* Norman: University of Oklahoma Press, 1955.

———. "The Nez Perce Tribe Versus the United States." *Idaho Yesterdays* 8 (Spring 1964).

Haines, Francis, George Hatley, and Robert Pekinpah. *The Apaloosa Horse.* 3rd Edition. Moscow, ID: News-Review Publishing, 1957.

Hatch, Thom. *The Custer Companion: A Comprehensive Guide to the Life of George Armstrong Custer and the Plains Indian War.* Mechanicsburg, PA: Stackpole Books, 2002.

Hawthorne, Julian, ed. *History of Washington, the Evergreen State: From Early Dawn to Daylight; With Portraits and Biographies.* 2 Vols. New York: American Historical Publishing, 1893. Also accessed at http://www.archive.org/search.php?query=publisher%3A%22New+York%2C+American+Historical+Publishing%22.

Heitman, Francis. *Historical Register and Dictionary of the United States Army, from Its Organization, September 29, 1789, to March 2, 1903.* Washington, DC: National Tribune, 1890.

Highberger, Mark, ed. *The Death of Wind Blowing.* Wallowa, OR: Bear Creek Press, 2000.

———. *The Soldiers' Side of the Nez Perce War.* Wallowa, OR: Bear Creek Press, 2006.

Howard, Helen Addison, and Dan L. McGrath. *War Chief Joseph.* Lincoln: University of Nebraska Press, 1941.

Howard, Oliver Otis. *My Life and Experiences among Our Hostile Indians.* Hartford, CT: A. D. Worthington, 1907.

———. *Nez Perce Joseph: His Ancestors, His Lands, His Confederates, His Enemies, His Murders, His War, His Pursuit and Capture.* Boston: Lee and Shephard, 1881.

Hunter, George. *Reminiscences of an Old Timer.* San Francisco: H. S. Crocker, 1887.

Hutton, Paul. *Phil Sheridan and His Army.* Norman: University of Oklahoma Press, 2003.

Idaho Military Historical Society. "The Battle of White Bird Cañon." Part 1. *Pass in Review.* 3rd Quarter (October 2001): 1-6.

———. "The Battle of White Bird Cañon." Part 2. *Pass in Review.* 4th Quarter (December 2001): 1-6.

———. "The Cottonwood Skirmishes." *Pass in Review.* 3rd Quarter (September 2004): 1-9.

———. "Idaho File into History." Part 1. *Pass in Review.* 3rd Quarter (October 1999): 1-5.

Idaho State Historical Society. Reference Series. *Early Nez Perce Country.* No. 334, August 1963.

———. *Indians and Whites in the Nez Perce Country.* No. 89, August 1964.

———. *The Lolo Trail.* No. 286, August 1970.

———. *The Nez Perce Trail.* No. 285, August 1972.

Idaho Yesterdays 4 (Fall 1959). "Nez Perce Horses."

Jessup, John E. Jr., and Robert W. Coakley. *A Guide to the Study and Use of Military History*. Washington, DC: US Government Printing Office, 1982.

Johnson, Robert Underwood, and Clarence Clough Buel, eds. *Battles and Leaders of the Civil War*. Vol. 3. New York: Century, 1887.

Josephy, Alvin M. Jr. *The Nez Perce Indians and the Opening of the Northwest*. New Haven, CT: Yale University Press, 1965.

Keenan, Jerry. *The Life of Yellowstone Kelly*. Albuquerque: University of New Mexico Press, 2006.

Kelly, Luther S. *Yellowstone Kelly: Memoirs of Luther S. Kelly*. New Haven, CT: Yale University Press, 1926.

Laughy, Linwood, ed. *In Pursuit of the Nez Perces: The Nez Perce War of 1877*. Kooskia, ID: Mountain Meadow Press, 1993.

Lavender, David. *Let Me Be Free: The Nez Perce Tragedy*. New York: HarperCollins, 1992.

Lewis, Bonnie Sue. *Creating Christian Indians: Native Clergy in the Presbyterian Church*. Norman: University of Oklahoma Press, 2003.

Lowie, Robert. *The Crow Indians*. Lincoln: University of Nebraska Press, 1983.

Lyman, William Denison. *Lyman's History of Old Walla Walla County*. Vols. 1 and 2. Chicago: H. J. Clarke, 1918.

McDermott, John D. *Forlorn Hope: The Nez Perce Victory at White Bird Canyon*. Caldwell, ID: Caxton Press, 2003.

McFeely, William S. *Grant: A Biography*. New York: W. W. Norton, 1981.

McLuhan, T. C. *Touch the Earth*. New York: Promontory Press, 1971.

McWhorter Collection. Manuscripts, Archives, and Special Collections. Washington State University, Pullman.

McWhorter, L. V. *Hear Me, My Chiefs!: Nez Perce Legend and History*. Caldwell, ID: Caxton Press, 1952.

———. *Yellow Wolf: His Own Story*. Caldwell, ID: Caxton Press, 1940.

Miles, Nelson Appleton. *Personal Recollections and Observations of General Nelson A. Miles*. Chicago: Werner, 1896.

———. *Report of Colonel Nelson A. Miles on Final Operation*. Field, Bear's Paw Mountain, MT: US Army, 1877.

Nerburn, Kent. *Chief Joseph and the Flight of the Nez Perce*. New York: HarperCollins, 2005.

Nunnally, Michael L. *I Survived Custer's Last Stand!* N.p.: Moon Wolf, 2005.

Painter, Robert. *White Bird: The Last Great Warrior Chief of the Nez Perces*. Fairfield, WA: Ye Galleon Press, 2002.

Pfau, Scott E. "The Nez Perce Flight to Canada: An Analysis of the Nez Perce-US Cavalry Conflicts: Applying Historical Lessons Learned to Modern Counterinsurgency and Global War on Terrorism Operations." Master's thesis. US Army Command and General Staff College, 2006.

Potucek, Martin. *Idaho's Historic Trails*. Caldwell, ID: Caxton Press, 2003.

Report of the Commissioner of Indian Affairs, 397-728. In *Report of the Secretary of the Interior*, 1877. House Executive Document 1, part 5, vol. 1. 45th Cong., 2nd sess. Washington, DC: US Government Printing Office, 1877.

Report of the General of the Army, 330-415. In *Annual Report of the Secretary of War*. Vol. 1. Washington, DC: US Government Printing Office, 1877.

Roe, Frank Gilbert. *The Indian and the Horse*. Norman: University of Oklahoma Press, 1955.

Romeyn, Henry. T*he Capture of Chief Joseph and the Nez Perce Indians*. Contributions Vol. 2. Helena, MT: Historical Society of Montana, 1896.

Ruby, Robert H., and John A. Brown. *Dreamer-Prophets of the Columbia Plateau: Smohalla and Skolaskin*. Norman: University of Oklahoma Press, 2002.

Schmidt, Thomas. *National Geographic's Guide to the Lewis and Clark Trail*. Washington, DC: National Geographic Society, 1998.

Schullery, Paul. *Searching for Yellowstone: Ecology and Wonder in the Last Wilderness*. Helena: Montana Historical Society Press, 2004.

Shaver, F. A. *An Illustrated History of Southeastern Washington*. Spokane, WA: Western Historical Publishing, 1906.

Shields, George O. *The Battle of the Big Hole: A History of General Gibbon's Engagement with the Nez Perces Indians in the Big Hole Valley, August 9th, 1877*. New York: Rand McNally, 1889.

Shoup Letters. Special Collections Department. Eli M. Oboler Library. Pocatello: Idaho State University, 1877.

Tchakmakian, Pascal. *The Great Retreat*. San Francisco: Chronicle Books, 1976.

Trafzer, Clifford E., and Richard D. Scheuerman. *Renegade Tribe: The Palouse Indians and the Invasion of the Inland Northwest*. Pullman: Washington State University Press, 1986.

Utley, Robert M. *Frontier Regulars: The United States Army and the Indian, 1866-1890*. New York: Macmillan, 1973.

The Washington National Guard in the Philippine Insurrection. Vol. 4 of *The Official History of the Washington National Guard*. Camp Murray, Tacoma: Washington National Guard State Historical Society, n.d.

West, Elliott. *The Last Indian War: The Nez Perce Story*. New York: Oxford University Press, 2009.

Williams, Mathyn. "Indian Wars: Failings of the United States Army to Achieve Decisive Victory During the Nez Perce War of 1877." Master's thesis. US Army Command and General Staff College, 2004.

Wilmot, Luther P. *Narratives of the Nez Perce War*. Manuscript. Special Collections. University of Idaho, Moscow.

Wilson, E. T. "Campaign Against the Nez Perce Indians: The Year 1877." *East Washingtonian*. June 16, 1914. First Garfield County Pioneer Edition. Section 3.

———. *Hawks and Doves in the Nez Perce War of 1877*. Helena: Montana Historical Society, 1966.

Wood, Charles Erskine Scott. "Chief Joseph, the Nez Perce." *The Century* 23, no. 1 (1884): 135-142.

Index

Page numbers followed by *f* refer to items in illustrations.

Acknowledgments

Grateful acknowledgement is made to the following individuals and organizations who contributed to the development, research, and illustrative materials for this book:

Washington State University houses wonderful archives of Native American materials. I obtained much of the native oral tradition of the conflict from these archives, particularly the Lucullus V. McWhorter Collection. I wish to thank the curators and staff of the Washington State University Library's Manuscripts, Archives and Special Collections (MASC): Pat Mueller, Julie King, Jennifer Jouas, Mark O'English, and Cheryl Gunselman.

Likewise, the University of Idaho Library Special Collections and Archives were extremely helpful in finding period documents and sources. Thanks to Garth Reese and his staff, especially the efforts of Julie Munroe.

Thanks to Karen Kearns at the Idaho State University Library Archives for assistance with documents relating to the Nez Perce in southern Idaho. Thanks to Daisy Njoku at the National Anthropological Archives of the Smithsonian Institution and to Bill Huntington at Whitman College in Walla Walla, Washington, for their assistance.

I also want to acknowledge and thank Dell Montoya for his valuable advice on writing structure and continuity, and also recognize the contributions of poet Mark A. Johnson who provided his knowledge and encouragement during the creation of this book.

Finally, grateful recognition is made for my publisher Bruce H. Franklin and the skilled editorial assistance of Ron Silverman.